Finding Common Ground

A Guide to Personal, Professional, and Public Writing

SECOND EDITION

Carolyn P. Collette
Mount Holyoke College

Richard Johnson
Mount Holyoke College

LONGMAN

An imprint of Addison Wesley Longman, Inc.

New York • Reading, Massachusetts • Menlo Park, California • Harlow, England
Don Mills, Ontario • Sydney • Mexico City • Madrid • Amsterdam

Executive Editor: Anne Smith
Developmental Editor: Matt Rohrer
Cover Designer: Mary McDonnell
Project Coordination and Text Design: Ruttle, Shaw & Wetherill, Inc.
Electronic Production Manager: Angel Gonzalez, Jr.
Manufacturing Manager: Willie Lane
Electronic Page Makeup: Ruttle, Shaw & Wetherill, Inc.
Printer and Binder: R. R. Donnelley & Sons Company
Cover Printer: The Lehigh Press, Inc.

For permission to use copyrighted material, grateful acknowledgment is made to the copyright holders on pp. 224–225, which are hereby made part of this copyright page.

Library of Congress Cataloging-in-Publication Data
Collette, Carolyn P.
    Finding common ground : personal writing and public discourse /
  Carolyn P. Collette, Richard Johnson. —2nd ed.
        p.   cm.
    Includes bibliographical references (pp. 220-223) and index.
    ISBN 0-673-98214-9
    1. English language—Rhetoric.   2. Discourse analysis.
  I. Johnson, Richard, 1937–   . II. Title.
PE1408.C54368   1997
808'.042—dc20   96-20573
                                                          CIP

ISBN 0-673-98214-9

2345678910—DOC—99989796

For
Matthew and Andrew
and for
Nick and Tina, Patrick and Jelena,
Hong, and Loeun and Sidavi

Table of Contents

Preface

This book is designed to show writers ways of maintaining a personal presence in their writing no matter what the subject, audience, or discourse. Whatever you write and however you write about it, you write best, we believe, if you think about writing as an interaction between yourself and your reader. Ultimately the decisions you make about your presence in your writing and your interaction with your reader are a matter of writing not only effectively and persuasively but also responsibly.

We intend this book for those interested in enlarging the scope and effectiveness of their writing, for students in advanced writing courses with different approaches and styles of writing, and for writers who have already declared themselves interested in making writing a part of their lives. We assume that you want to write well about subjects you care about, whether philosophy or your childhood, the environment or taxation, electrons or an aunt whose life didn't turn out well. We also assume that you are seeking ways to invest your writing with a sense of your own commitment to the subject and to communicate directly with your reader as one person speaking to another.

Much of what we offer consists of practical advice about writing drawn from short, vivid pieces that represent a broad spectrum of viewpoints, situations, styles, and subjects. Part of our goal is indeed simply to offer useful tips, to show how certain tools of composition can be used, and to provide an opportunity for practicing their use. But our larger goal is to challenge the assumption that writing personally and writing professionally or publicly are necessarily opposed to each other.

PERSONAL WRITING

Writing exists to communicate ideas and information, feelings, and opinions. In every case a person—the writer—is responsible for shaping the idea or for organizing the information to inform or persuade a reader. In Part I, "Personal Presence," we discuss several ways of making yourself present in your text. In Chapter 1, "Transforming Experience into Words," we concentrate on asserting presence by using details and analogies. Chapter 2, "Orienting the Reader," discusses several ways in which writers give readers a sense of where they—both the writer and the reader—are. Chapter 3, "Creating a Common World of Feeling," discusses the presence of writers and their connection with readers through humor and anger. Chapter 4, "Leading Your Reader Through That

World," discusses large-scale patterns of movement. Chapter 5, "Moving Through Words and Sentences," looks at smaller-scale patterns of movement governed by word choice and sentence construction.

To accomplish their goals, writers need to be aware not only of their material and the "rules" of good writing but also of the possible ways in which they interact with their readers. Presence does not depend on craft and structure alone; it also derives from your own commitment to your subject and from thinking about how close or distant you want yourself and your reader to stand as you view your topic. A carefully constructed text that reaches out to readers and draws them along its lines of thought, argument, and evidence makes a statement of the writer's sense of the importance of the subject.

PROFESSIONAL VOICES

Wanting to invest your writing with your presence does not mean turning away from the more "impersonal" modes that characterize professional and academic discourses. In Part II, "Professional Voices," we consider ways of being present in kinds of writing that have been defined by conventions of relative impersonality. Chapter 6, "Reading and Writing in Professional Worlds," discusses why disciplinary and other specialized discourses exist and how they do or do not communicate succinctly and effectively. Chapter 7, "Working with a Range of Discourses," discusses ways in which writers can break out of their conventional discourses to signal their personal involvement in, for example, a new idea, a different way of thinking, or dissatisfaction with the limitations a particular set of discursive conventions may impose.

Developing a presence in your writing for either professional or large-scale public purposes can make your arguments more persuasive, but that is not the only or even the most important issue. Presence implies commitment and invites conversation; these seem to us to be matters of the deepest importance to anyone who writes.

PUBLIC VOICES

Perhaps paradoxically, to make yourself present in your writing almost inevitably leads to thinking about your audience and about your relation to discourses that are often socially or professionally defined. To be yourself inevitably leads to thinking beyond yourself. Whereas the personal voice represents the writer as a unique individual and the professional voice represents the writer as a member of a group, the public voice is a larger mode of self-representation.

In Part III, "Private Voices Made Public," we consider ways in which writers move into public worlds without losing a sense of who they are. Such a movement often leads to fuller realization of oneself. We begin, in Chapter 8, "Creating a Public Self," by looking at ways in which writers create "personae," or verbal personalities, and in Chapter 9, "Connecting with Readers," at ways writers can reach out to readers by cultivating particular kinds of responses. Chapter 10, "Finding a Voice," discusses how writers realize their voices by listening to their own cadences, by listening to other writers' voices, and by drawing on memories.

Chapter 11, "Writing with Responsible Authority," discusses the verbal foundations of achieving a measure of public authority in writing. Writing about a school bond issue, I may speak as an isolated individual who is protesting an increase in taxes or as an educator who brings my interests and expertise to bear on the problem, but I may also speak as someone whose concerns are in some sense larger than personal interest or professional expertise. As you move toward establishing a public voice you do not necessarily leave private interests or professionalized knowledge behind; your voice may indeed be a medley of all these voices. By your public voice you represent yourself within the larger debates of communities you belong to.

INTERACTION BETWEEN THE PERSONAL AND THE PUBLIC

While we use the term *personal writing,* it is not our purpose to come down on one side or the other of a debate between those who value intense concentration on the personal element in writing and those who see writing in terms of mastery over particular discourses. The personal, the discursive, and the public are parts of a constellation that defines all writing. We wish to throw light on what one of our readers called "the vital, complex interaction between the personal and the public" in writing. Our goal is to promote awareness of the different ways in which you can respond to different writing situations with the tools that are available to writers for expressing their intentions on specific occasions.

Our deepest intention is to suggest that the recognition and use of these tools should not be divorced from questions of purpose and commitment. The structure of the book is intended to move the reader more and more fully into the ethical and political spheres of writing. Thus we move from specific advice about how to use detail, figurative language, grammar, and structural organization to questions of voice as essential to public discourse. The relative weight we have given Part I may seem to indicate that we are favoring personal writing over more public forms. Or, conversely, the movement from the personal through the professional to the public may create the opposite impression, that we have favored public concerns over private ones.

Neither of these inferences would be correct. In organizing the book as we have, we mean to create a simple and usable structure. We work from the personal to the public because we feel that coming to terms with your own voice and your own experience provides a useful base for developing a professional and a public voice. At every juncture, however, we want to interweave the writer's responsibility to his or her own experience with awareness of the writer's readership. The personal and the public are two directions on a two-way street. When you are writing in the most public or professional manner it is still useful to remember that you are a person, however you decide to show it in your text. When you are writing about your private experience and feelings, as soon as you think of someone reading that writing you begin to move toward the public realm.

To be aware of the interaction among these three voices that we have described is not only a matter of practicality. As you think about the interactions between writer and reader that occur whatever the mode, we suggest that questions of personal responsibility and public commitment do and should arise and need to be faced. Writing to persuade a reader without considering the political and ethical propriety of that persuasion seems to us short-sighted. Writing about oneself without considering the larger implications of what one says runs the danger of self-centeredness and narcissism. In short, to think persistently about the relation of reader to writer should lead to thinking about political commitment and ethical obligations.

ACTIVE READING

A final note: using this book as a writer means a commitment to becoming an active reader. The examples that we discuss provide useful insight into how writers achieve a variety of effects in their writing. The analyses of exemplary passages also provide a guide to alert reading, that is training in how to recognize both the form and the substance of a text. We hope that reading this book will encourage you to become an active reader of whatever text you pick up. If you want to develop your writing skills, we believe, you will need to develop your habits of reading. If you find a piece effective, ask yourself what makes it so. What is it that stimulated your interest or imagination? If the text is boring, you can learn something about your potential readers' possible reactions to your writing by looking at what bored you in the piece at hand. Often, the problem is not the subject but the approach. Once you begin to identify what interests you in writing, or what failed to, you can adapt successful techniques to your own purposes.

We offer a book that is suggestive rather than prescriptive. We identify a number of techniques and explore a variety of patterns and strategies. We ask you to read it actively; to try the writing exercises we have constructed where they seem relevant; and always, both with our words and with the passages we discuss, to be ready to disagree, as well as to agree. Creating your own ways of being present to and interacting with readers, and your own voices, will ultimately be up to you.

ACKNOWLEDGMENTS

Many students, colleagues, and other friends have given us suggestions, criticism, and encouragement in the writing and revision of this book. It is a pleasure to be able to thank some of them publicly; we hope others will recognize their contributions and our silent but heartfelt thanks. The columns of Anna Quindlen, from which we quote amply in our text, first focused our attention on making public the private voice as a way of teaching writing and provided continuing inspiration for our approach as it developed into book form. Constance Rajala responded to our ideas with enthusiasm and with practical suggestions that marked our path of composition. Elaine Beilin, Anne Boutelle, Robert Brown, Robert Hosmer, Patrick Johnson, Anne Jones, Nancy Keyes, Mary McHenry, Mark McMenamin, Michael Pettit, and Stan Rachootin responded to our early proposal with criticisms and with suggested topics and readings. Peter Elbow, Penny Gill, Nick Johnson, Jessamyn Spears, Mary Alice Wilson, and Annie Woodhull read drafts of the first edition of the book with numerous suggestions for its improvement, as did these reviewers:

Linda Callendrillo, Bradley University
William Covino, University of Illinois at Chicago
John Dick, University of Texas at El Paso
Kate Frost, University of Texas at Austin
Peter Grudin, Williams College
Anne Matthews, Princeton University
Jack Prostko, Stanford University
Jeff Rackham, University of North Carolina at Asheville
Karen Rodis, Dartmouth College
Bob Schwegler, University of Rhode Island

Rolf Norgaard of the University of Colorado made many helpful suggestions for the revised edition, as did Barbara Connor and Marilyn Dwyer.

Students in our course Writing from the Inside Out have given us feedback about the first edition that has proved invaluable in revising. We are grateful to a number of instructors who have used the book, notably Penny Gill and Andrea Sununu, for their suggestions and support as we have worked on the new edition.

The Academic Computing staff at Mount Holyoke College gave us extraordinary assistance with preparing the manuscript. Jennifer Lonoff guided the manuscript of the first edition and the authors with tact and precision, constructive criticism, and encouragement through the various drafts. Anne Smith worked with us throughout on the second edition, and we are deeply grateful for her insights and her support. We are responsible for remaining errors or infelicities; but had all of these people not helped us, there would be many more. Yvonne Nicholson proofread texts and quotations, compiled bibliographies, checked citations, and helped us gain permission to quote copyrighted materials. David Collette and Kay Johnson, our spouses, gave us every imaginable support, including that of irreverent criticism, and gave the manuscript its two most thorough and helpful readings. To all, thanks.

Carolyn P. Collette
Richard Johnson

PART I

Personal Presence

CHAPTER 1

Transforming Experience into Words

When we read we transform words into experience. When we write we reverse the process, transforming experience into words. We do this all the time, as, for example, when we eat a piece of cake and exclaim, "What a wonderful piece of cake!" The eating and the experience of eating almost become the words used to describe them. Writers use language to create experience so powerfully for the reader that words become the reader's experience as much as the writer's. One place to start thinking about this process of transformation is with small units of experience and of language—details. Details help to focus both the reader's and the writer's attention on the nature of an experience. They provide the color, the imaginable information that a reader uses to work with the writer to re-create the writer's experience. In this chapter we discuss how to select and use details. As we write about them, we're aware that details very often have a life of their own. Writers start with literal descriptions of experience and find that almost immediately they get into not only what an experience was but also what it was like. Thus we see analogies, that is, all sorts of verbal comparisons, as closely related to details. We discuss them with details in the pages that follow because we believe that they are basic to successful writing.

1 USING DETAILS

We begin with details simply because they are basic units of experience and writing. You've probably been told dozens of times to use a lot of details in your writing, to be concrete, so our advice to pay attention to details will not come as news. How many? What kind? How to arrange them? There are no simple answers to these questions, and, indeed, a single detail can sometimes "say everything," while a welter of particulars leaves you confused. Our point is not that more details are better or worse but that the way to think about them is in terms of the reader, in terms of what you want your reader to see, feel, and think.

Look at this example from George Orwell's account of the Spanish Civil War, as a soldier fighting on the Loyalist, anti-Fascist side:

At this moment a man, presumably carrying a message to an officer, jumped out of the trench and ran along the top of the parapet in full view. He was half-dressed and was holding up his trousers with both hands as he ran. I refrained from shooting at him. It is true that I am a poor shot and unlikely to hit a running man at a hundred yards. . . . Still, I did not shoot partly because of that detail about the trousers. I had come here to shoot at "Fascists"; but a man who is holding up his trousers isn't a "Fascist," he is visibly a fellow-creature, similar to yourself, and you don't like shooting at him.

("Looking Back on the Spanish Civil War," 199)

The life of Orwell's enemy may have been spared because Orwell noticed a detail, the man holding his pants up with both hands—an awkward, slightly comical, and bizarre detail; lifelike in the extreme; seeming to illustrate a cliché about getting caught with your pants down. We understand why Orwell did not shoot. Orwell could no longer think of him as a type, could no longer apply a label like "Fascist" or "enemy," but suddenly saw the man specifically, an individual human being in an awkward position. Orwell doesn't tell us much more—he certainly doesn't bore us with what color the man's uniform was or how short or tall he was—but simply gives what's needed to reclassify the man.

Orwell uses a single, representative detail that conveys a powerful truth—similarity to himself, that is, fellow-creaturehood—without much elaboration. The detail signifies something; it stands for the concept fellow human being. What happens if you rewrite the passage in your mind so that the generalization takes the place of the detail? The second sentence might read, "He was a fellow creature, similar to myself"; the fourth, "I did not shoot him because of the general idea of his being like myself." Something vanishes—not the idea, but the immediacy of the idea. Orwell's point, then, is that for him, both as a writer and as a soldier, detail has an immediacy that generalization does not. The generalization is there, but it is carried by the one carefully observed and selected detail.

To use details we must learn to observe, to focus, and to select. We process innumerable perceptions all the time, especially with those extraordinary sensory vacuum sweepers, our eyes and ears. We mix them with our memories, similarly composed of countless individual perceptions, and catalog them with our minds and our language. From all that richness and confusion we can select and arrange a few details to draw our readers closer to our experience, to give them a sense not only that they know what we think or feel but also that they have thought and felt it with us.

How? Think about the way in which a filmmaker uses details. Movies are so full of details that they seem nearly indiscriminate. In fact, cameras focus on certain details, exaggerate them, and move from distant views, which comprehend broad patterns, to close-ups, which exclude all but a few crucial details. They give us a sense of being there—we are not sitting in a movie theater, perhaps with cramped necks from looking around the bulky fellow in front of us, but in a café in Casablanca, looking at a clash between strident evil and lethargic goodness. The cameras do that, and they give us a sense of what is significant. A gesture, an inflection or emphasis in a sentence, a piece of clothing like a white dinner jacket, a tune, or a body movement even as small as a lifted eyebrow or a deep breath helps sketch the inner life of a character or the relationship between two people. All of these represent ideas and interpretations, how the film director has seen the characters and actions.

Like the director or cameraman, the writer starts by observing and focusing, then by selecting and judging. We can see these processes at work in a piece of writing by William Least Heat Moon:

> I couldn't see how anyone could survive a year in this severe land, yet Hopis, like other desert life, are patient and clever and not at all desperate; they have lasted here for ten centuries by using tiny terraced plots that catch spring rain and produce a desert-hardy species of blue corn, as well as squash, onions, beans, peppers, melons, apricots, peaches. The bristle-cone pine of American Indians, Hopis live where almost nothing else will, thriving long in adverse conditions: poor soil, drought, temperature extremes, high winds. Those give life to the bristle-cone and the Hopi.
>
> (*Blue Highways: A Journey into America*, 175)

Heat Moon offers a profusion of details, all exemplifying species that not only survive but also thrive in the desert, species that include the Hopi. The Hopi know how to bring life out of the desert; the Hopi themselves are a species of life brought out of a desert. The single detail of the man holding up his pants does the trick for Orwell; Heat Moon, by the very nature of the statement he is making, needs many details—blue corn, squash, onions, beans, peppers, melons, and so on. Heat Moon's point is profusion: lots of things manage to flourish under apparently inhospitable circumstances—the Hopis, the things they tend, and other species like the Hopis. Orwell's point is singularity: the one experience that reveals something to him, the singularity of each human being. Both techniques can be seen as answers to the question of what the reader needs to see in order to comprehend the point as the writer sees it.

In any piece of writing, more is left out than included. It may look as if Heat Moon is being less selective than Orwell, but if we think about it for a moment it will be clear that he, too, is selecting and focusing, as well as observing and collecting. He has not told us everything. Rather, he has selected an area on which to concentrate the reader's attention; in doing so he has also chosen not to focus attention on certain other areas. As a writer he is present in his own text, shaping it. When you are writing from any point you can decide whether or not to go into more detail. You can say, "She stayed in Seattle that night" or "She stayed at a motel in Seattle that night" or "She stayed in a Ramada Inn in Seattle that night." And so on. It isn't just a matter of "what she did"; it's what, from the many things she did, you want your reader to focus on. You may well decide that "she stayed in Seattle" is enough and save your details for somewhere else; it depends on where you want to direct your reader's attention.

At this point you may be thinking, it's fine to say how professional writers like Orwell and Heat Moon do things; I can see and appreciate their art. But I'm an amateur; I can't do that, or at least, how do *I*, a relative novice, do that? In fact, the selection of details, like all the tools and tactics we offer, is not particularly esoteric or difficult; mostly, it is a matter of common sense. Once you think about it, you realize that you do this all the time. You observe details; you select and arrange. The point is to sharpen your awareness of this habit, to hone it for use in writing. Train yourself to develop the capacity of isolating the significant detail. Try this exercise.

✎ **Writing**   Look at the place where you are now. Let your mind's eye be a camera taking snapshots of the scene. Now imagine yourself making a small album of those snapshots aimed at giving someone who has no knowledge of where you are a sense of what it is like. Select six representative details. From all the images in your mind choose and arrange six imaginary snapshots that will convey to someone else what was important to you as you saw the scene. Note that this process concentrates your attention on how to construct a pattern of details that will, in effect, guide the reader in reconstructing your experience. Write a brief paragraph or two that describe your location through these "snapshots" of details.

Using Details to Evoke

Details not only help the reader to see things as the writer does, but they also enlist the reader's help in creating meaning. You can see how this works in an essay called "Writing and Remembering" by William Zinsser, which introduces a set of reminiscences about childhood by several different writers.

> Mine was the most privileged of the five boyhoods. In 1920 my parents had built a large and unusually pleasant house—one of those summery, white shingled houses with a lot of screened porches—on four acres of hilly land near the end of King's Point, overlooking Manhasset Bay and Long Island Sound. Boats and water were my view; I thought it was as beautiful a location for a home as any child could ask for. My father's business in New York withstood the Depression, so my three older sisters and I were sheltered from its cold winds, and we grew up in a happy family, well loved and well provided for. (12–13)

In one way, the passage is full of details; in another, it is not really all that specific. Rather than attempt to describe in full detail the house that clearly meant so much to him, Zinsser selects a few images on which he focuses the power of the reader's imagination, asking the reader to build the fuller picture out of them. Some readers might criticize Zinsser for not telling how large the house was, how many porches, what kind of boats, and so on—in the belief that the more specific the details, the better. Zinsser's technique, however, is to choose a few details for their ability to represent the essence of the experience and through them to reach out to the reader, to enlist the reader's imagination in creating the scene out of the reader's lived, vicarious, or imagined experience.

Later in the essay, after re-creating his childhood in a series of detailed images, Zinsser returns to the house. Once more the passage that seems so detailed is actually more evocation than literal description. It evokes what for many readers are their own memories of similar, familiar experiences; it asks for the reader's imaginative cooperation to bring its carefully selected details to life and to fill in the whole, which he just sketches:

> I described the house, with its sunlit rooms and its big windows and its agreeable porches that enabled us to watch an endless armada of boats: sailboats, motor boats, excursion boats, launches, freighters, tankers, trawlers, tugs and barges, navy destroyers, and every night at six, one of the two night steamers of the Fall River Line, aging belles named the PRISCILLA and the COMMONWEALTH. I described the sounds of the water that were threaded through our lives: the chime of the bell buoy, the mournful foghorn of Execution Light, the unsteady drone of an outboard motor, which, even more than the banging of a screen door, still means summer to me. I described the hill in front of the house that we sledded down on our Flexible Flyers. (18)

In spite of the apparent detail in the list of types of ships, Zinsser is more interested in conveying the sense of the place, the sense of his memory of the place, than in trying to describe it fully. Here the list of boats serves not so much to specify the view as to suggest the magic and excitement of the house and the boyhood lived in it. Through a few specific details Zinsser creates a whole world of seeing (the house with its sunlit rooms and big windows), hearing (the sounds of the water, the chime of the bell, the banging of a screen door), and feeling (agreeable porches, mournful foghorn).

✎ **Writing**   A good way to practice this skill is to try your hand at a short evocation of an event you are seeing or participating in with several other people, who will also write descriptions of it. It might be the opening convocation of a school year, a party, or a trip to the movies.

Choose the details carefully with the two principles in mind: evocation and enlisting your reader's imagination. After you've written, compare your sketch with the others. Note the differences. Discuss why each of you chose the details you did.

Using Details in Less Personal Kinds of Writing

So far, the examples we have used are based on personal experience, but as we will keep saying in other parts of this book, details are useful in all sorts of writing, as you can see in this passage from a biography of Ulysses S. Grant. The passage narrates an often-described event in American history, the end of the Civil War:

> April 8 was a day of more fighting and more deaths, and of great psychic strain on Ulysses Grant. That evening, having still not heard from Lee, Grant rode on his horse Cincinnati into that night's makeshift headquarters, and uncharacteristically greeted Meade with an affectionate "Old Fellow." Meade, pleased, was gentle in reply, knowing Grant "had one of his sick headaches, which are rare, but cause him fearful pain, such as almost overcomes his iron stoicism." The two staffs, Grant's and Meade's, shared a farmhouse, and one of the officers was pounding the piano he had discovered there. Music was noise to Grant; he sat bathing his feet in hot water and mustard, and putting mustard plasters on his wrists and the back of his neck. His headache was severe. About midnight, when the farmhouse had at last quieted and Grant rested on a sofa in the front room, a message from Lee finally arrived. Horace Porter and John Rawlins were reluctant to disturb Grant, hoping he had managed to fall asleep, but when Rawlins pushed open the general's door quietly, Grant immediately called to him to come on in; the headache had kept him awake. He sat up and read Lee's note by candlelight. . . . Grant did not like to be preached to; he wanted one thing and one thing only—the surrender of Lee's army. He would not talk of terms; he would not negotiate a peace. He lay down on the sofa again, telling Rawlins and Porter that he would reply in the morning.
>
> When Porter went to check on Grant at four in the morning, the room was empty, and going outside, he found Grant pacing back and forth, his hands pressed against his head. His migraine was excruciating, and Porter and Rawlins got him some coffee. When the throbbing abated a bit, he wrote Lee, "I have no authority to treat on the subject of peace; the meeting proposed for 10 a.m. to-day could lead to no good." He did add a plea for a battlefield surrender without any talk of the general political situation: "I will state however, general, that I am equally anxious for peace with yourself, and the whole North entertains the same feeling." The eloquence of his statement, but perhaps not its persuasiveness, was diminished by his comment that the surrender would save not only "thousands of human lives" but also "hundreds of millions of property not yet destroyed." In all, the message that went out early in the morning of April 9 had a decidedly urgent tone.
>
> Grant told Horace Porter that morning, at the start of the greatest day of his life, that the best thing that could happen to him that day would be for

the pain of the headache to clear. It was still torturing him, but he turned down an ambulance, mounted Cincinnati, and rode off. One would expect that with hopes so high for an affirmative message from Lee, he would have alerted officers to his whereabouts at every imaginable point. Instead, finding one road blocked, he went off with Rawlins, Porter, and Babcock to look for another, without leaving word of his destination. Perhaps there was a curious want of confidence at a moment when none but Grant could imagine such a thing; perhaps he dreaded still another rebuff by Lee.

(William S. McFeely, *Grant*, 217–218)

As befits historical writing, there is a great deal of detail here: the name of Grant's horse, what General Meade said to him, exactly where he was and what he did, and so on. As readers, however, we focus on Grant's headache, which becomes a common thread throughout these paragraphs. We understand implicitly that the headache is not just an accidental malady but the result of the psychic strain of a long and terrible campaign, with much suffering and many deaths. It provides readers with a place on which to focus their attention, and it reveals a great deal about the moment and the character without long-winded explanation.

You can use details not only to convey meaning, as McFeely does here, but also to say a lot economically. McFeely the historian notes the detail that Grant had a headache during those crucial days; McFeely the writer uses the headache to focus the reader's awareness on the pain and suffering of these terrible last stages of a bloody war and on Grant's anxiety. There are, no doubt, accounts of this event in which the headache is not even mentioned. This account focuses our awareness on everything that has been going on, perhaps even the pain and suffering of these terrible last stages of a war full of suffering and death and Grant's anxiety to end it. It allows McFeely to summarize both the physical and the psychic atmosphere. After giving detailed accounts of further negotiations by mail the next day that lead finally to the agreement to meet at Appomattox Court House, McFeely concludes: "The headache was gone."

Again, though McFeely is a prize-winning writer of history, his art is in principle not different from something you do all the time but might not be fully aware of or value very much. Why not? In part it may be because our culture, generally, places a high value on abstraction, on analyzing in order to extract principles that can be applied broadly. Academic conventions pressure writers to flatten their prose, to state things in general terms. These conventions, as we will see, have their uses, but it's worth making an effort to free yourself from their tyranny: you don't have to do it that way all the time. It's worth noting that, paradoxically, good academic writers know what every good storyteller knows, that it can be very effective to focus on material aspects of a subject and then to select a few images as focal points for what you are saying. Even in this kind of material, detailed specificity is absent from your writing; although it's probably there in your speech, particularly in your storytelling. Bring it back into your writing by consciously trying to anchor your generalizations in the world of your own observed, material phenomena.

Working from Generalizations to Details

Generalization is an enormously powerful tool, something we use all the time, something that it is almost impossible to do without in any kind of writing or, indeed, thinking in Western culture. It allows us to get beyond the single instances and deal with experience over a broad range, to classify and sort out patterns and causes. But there are dangers in generalizing, dangers of getting away from the source of the generalizations; giving details allows you to show your generalization as something that's still connected to its source in experience. For example, here is a brief excerpt from an article about politics in India by the novelist Anita Desai:

> Rajiv Gandhi's brief term in power between 1985 and 1989 saw the coming to bloom of the new commercialism in India, and the establishment of the new middle class—the small shopkeepers and petty traders of the past breaking into the new era of enterprise and entrepreneurship. The cities became filled with the rural poor desperate for a share in the new wealth, streets became noisy with the urgent little Maruti cars, marketplaces overflowed with goods, shoppers jostled to buy what they had seen advertised on television the night before—Wrangler jeans, Benetton shirts, track shoes, and Pepsi-Cola.
>
> ("India: The Seed of Destruction," 3)

The complex social changes described first in broad generalizations—new commercialism, new middle class, new era of enterprise and entrepreneurship—are translated into specific images and details: streets crowded with a certain kind of car, shoppers bumping into one another, and the products the shoppers are buying. The writer, fine novelist that she is, is pinning down her general statements so that her readers can see them in terms of an urban scene filled with recognizable human beings.

And one final example, this from a book about cities:

> As cities grow, they replace the imports which they earn from neighboring cities, as well as from outside their nations. For reasons we shall come to, the process of replacing imports is apt to cause cities to grow explosively. Episodes of explosive growth can recur again and again during the life of a city as new and different imports are earned, then replaced. But before going into that, let us examine a little more closely just what happens when a city replaces an import with new local work, as Tokyo did with its bicycles.
>
> First of all, before the process could occur at all, two sorts of events had to have taken place. Tokyo had already become a good market for imported bicycles; and this meant it was becoming a place where it was worthwhile for somebody to make them. Also, before the bicycles were actually manufactured there, workmen in the city were learning how to manufacture them,

even though their work at first had a different purpose. The production of bicycles could be logically added to work that was already being done in Tokyo.

(Jane Jacobs, *The Economy of Cities*, 146)

For our purposes the important words here are "let us examine a bit more closely." And, indeed, in the course of this chapter, the reader learns a good deal about the manufacture of bicycles in Tokyo as an example of a certain kind of manufacturing that produces a certain kind of growth in cities, anywhere and any time. Jacobs is asking us to look a little more closely; she is giving us a close-up, a detailed example of what she is generalizing about, and it is worth noting that this kind of detailed work is crucial to successful writing of a general sort—knowing the value of moving the reader closer to a detailed example of what you are generalizing about. Details make generalizations work.

✎ **Writing** Use as a point of departure this aphorism of Robert Morley: "The human body is an ingenious assembly of portable plumbing" If you like you may substitute any descriptive phrase you prefer for "portable plumbing." Then give a detailed explanation of what you mean by the generalization.

In all cases, we suggest, details provide you with something quite analogous to the close-up in filming, a means by which you can draw your reader close to your subject. We can distinguish at least five overlapping uses of this device of close-up that will give you an idea about the range of its usefulness. (1) You can use it to concentrate attention on a particular fact or idea, as Orwell and McFeely do, to focus the reader's awareness on a central idea represented by an image or other detail. (2) You can give your reader a sense of location, of being in a particular place, as Heat Moon does. (3) You can use it to evoke a feeling, as Zinsser does. (4) You can use it to anchor a general discussion, to give a sense that the general statement has a grounding in reality, as Desai does. (5) And, closely related, you can use it to illustrate a generalization, to give specific examples, as Jacobs does.

Having said this much about how details work in writing, we can now give both some general advice about learning how to use details and some specific techniques for doing so. Begin by being an observant reader, watching the ways in which different writers use details and looking for the "gear shifts" from general to specific and specific to general. Notice how "telling details" are used and, particularly, the selection processes—how one writer focuses on a few details and how another uses details to give you a feeling, as Zinsser, Heat Moon, and Jacob's do, of a wealth of experience.

It seems idle to say, "Be more observant," but you can in fact train yourself to notice details around you, simply by being conscious of what you are seeing. As you walk about, think of yourself as a camera; look at the world as if through a lens, and note where your attention naturally leads you. Remember that certain details come to signal or stand for experiences. Think of someone who has recently caught your attention, for example, or someone you know well, and see if your mind has automatically focused on some details—a manner of speech, a piece of clothing, a way of walking or eating, a repeated phrase, or the way hair was combed—that characterize the person in your mind. Look also for the surprising detail, the little peripheral gesture or habit that reveals much without being obvious. Then, imagine describing that person to a friend: think about what details you might use to catch the reality of the person you are describing.

Detail comes, originally, from a word meaning "to cut," and is closely related to "tailor." You can think of using details as a kind of tailoring, of yourself carefully cutting selected pieces from the immense fabric of your experience or your reading in order to fit the particular needs of your reader. Even the most detailed writing uses relatively few details, in comparison to the wealth of details that filter through our senses and memories at any given time. Make that selection process conscious, while at the same time trusting your powers of observation, memory, and selection to provide the materials.

More than anything else, be aware of at least an imaginary reader or audience present with you as you work with details. That is, you are not merely putting details onto paper; you are also focusing a reader's attention, and doing so for a given purpose. You can practice this as a specification exercise, writing on a subject generally, then going back and thinking about places where you want to have a close-up, where you want to have the reader "examine things a little more closely." You can practice this informally with friends, asking them to serve as "straight men" as you present ideas or experiences, breaking in to ask where they need more explanation, more details, in order to understand. But remember also that you are in control: you are not merely responding to your reader's wishes but also directing your reader's attention, using close-up as a tool of emphasis.

2   DRAWING ANALOGIES

We live in a world of things and actions rendered distinct and distinguishable because they have names or, more precisely, because we have constructed a system of naming and signifying called language. To speak or write, in this view, is to use and connect those names: *trees, tables, ions, giraffes, love, money, saw, eat, spend,* and so on. Trying to re-create our experiences for other people, however, we discover that some of those experiences elude our language as we have just described it, which is perhaps why we fall back on *filler* phrases, *you know, sort of, kind of, I mean*, and, almost universally, *like*. When we can't quite say what something *is*, we instinctively compare it to something else; we say what it *resembles*; we define it by likening it to and distinguishing it from something else.

> Shall I compare thee to a summer's day?
> Thou art more lovely and more temperate. . . .
>
> (Sonnet 18)

Such comparing is one of the central impulses behind poetry, as in the opening of this sonnet by William Shakespeare. But it is also something we do every day: we use language to compare; we make analogies; we use metaphors and similes and other figures of speech that expand the resources of language beyond literal description.

Doing so can be the homeliest thing in the world; it can also have substantial consequences. In an essay called "How Lincoln Won the War with Metaphors," James McPherson, a historian, compares Lincoln's use of language with that of Jefferson Davis, president of the Confederacy. By background and training, Davis should have been the more skilled user of words; he had

> excellent training in the classics, in rhetoric, logic, literature, and science. He should have been a superb communicator. . . . He could write with vigorous logic, turn a classical phrase, quote the leading authorities on many a subject, and close with a rhetorical flourish. (94)

But although Davis was skilled "by the standards of the day," it was Lincoln, in fact, who won the war of words and may, McPherson suggests, have won the war *with* words.

Why? McPherson argues that it was particularly Lincoln's skill with figurative language that made him so capable of inspiring and communicating with people, and that these in fact may have come because he had the good fortune to spend a lot of his time as a young man reading

> the King James Bible, *Aesop's Fables, Pilgrim's Progress,* and Shakespeare's plays. What do these four have in common? They are rich in figurative language—in allegory, parable, fable, metaphor—in words and stories that seem to say one thing but mean another, in images that illustrate something more profound than their surface appearance. (95)

Perhaps the central power of metaphor, then, is its ability to express something that is complex, elusive, or abstract in terms of something that is concrete, immediate, and familiar. Whereas Davis spoke in "abstractions and platitudes," Lincoln spoke in tangible images and arresting stories. And his ability to do so came from reading and from direct experience—and from a willingness to put ideas into tangible terms.

Lincoln's genius lay in his innate recognition that all figurative language has a remarkable ability to bring to abstract ideas a powerful sense of immediacy and of human experience. One theorist, Paul Ricoeur, has said:

> The very expression "figure of speech" implies that in metaphor . . . discourse assumes the nature of a body by displaying forms and traits which usually characterize the human face.
> ("The Metaphorical Process as Cognition, Imagination, and Feeling," 144)

Figurative language is the human face of generalization and abstraction. Often, if not always, the effect of figurative language is to provide readers with something like first-hand experience, things they can see and feel, as a way of drawing them into a text and toward shared understanding. Often, figurative language connects our private arguments or feelings or experiences with external or otherwise shared worlds of perception. Figurative language embodies thought, feeling, and experience, and by its very nature it involves reader and writer or, as in Lincoln's case, speaker and listener in a common enterprise.

In the following section we discuss metaphor and, more briefly, a few other kinds of figurative language. Like details, they can give a reader a quick picture of what you're talking about, a sense of direct experience; but they differ in that they involve a principle of conversion, a "jump" from one thing to another and a willingness to make connections between relatively dissimilar things.

Metaphors and Similes

Metaphor begins in comparison, in likeness and difference, and ends up as a way of knowing, a tool of discovery. We use the familiar to describe the unfamiliar, the visible to describe the invisible, the tangible to define the intangible. Here is the beginning of the essay "On Metaphor" by the late Howard Nemerov, a poet and teacher of literature:

> While I am thinking about metaphor, a flock of purple finches arrives on the lawn. Since I haven't seen these birds for some years, I am only fairly sure of their being in fact purple finches, so I get down Peterson's *Field Guide* and read his description: "Male: About size of House Sparrow, rosy-red, brightest on head and rump." That checks quite well, but his next remark—"a sparrow dipped in raspberry juice"—is decisive: it fits. I look out the window again, and now I *know* that I am seeing purple finches.
> That's very simple. So simple, indeed, that I hesitate to look any further into the matter, for as soon as I do I shall see that its simplicity is not altogether canny. Why should I be made certain of what a purple finch is by being led to contemplate a sparrow dipped in raspberry juice? Have I ever

dipped a sparrow in raspberry juice? Has anyone? And yet there it is, quite certain and quite right. Peterson and I and the finches are in agreement. It is like being told: If you really want to see something, look at something else. If you want to say what something is, inspect something that it isn't. It might go further, and worse, than that: if you want to see the invisible world, look at the visible one. If you want to know what East really is, look North. If you have a question concerning the sea, look at the mountains. And so on. (114)

As Nemerov notes, there is something magic, something uncanny, about how a metaphor works. Something we've never in fact seen—a sparrow dipped in raspberry juice—ensures a quick, sure identification of the finch before us; it is decisive and quick, a knockout blow because of the extraordinary power of the imagination to "see" what in this case it has never seen, a sparrow dipped in raspberry juice.

But as McPherson suggests, it is not just poets—or bird guides—who use metaphors. Metaphor is a universal quality of mind and language. Here is a passage from a book by Hashim Khan, perhaps the greatest squash player ever:

> What can one say about ball? You can see it is a small black rubber ball, less than one ounce. Important thing you do not see. Hollow, this ball. When it is cold, it is hard, it sleeps, it does not wish to play. But you knock it up a bit, air in hollow inside warms up and pushes to get out, it becomes like a spring. Now this ball bounds with joy.
>
> *(Squash Racquets, 50)*

Everything is straightforward until midway through the fifth sentence, when an inanimate object starts doing things that only animate objects do: sleeping, not wishing to play, bounding for joy. That's Khan's point: when you've hit the ball for a while, it almost has truly become animate. Its animation becomes real enough that we can usefully speak of it as if it were genuinely so. We say that the ball is not literally alive, but it acts that way; it's *figuratively* alive, or alive *in a manner of speaking*. Indeed, metaphoric language can have extraordinary reality. So effective is it, we reliteralize the metaphor and stop seeing it as metaphor: a ball isn't *like* a living thing; it is *lively*.

It may be useful here to go back to a familiar schoolroom distinction, that between metaphor and simile. Similes make comparisons explicit by using *like* or *as*: she is as quick as lightning; he runs like a deer; my love is like a red, red rose. Metaphors, in the narrow sense, work by a kind of substitution, replacing the thing you're talking about with something else: he's a pig; you're gobbling your food; she's just pecking away at her dinner. Nemerov suggests that the essential difference between the two is this: "The simile isolates for you the likeness in virtue of which the comparison is made; the metaphor leaves it up to you to isolate the likeness or for that matter not to isolate it" (116). Metaphor goes the whole way with comparing: *x* is so like *y* that, for this instant, we might say let *x be y*. (We will, however, be following the common usage that lets metaphor refer to both metaphor and simile; that is itself a figure of speech, metonymy, as we point out on page 21.)

It is amazing how easy it is to neglect the kind of double vision that allows us to see one thing as another, in effect to pretend that a ball is alive for certain purposes. And that is where you should begin with metaphor: just noticing how much of it is embedded in your speech and writing, in what you read, in what people say to one another, in the popular songs one hears. Doing so, you will undoubtedly notice a good many stale metaphors and dead metaphors, but you will also probably notice how common a tool metaphor can be. You don't have to invent metaphors: our language, and your mind, are full of them. Reading quickly, you might pass over a passage like the following without really seeing the metaphors within: "A Federal Reserve Board survey of national economic conditions on the eve of war in the Middle East depicted an economy limping along with few regions or industries displaying much strength" (Paul Duke, Jr., "Survey Finds Limp Economy on Eve of War," A2). The "limping economy" is a powerful metaphor: you might see a giant with a badly injured leg. Notice also that there are other, rather half-developed metaphors here: "eve of war," "depicted," "displaying." To read for the metaphors, as well as for the meaning, is rather like the difference between hearing a melody and hearing a fully orchestrated arrangement of it. We can skim over the metaphoric facet of language quickly, in order to get the point, or we can get our minds used to following the metaphors, as well as the abstract meaning, or better yet, to following the abstract meaning *by* looking at that web of images. When you write about a star player, see a heavenly object. When you have a gut feeling about something, think about anatomy. When you're hopping mad, think about jumping up and down.

Verbs and Metaphor

Sometimes, elements of metaphoric language are so deeply embedded in our language that the reader can quickly "see" the point without ever really articulating it consciously, as in this passage from a novel by Jane Austen:

> A few minutes were sufficient for making [Emma] acquainted with her own heart. A mind like hers, once opening to suspicion, made rapid progress. She touched—she admitted—she acknowledged the whole truth. . . . It darted through her, with the speed of an arrow, that Mr. Knightley must marry no one but herself!
>
> (*Emma*, 407–408)

As the critic George Steiner has pointed out ("Eros and Idiom," 95), the metaphor—darting, speed of an arrow—is so familiar that it is hardly noticeable: *arrow* and *dart* are common words for speed. More faintly, we recall a myth, still widely invoked on Valentine's Day, that love arrives when blind Cupid shoots arrows into our hearts. Here is a variation on that. The arrow is going through the mind of the heroine, not through her heart. This is a moment of self-recognition; she is understanding her own feelings, and the metaphor, deftly used, is the vehicle of her self-awareness. But notice also that Austen is using other kinds of partially submerged metaphors located in verbs: talking about her heroine "becoming acquainted with her heart," as if they were two people meeting, and of her mind "opening," "making progress," and "touching the truth."

Here is another example of a surface controlled by metaphors that are only lightly touched:

> But [Richard] Hoggart's calm prose only makes me recall the urgency with which I came to idolize my grammar school teachers. I began by imitating their accents, using their diction, trusting their every direction. The very first facts they dispensed, I grasped with awe. Any book they told me to read, I read—then waited for them to tell me which books I enjoyed. Their every casual opinion I came to adopt and to trumpet when I returned home. I stayed after school "to help"—to get my teacher's undivided attention. It was the nun's encouragement that mattered most to me. (She understood exactly what—my parents never seemed to appraise so well—all my achievements entailed.) Memory gently caressed each word of praise bestowed in the classroom so that compliments teachers paid me years ago come quickly to mind even today.
>
> (Richard Rodriguez, *Hunger of Memory*, 49–50)

It is hard to draw a line between the kinds of metaphors that we use all the time and that are part of the language and those that are conscious inventions of a writer. We are, for example, used to hearing about "dispensing facts" and of someone "grasping" them, but in fact Rodriguez displays a light touch there, treating these intellectual objects as if they were little pieces of something that could be dispensed and grasped. When we hear of opinions being *trumpeted* and memory *gently caressing*, we are perhaps more keenly aware of metaphor, but we still would probably not think of the passage as being ostentatiously figurative.

The example Rodriguez sets is one any writer can follow. At the heart of his method lies a way of looking. He sees ideas as if they were activities. We all do that to an extent, as when we say, "That movie really bowled me over"; we only need to extend this native capacity. More to the point, Rodriguez recognizes that this knowledge can be conveyed particularly well through verbs: *facts* are *dispensed*, then *grasped*; *opinions* *trumpeted*; *words* of praise *caressed*. That is, Rodriguez uses a verb that suggests concrete action to describe something that a less concrete subject does. You can do the same with nouns and adjectives, but it works particularly well with verbs. What results from this method is not so much a feeling of artificial metaphor but of concreteness and activity.

You can use this method of letting verbs imply metaphors to deal with even quite abstract materials; in fact, it is a particularly useful tool when writing about an abstract subject. Here is a paragraph from a book by a historian:

> In a society in which the dream of success has been drained of any meaning beyond itself, men have nothing against which to measure their achievements except the achievements of others. Self-approval depends on public recognition and acclaim, and the quality of this approval has undergone important changes in its own right. The good opinion of friends and neighbors, which formerly informed a man that he had lived a useful life, rested on appreciation of his accomplishments. Today men seek the kind of approval that applauds not their actions but their personal attributes. They wish to be not so much esteemed as admired. They crave not fame but the glamour and excitement of celebrity.
>
> (Christopher Lasch, *The Culture of Narcissism*, 116)

Look at Lasch's verbs: *drained, measure, depends, informed, seek, crave.* We are not aware of conscious metaphor, but of physical action, even in the realm of ideas and opinions. Things are happening.

✎ **Writing**   Here, for example, are some sentences from a national weather forecast. They show that finding the right verb can enliven even the dullest and most abstract writing.

> Heavy thunderstorms will roam eastern Texas this afternoon. Moist air percolating upward in the afternoon heat will be further lifted by a disturbance in the jet stream, causing heavy downpours, lightning and gusty winds.
>
> Showers will attend a cold front advancing through eastern New England. West of the front a trailing pool of cold air at 18,000 feet will foster scattered thundershowers. . . . Patches of dense fog will yield to bright sunshine.
>
> (*New York Times*, June 28, 1987)

Look for a passage of dry writing, and convert it to active, metaphorically enriched prose by working with the verbs.

Constructing Multiple Metaphors of Experience

To explore how metaphor can be used to convey complex feelings and relations, we will look in some detail at a passage from the memoir of an Irish writer, Polly Devlin, who is explaining the relationship of her sisters and herself to the town in a remote corner of Ireland where their father's family has lived for many generations:

> What happened to our immediate forbears and affected us profoundly is what usually happens only to people who have left their native place of birth, and met and married someone from different stock and background. Each new partner then acquires the preoccupations, priorities, memories, the new

ways of family of the other. In the pooling of these they make for themselves in the new place a new life, fueled by a new energy, and thus give themselves a different future. But the making of the new blood-line and that different future has been accompanied by the febrile, disruptive shock of leaving home, of pulling up old roots.

(*All of Us There*, 11–12)

At this point the metaphors are perhaps the most familiar ones for discussing family background: even though her mother and grandmother came from other parts of Ireland, her family was *deeply rooted* in the *soil* of a particular town. A family is like a plant or tree, and the place is like the earth. We are so used to this kind of metaphorical language that we think of it as being quite literal, as when we talk of family trees and roots. Family relations, relations of people to place, and relations among generations can be complicated and difficult to explain. Here they are given the power of familiar, concrete experience. We can see them as roots clinging to the earth, as plants extending above the earth.

"But," Devlin goes on to say, "something else"—something other than relocation—"was disturbing those roots." That something was the twentieth century, which arrived 50 years late in this remote place. To represent the change Devlin appropriately changes the metaphor. The twentieth century "was encircling our community, about to invade it, weapons and barter goods at the ready: trinkets for the natives, electricity, wireless and television and, most dazzling of all, Social Security" (12). Here the metaphor is military and colonial; the century is personified as an army, the community as natives to be subdued by arms and pacified with trinkets. To describe the effect of this invasion Devlin again changes the metaphor:

> We grew up in that moment between the death throes of the oldest kind of social security and the beginnings of a new dispensation, living in a left-over place operating on a time-scale of its own, with a way of life that still clung softly to the earth, nourishing it and being nourished by it like the fleece on a sheep. (12)

The "oldest kind of social security" is families taking care of their own members, and friends taking care of each other, the kind of caretaking that flourishes in isolated agricultural villages. Devlin's particular concern here is the carryover from the old way of life, the pocket of the old existing within the new, which she likens to the fleece of a sheep. Notice that she begins the comparison by using a term from the earlier one, *nourishment*. The fleece is like a plant; it draws nourishment from the earth, and even nourishes in return.

In the next paragraph, Devlin gives this metaphor a quite amazing twist:

> When fleece is cut from the sheep and collected at nightfall, the fleeces are still live and warm. If the summer night is cold after a hot day, a mist like the haze on the Lough clouds the wool and the cooling fleeces stir slightly all

> night through. In an old wool-room you could hear the fleeces stirring—a
> faint sound like soft breathing. Our generation in Ardboe were like fleeces
> cut from the last of the flock. (12)

Even though cut, the fleece seems to move and breathe. The fleece is a
whole generation of deeply rooted people and a way of life, living on as if
still attached but with a sure end in front of them.

Notice, too, that the metaphor carries considerable emotional
weight, partially because it is at the end of a series. The reader is prepared
to engage it because of having been led through a series of metaphors,
asked to think creatively, and invited to participate. This generation still
lives, but the old ties have been severed. If readers merely let themselves
follow the images, they will experience that emotion of loss, though it is
never stated as an emotion. And this, too, is one of the powers of
metaphor. It is often closer to feeling than the words we use to express
emotion directly, words of sadness or loss.

✎ **Writing**   Write about a moment of emotional intensity that you have
witnessed or experienced; try to use several metaphors that will economically convey your feeling(s) to your reader or listener. You may want to
do what Devlin has done and draw on your experience of personal or
family relations.

Looking for Metaphors

Devlin's figures of speech originated in careful observation and were developed in a patient willingness to listen to her own inner voices, to trust
her own inner vision. It is important to see that metaphorical thinking is
a common and natural if not always observed part of our speech, language, and thought, and at the same time a different way of thinking
from what usually goes by that name, something that may well involve a
different part of the mind from that which we use in sequential, analytical thinking. Metaphorical thinking is sideways thinking, moving from
one area of thought to another, from family and generational thinking,
for example, to the fleece of a sheep. Its essence is very simple: you begin
by thinking what you want to say about your subject: then, if you want to
move to metaphor, see if you can substitute the thing it is like for the
thing itself. (Sometimes you'll find that the metaphor comes first.) Deflection always plays a part in metaphor, as we talk about one thing by
experiencing another; but it is not always obvious deflection since, if the
metaphor works, we see the subject in terms of the image to which it is
implicitly compared.

Although different people draw on their own inner images in different ways, our view is that metaphors are in fact within all of us, within
our instinctive ways of understanding the world. Whatever we think of

our natural gift for making metaphors, the ability to think metaphorically is well worth cultivating, for it provides roads into ourselves and bridges between ourselves and others. Thinking metaphorically provides a common ground between writer and reader. Again, the story of Lincoln and Davis instructs us. Lincoln did it instinctively; he was able to find a brilliant way of making complex ideas of government available to people by drawing on the things he knew particularly well and shared with most of them: common labor, nature, the seasons, animals. Turn first to what you know well—it might be horseback riding, cooking, mountain climbing, computers, sailing, basketball, or almost anything. Try explaining other topics in terms of those areas of direct experience.

A good place to begin looking for similes and metaphors, then, is in your own mind and memory and experience. Look very carefully at what you are actually thinking and feeling. Our minds are full not only of ideas and stories but also of pictures and sounds and smells. Almost inevitably each of us associates certain ideas with certain sensory experiences. Let those personal associations develop. Trust the imaging part of your mind.

Other Kinds of Figurative Language

Metaphorical language is not the only kind of figurative language; you can also use other kinds of figurative language, which have been cataloged with minute and painstaking thoroughness by rhetoricians over the centuries, to reach out to your reader. Here we will mention only a few kinds that are particularly related to this book.

One kind we have already referred to is called *metonymy*; a major subtype of it is called *synecdoche*. Metonymy means talking about something by talking about an associated entity or quality, which is why your eyes can be bigger than your stomach. A London Cockney was asked about a respiratory illness Winston Churchill was suffering from on the Riviera. "Get 'im back to the fog an' 'e'll be alright," the Cockney said. "Fog" here is Cockney slang for London (and there is of course some irony in thinking that London's thick, then heavily polluted, smog was the best cure for bronchitis; but he was also saying that being home has curative powers, whatever the conditions). "The Red and the Black," as representations for military and religious life, is metonymy, as are "according to the White House, Baghdad has been delaying its compliance" and "I have read all of Shakespeare," meaning all of his works. (Think of how many products we identify by place of origin: china, hamburgers, frankfurters, madras, jodhpurs, ottomans, muslin, and so on. These too are metonymies.) Synecdoche is closely related. It substitutes the part for the whole, as in "Give me a hand" or "50 head of cattle" or "nice wheels," meaning "I like your car." Material can stand for product, as when we call clothes "threads" or a football "the pigskin." When we use a genus or subset to represent a species or set (or vice versa), we are also using synecdoche (that is how "metaphor" gets to stand for "figurative language"). An extraordinary synecdoche that gives writers a lot of trouble is the one by which "man" has come to stand for "human" and "he" for "a person whose sex has not been specified." That is, the part chosen to stand for the whole reveals a great deal about what we assume to be the dominant or identifying characteristic.

Without saying so, we were often talking about operations like synecdoche and metonymy when we discussed the use of details in the first section. Inevitably, writers focus on certain details that represent something broader than themselves or look for details that represent the whole as they wish the reader to see it. McFeely's use of Grant's migraine was not idle: he was asking us to look at Grant, as well as war, in a particularly human way, as being full of excruciating pain. Zinsser's house, with its innumerable porches, stood for privilege and secure childhood in a similar way.

Irony and exaggeration are other kinds of figurative language. In irony, we say something in such a way or in such a context that we prompt the hearer to reverse the meaning. We say to a friend, "Mary says she'll call you," and the friend says, "Sure." The slightest elevation of the eyebrow, nod of the head, or exaggeration of tone cues us to read "Sure" as "Totally doubtful." Through irony, a statement can mean the opposite of itself. Note that irony particularly involves a bond of awareness between writer and reader and speaker and listener: you have to catch the cues to be able to understand the meaning; the writer offers the reader a chance to participate in a sly or hidden meaning that others, lacking awareness of the cues, will miss.

But this kind of bond occurs in all forms of figurative language. The five kinds of figures of speech we have been talking about form a kind of spectrum. In synecdoche, a part of x represents all of x. In metonymy, something associated with x represents x. In simile, something other than x is likened to x. In metaphor, something other than x is substituted for x. And in irony, x stands for the inversion of itself, for y. Irony and metaphor, the two with which we are likely to be most familiar, are also the most difficult and the riskiest; yet they also have the greatest potential for bringing you and your reader closer since they clearly depend on the fact that your readers will "get it"—will know that you and they are on common ground.

CHAPTER 2

Orienting the Reader

Details and metaphors offer readers a way into a writer's mind and meaning, but they are momentary connections. This chapter is about the more sustained kinds of connection that every writer establishes with the reader at the beginning of a text. It may be helpful to think of the bond between writer and reader at the opening of a text as being like a bridge the writer builds out of words. The purpose of the bridge is to offer a shared platform from which both writer and reader can look at the topic at hand.

The goal of all writing is communication, a word derived from the Latin root *communis*, meaning "common." To communicate is for reader and writer to aspire, at least for the moments of reading, to common perceptions, common understanding, common thoughts. Almost everything we talk about in this book is meant to foster those commonalities. In this chapter we focus on three particular ways to bridge the gaps between yourself and your readers as you begin writing: using anecdotes, establishing mental settings, and defining perspectives. These are by no means the only ways of achieving commonality, but they are three important topics every writer should consider in constructing the opening of a text.

1 TELLING STORIES

A metaphor is a way of putting an idea into concrete form by creating an image in your reader's mind. A metaphor is a peg to hang your idea on. Whereas detail stands on its own, evoking a brief, vivid impression, a metaphor invites the reader to extend an experience into an idea. An anecdote, a short narrative, or a story takes the elements of detail and of metaphor one step further, allowing readers to see ideas in time and space. Originally, *anecdote* meant "unpublished," something that might not get into an official account or authorized biography. The word suggests brevity, informality, irreverence—but also revelation and interest.

Many writers and speakers use anecdotes to catch attention. As the art critic E. H. Gombrich says, speaking of the little stories that tour guides tell travelers in museums, "The mind soon threatens to become blank unless it is given something to play with—a story, an anecdote, a bit of gossip or background information" (*Norm and Form*, 65). Stephen Hawking, an astrophysicist and mathematician, begins his book *A Brief History of Time* as follows:

> A well-known scientist (some say it was Bertrand Russell) once gave a public lecture on astronomy. He described how the earth orbits around the sun and how the sun, in turn, orbits around the center of a vast collection of stars called our galaxy. At the end of the lecture, a little old lady at the back of the room got up and said: "What you have told us is rubbish. The world is really a flat plate supported on the back of a giant tortoise." The scientist gave a superior smile before replying, "What is the tortoise standing on?" "You're very clever, young man, very clever," said the old lady. "But it's turtles all the way down!"
>
> Most people would find the picture of our universe as an infinite tower of tortoises rather ridiculous, but why do we think we know better? (1)

The story is not original and does not play any further role in the book, but it makes an effective opening. It uses humor to put the reader who is facing esoteric subjects at ease, and it makes us feel that the writer is someone who can talk to us directly and understands our ignorance and our anxiety—even shares them.

The force of well-chosen anecdotes and illustrations is often such that we feel we may know all about a subject from a single instance, that the story is so well selected and so aptly told that it seems to contain all truth about the matter at hand. This is so partly because anecdotes often come to us as first-hand experience to illustrate a point in an abstract argument. For example, here is a William Safire column that illustrates its main point by recalling a personal experience. Safire begins by clearly stating the premise of the column, passing easily from the general to the specific as an illustration, and then passing from the illustration to the wider argument of the column—the then recent Supreme Court decision about the constitutionality of "flag burning":

> The political exploitability of the flag—as a symbol to stir emotions of fierce patriotism and profound resentment—was brought home to me on a balmy summer's day in Indianapolis in 1968.
>
> Richard Nixon was reading an insert into his stump speech that I had suggested to underscore the need for new leadership. The rhetorical device was in three lines beginning: "Under new leadership," building up to a sure-fire applause line about respect for the Presidency.
>
> The second line, intended only as a bridge toward the applause line, read: "Under new leadership, no tin horn dictator is going to make a doormat out of the American flag." The candidate delivered those words and started the next line when the audience interrupted with a roar. Mr. Nixon stopped, looked around in some surprise, then nodded to his campaign aides: that hot-button line instantly became a permanent part of the stump speech, to be delivered hundreds of times—always to approving roars from the crowd, and to eye-rolling from the cynics of the press. On

Election Day, an irreverent colleague sent me the ultimate accolade: a do-it-yourself diplomacy package containing a large doormat and an American flag.

Marinated in that milieu, I can understand the glee with which some political operatives greeted the Supreme Court's reaffirmation of freedom of speech to the extent of flag-burning. What a natural—an amendment pitting the patriotic defenders of our values (80 percent poll support!) against the handful of flag-burners and the libertarian goo-goo defenders.

("Fourth of July Oration")

Safire goes on to argue in the rest of the column against such an amendment, basing his position on three principles: "Never touch the Bill of Rights," "Do not corrupt patriotism by mixing it with religion," and "Do not confuse symbol with reality." Safire's use of anecdote here is a bridge from the very general point to a related but more narrowly defined issue. In effect he uses the anecdote to bring personal experience into the world of the column—as a way of attesting to the "real-life" truth of the general principles and observations he will be discussing. (In this case, he seems to be saying, these political speeches about flag-waving originated with me, so if I'm against this amendment, you should listen to me.) Anecdote validates and authenticates; it offers personal witness. Note that Safire's argument gains no validity per se by his having been there when Richard Nixon discovered the political volatility of the flag-burning issue nor from having written a speech that incidentally helped get it started. But it seems to.

At perhaps a less complex level, readers simply like to know where in a person's experience an idea has come from, in what personal circumstances the main subject of attention originated. Here is the opening of a story about what turned into an important discovery about a drug:

At the police reserve academy in Napa, California, my teachers drummed into me and my classmates that there's no such thing as a "routine" traffic stop; a silver bullet with our name on it could be waiting for us every time we pulled over a car.

I've learned that reporting is no different. But the silver bullet in what began as a routine flu story turned out to be a Pulitzer Prize in specialized reporting.

More importantly, the series of articles linking a rare blood disorder with a supposedly benign dietary supplement may even have saved a few lives.

The story had an innocuous enough beginning. My editors at *Journal North*—a zoned edition put out by *The Albuquerque Journal's* Santa Fe bureau, where I work—had been swapping stories with some stringers during a meeting about the upcoming Christmas insert.

One of the stringers mentioned that he knew of several people who were suffering particularly unusual symptoms in what was already an unusual strain of flu. He also thought at least two of them may have been taking L-Tryptophan, a synthetic form of one of 22 essential amino acids that form the building blocks of protein.

Tim Coder, managing editor of *Journal North*, dropped by my desk after the meeting, gave me a quick rundown of what the stringer had told him and said, "Check it out."

(Tamar Stieber, "L-Tryptophan—A Medical Puzzle," 453)

The brief anecdote about the police academy, which presents in personalized form the idea that routine work can become important, either for good or for ill, is followed by a second story, of the reporter's coming across the idea that led to her important discovery. We know where the story started, and that knowledge makes the story more human. It is not a device that is appropriate for all occasions and purposes, but it is useful as a way of establishing contact with your readers, showing them how your interest in the subject began.

Your own experience, then, can serve as a bridge to your readers, suggesting that what you're saying is not a detached set of thoughts but something that happened to a real person.

✎ **Writing**   Find something you or someone else has written previously, something whose opening perhaps needs to be enlivened. Look for an anecdote to serve as an entry to the story. If one doesn't readily come to mind, think of someone else's. For example, think about family or other group occasions, perhaps Thanksgivings or reunions or regular dinners, at which stories are told.

Finding the Typical in the Personal

Anna Quindlen, a writer whose observations on life in America nearly always begin with a brief anecdote from her own experience, is careful always to underscore the fact that the anecdote and the experience it recounts are valuable not because they are unique to her life but because they are typical of life at the end of the twentieth century in America. She began a column on April 28, 1988, about the constraining artifices that govern our lives in general, and the relations between men and women in particular, with the following anecdote:

At dusk the deer come down the hillside like bridesmaids, stately in their single file, their eyes straight ahead, their path sure. From the crest of the mountain they cut a diagonal to just above the barn, then disappear into the stand of pines near the center of a field of high grass. Each night for a month, they do this at exactly five minutes to 5, the sky to one side of them turning from hot pink to ashes of roses as they descend. Now, they are nowhere to be seen.

This was my favorite part of the weekend, the parade of the deer, and I have spent some time trying to understand why it came to an end, whether we despoiled the hillside with scent of humans or dogs or talked too loudly as we watched them from the window. Perhaps there is a reason, but I suspect that all of this was beyond our control; that when they paraded down the mountain in January, the deer were doing it instinctively, and when they stopped, the same was true. They were doing what comes naturally, just as certain birds arrive at the feeder in the morning and others won't eat until lunchtime rolls around.

This is what I like most about wild animals: that dumb instinct, that sense of natural behavior that human beings in the latter half of the 20th century have effectively and relentlessly obliterated from their lives.

("Life in the 30s")

Like Safire, Quindlen uses the anecdote to underscore the personal experience that gives rise to her need to write, that creates the urge to communicate the personal experience to a wider public. But more than that, you can see in the way she describes the deer that her language pays respect to what the deer are and to what they represent within the context of the column; she uses language that is quiet, dignified, and somewhat more elevated than the lively and humorous twists her style adopts later.

Her anecdote here is all the more remarkable because it is not at first obviously related to what follows. It's only after you read the whole column that you see that she has traced her thinking for you, sharing with the reader the gaps and jumps that characterize a lot of the associations we make between observed or lived experience and the sense—the theory or significance—we make of it all:

It occurs to me sometimes that while we once thought, romantically, that the entry of significant numbers of women into power breakfasts would put a crimp in this manipulative Machiavellian style [of planning every move], quite the opposite has turned out to be true. Since women feel outnumbered everywhere but on nursing staffs and in convents, many feel obliged to jump into this nonsense feet first. If a man tries to work against it, he is considered a maverick. But a woman who won't play ball is usually assumed to be someone who throws like a girl.

Quindlen's anecdote seems at first glance remote from what follows in the article: on the one hand, the deer, stately, instinctive, inscrutable; on the other hand, humans, comic, artificial, and often all too transparent in their motives. The anecdote represents being close to instinctive, natural, even impulsive behavior; the rest of the column is an argumentative, at times analytical, commentary that tries to explain why we have gotten so far away from what the deer represent. In this case, then, the anecdote is not simply a quick story to make an abstract point more palatable by adding humor or human interest. Rather, it conveys a way of living and perceiving that the rest of the article suggests is vanishing.

The trick is not to make up a good story for the occasion but to be alert to the connections between your experiences, to events and ideas that can be joined in narrative. Too often composition courses deflect or minimize this natural gift. Recognized and cultivated, the ability to use narrative, to tell the illustrative anecdote, can be a powerful tool to bond reader and writer. Start to look for stories that naturally associate themselves with your ideas. Try deliberately to correlate lived experience, events, and people with abstract thought. Move back and forth between material things and intellectual things, thinking of one in terms of the other. Remember, you can use a story as a way of getting started in writing, even if you don't include the story in the final draft.

✎ **Writing**   Make a list of topics about which you would like to deliver your opinion—say, five of them. As you are thinking about what you want to say, think about an occasion when your interest in the topic has been whetted or your opinion shaped by something you saw, heard, read, or did. Construct the anecdote. Write down the story.

Anecdote as Narrative Metaphor

In the Quindlen column, the anecdote is richly involving, and the rest of the article is a commentary on what is learned through the anecdote. In the example that follows, the anecdote is the whole story, and we can see how writers sometimes can make their points only through anecdotes.

> Here in the darkroom faces take form under red light. For 30 long seconds there is nothing. Then slowly the gentle rocking of fluid over paper brings a sharpening of lines, shadows, shapes. My brother Jim stands dressed in gray beside his lady in white on the chapel steps. I try again. Find them frozen in step down the aisle. Now posed with parents.
>
> In this darkroom I print the photographs of my brother's wedding—my gift to him and his bride. On a cord stretched across the room my family hangs drying from clothespins. I tone their images, increasing contrast, cropping distraction, enlarging the scenes that please me most. Here I can pretend to be the master of memory.
>
> But the photos finally disappoint. I find only the expected pictures I have seen before in my parents' album; pictures that surely appear in everyone's album. Perhaps only years from now will they become dusted with the mystique of age like the photos I now treasure most, photos of ordinary moments from a time when we were closer. I try to picture my brother's children and their children lifting the album from some trunk, and I wonder how many generations will flip through the pages before somebody questions: "Who are they?"
>
> I make new prints. They float one upon the other, rinsing in water. I search in vain for a photo I know is not here, but is one I want most to give and to keep. It was after breakfast at the inn, Jim was scrambling about the bedroom, searching for cuff links, fretting about the first waltz he would have to lead. We had not danced a waltz since sixth-grade lessons after school in the gymnasium. He moved a towel aside from the floor and took my hand, put an arm around my back. In stocking feet we shuffled awkwardly to a mumbled, "one, two three . . . " remembering as we went.
>
> It was the only moment we shared, just we two, before the wedding. For the rest of the day I fiddled with *f*-stops and lenses, trying to capture moments that seemed strangely distant. When I clicked the shutter and froze Jim and his bride on the chapel steps, I felt as removed as a passenger in a car

driving by. My brother drew the attention and was drawn in by it. It was his day. And these are his photos; I appear in none of them.

I develop prints for hours without rest, keeping watch for what no chemical can sharpen onto paper, looking for what I already know will not be found here. Only in my memory can I focus on that instant when a big brother and his little sister danced once more.

(Christine Schultz, "A Sister's Gift," 144)

Schultz never fully explains to the reader the "message" of her essay. She ends with a reference to another anecdote, a story of how her relationship to her brother, once so close, had entered a new dimension in which she was observer-creator. If she hadn't lived the relationship, hadn't documented it in photographs, it would never exist as it now does, a matter between them and a public record preserved for posterity through images. Yet at the same time, emotionally she finds herself to be, like the photographer, on the margins, a participant-observer who is not really in the picture even though she creates it.

The opening anecdote (in paragraphs 1 and 2) establishes this idea through specific, vivid details: "The gentle rocking of fluid over paper"; "Jim stands dressed in gray"; "on a cord stretched across the room my family hangs drying from clothespins." And through metaphor she creates the photographer as puppet-master, or director: "I tone their images, increasing contrast, cropping distraction." So, the story is about photography, about relationships between family members, about memory. Perhaps more than anything else, the story embodies a particular feeling, a tenderness between brother and sister that goes back to their childhood and that has become embodied in the awkward dance in the hotel room, something memory can keep but photographs cannot capture. Explanation is sparse; details and moments carry the weight of meaning.

What do all these writers' uses of anecdote have in common? More to the point, how can any of this analytic description of what they do help you to adopt their techniques? First, each writer, at the outset of his or her attempt to describe complex emotion, a touchy political topic, or the web of ideas, impressions, and feelings that creates the fabric of any experience, has recognized the value of the story as a means of enlisting the reader's interest, sympathy, and participation. There is something about stories simply told without elaborate interpretation that stays in the readers' minds, that makes them read on, and that comes back after the book or magazine or newspaper is closed. Second, these writers do not explicate the anecdotes they use; all let the story stand as a compact, complete unit within the larger article. The symbolism is apparent if the writer has been able to find a proportional anecdote—that is, tell a story that fits the points and the shape of the writing to come. The writers trust their readers in the way that you trust friends who are in tune with you, even when, as in these cases, they do not know specifically who their readers are. Third, the writers also trust their own experiences to yield their stories. Draw on your own first-hand experience, which you almost automatically put into story form, and on your experience of storytellers, whom you have undoubtedly met.

✎ **Writing**   Write an essay that is all anecdote, using the anecdote as an extended narrative metaphor. In effect, talk about a subject by telling a story. Again, feel free to draw on other people's stories. The important thing is to let the story carry the weight of what you want to say.

2   ESTABLISHING SITES

Architects talk about "siting" a building, choosing the precisely appropriate spot for it and then designing the building so that it "sits" properly on that spot, almost, in some styles of architecture, so that it seems to be rooted in the ground. Writers have analogous techniques. They find ways of giving readers a sense of being located in a place where they can understand what the writer has to tell them. We call this establishing the mental site of your text. It is the second technique we want to discuss.

One of the most basic aspects of this technique is siting in a quite literal sense, letting the reader know where in time and space to locate what you are writing about. As examples of literal siting here are some openings from articles in regional magazines:

> Wet October snow chased Isaias Martinez and several other hunters into the warmth of the Los Pastores general store near Tierra Amarilla. Peering tentatively through the old storefront windows, the group seemed undecided on whether to return to the hunt or to linger by the hot wood stove.
> (Camille Flores, "Tierra Amarilla," 26)

> Silver City, the mining town where Billy the Kid once worked as a waiter, is looking for people who don't need jobs.
> (Frank Zoretich, "Silver City: Mining Its Historic Past," 58)

> Consider Salem, Massachusetts: a pretty place steeped in colonial charm, with a lush village green, historic harbor, prestigious museums such as the Essex Institute and the Peabody, a state college, and the nation's first urban National Park site.
> ("Bewitched, Bothered . . . and Bewitched," 10)

> We stopped in the middle of the road, straddling our bikes, and for a few moments cursed what we had just been praising. The warmth became heat. The solitude became isolation. It was lunchtime and we were hungry and lost on Prudence Island, in Narragansett Bay.
> (Pamela Petro, "The Ripe Age of an Island," 68)

It will be apparent at once what these writers are doing. They give you a clear sense of where you are, simply by naming the location. As with any use of details, the process is more selective than it might appear. There are many details that the authors did *not* give you, and already, in the opening sentences of these articles, the writers have begun the process of focusing your attention on information that will advance the attitude and theme they are developing. But at the outset, what is striking and useful is that the writers give you a firm sense of being located, a sense that you know where you are.

Note that the degree of explicitness will vary greatly according to what writers can assume about their readers. Writing for *New England Monthly* or *New Mexico*, as these writers all were, you already know a great deal about your potential readers; even the titles of the magazines offer readers common ground with writers; the titles of the essays will (and probably should) take you further.

Sometimes you will find that your readers need only a few light brush strokes to know where you want them to be because you and they already share a great deal of common ground. In other words, to say that carefully situating readers is important is not to say that long, laborious opening descriptions will usually be effective or necessary. Looking back at the examples we quote, you can see that the writers work economically, giving only the information needed to provide a sense of where they are, even while giving readers a sense that there is quite a lot of detail.

In situating your readers you need to ask three questions: Who are my readers? Where do I want them to be? What in particular and how much do I have to tell them to put them there? These are not always questions you can answer as you start your essay, and many writers will make substantial changes in their openings after they have finished saying what they want to say. Some writers will begin with a quite elaborate definition of their site, so that they feel themselves to be in the right place, but then return to the opening after they have finished and lop off most of what they started with, to get it down to the few hints that their readers need.

Two words of caution. First, it's important for a writer consciously and deliberately to develop techniques of siting because the reader will expect and look for hints about where what you say is happening. We would go so far as to say that it is a conventional expectation of all readers that the writer will sketch out location for them. If you don't do it, the reader will try to. The result may be that your reader literally misplaces your meaning.

Second, this process of siting a reader is often particularly difficult if you are a student who is writing a class assignment. Your reader, if a teacher, may well be serving a double role, that of the general reader and that of the teacher who formulated the assignment. To be candid, some of them may be a bit foggy about which of these roles they are playing. So, you may make a quite carefully situated opening in a paper for such a teacher only to be told that it was unnecessary because you could assume that your readers knew where they were; and the opposite may happen. This only illustrates the point that you need to define quite carefully who your readers are. As one more general piece of advice, however, we would emphasize the point that you cannot assume that your readers will immediately understand where they are; a few economical hints about site at the outset will often help the reader and rarely hurt. In the end, remember that you are in control of your essay, and ask, What do I want my readers to see? Where do I want my readers to be mentally and imaginatively as they read what I have to say?

A good way to approach this is by drawing on the suggestions we made in the last chapter about use of detail. Visualize the place you want to describe; then think about which few details convey the essence you have felt.

✎ **Writing**   Write about a public debate or controversy in terms of a place associated with it. For example, think about an argument that took place in your hometown or at your school or business. As you think about the issue in question, focus first on its locale—for example, a place where some of the debate has occurred or a scene that is central to the argument—and then move on to the debate itself. If you are writing about waste disposal, for example, describe the dump or the recycling center and perhaps the location of the public forum or a coffee shop where the issue is being debated. Use the sites of the issue to give your reader a full sense of the places in which it occurs; see if you can also find elements in the physical scene that will underscore particular aspects of the issue. You may decide to return to the scene periodically to continue to give readers a sense of where it's happening.

Mental Landscapes

What happens when the world the writer is creating is not tied to geography, to physical time and place, but to an idea or to the spirit of a particular historical period? A writer can also locate a reader in an intellectual milieu, as well as in a literal place. Consider the following opening, an example of siting in an era:

> I applied to college barely a year after the '68 student uprisings. It was a difficult time for my parents. I was opposed to the war in Vietnam in an uninformed way, and my parents were not opposed to it, with a kind of reflexive patriotism that most adults still had then.
>
> (Anna Quindlen, "Life in the 30s")

Quindlen gives her readers a sense of the atmosphere of a particular period, the late 1960s. The heart of her essay is a contrast between this original "site" and the present, a contrast between competing value systems, between different emotional outlooks. She sites the reader by briefly sketching the mood ("It was a difficult time") and the dominant issue of the period ("the war in Vietnam"). For those who lived through that period, the siting is complete there. For those who did not know or did not live through it, she provides a further bit of elaboration: "It's been 20 years since that unforgettable spring when all hell broke loose at Columbia." All of this is in preparation for her fundamental point, a criticism of the comparatively trivial anxieties of the late 1980s:

> In those days, my parents were worried about students having book-burning parties in professors' offices. Today, I'm more concerned about finding a school for my kids that won't turn them into avaricious little twits who believe that true hardship consists of wearing a shirt without an alligator on the front.

Recalling the turmoil of the 1960s—siting the reader in that historical landscape—allows her to make the point about the 1980s emphatically.

Sometimes, though, a writer must invite the reader into a mental landscape, one that is full of abstract ideas rather than of people and social issues. You've probably run into this situation if you've written many academic papers in the arts or social sciences. In such cases actual personalities and settings may be irrelevant. The writer is faced with the problem of creating a bridge for the reader out of ideas. Here's an excellent example of an interpretive opening written by the poet Adrienne Rich about her development as a writer:

> Ibsen's *When We Dead Awaken* is a play about the use that the male artist and thinker—in the process of creating culture as we know it—has made of women, in his life and in his work; and about a woman's slow struggling awakening to the use to which her life has been put.
>
> ("When We Dead Awaken: Writing As Re-Vision," 34)

You will notice that in this opening Rich establishes the common ground reader and writer will share as a particular viewpoint on Ibsen's play. She says the play is "about the use that the male artist and thinker . . . has made of women." Other readers of the play might disagree, might have their own interpretations. That is possible, but not within the world of the text Rich is writing. Within that world the writer and the reader begin from the common ground of this interpretation. The implicit promise here is that the rest of the text will develop from this point.

As a final illustration of a particularly imaginative way a writer finds to bring the reader into the world of a text devoted to explaining an abstract idea, we offer an example from the opening of a book about the Middle Ages, *Chaucer and Pagan Antiquity*, by Alistair Minnis. Minnis begins his book with a quotation that's halfway to being an anecdote:

> "The pagans are wrong and the Christians are right!", exclaims the hero of the late eleventh century *Chanson de Roland*. By contrast, in the *Roman de la Rose* (c. 1277) Jean de Meun assures his audience that "It is good to believe the pagans, for we may gain great benefit from their sayings". By Jean's time the pagans had attained a considerable degree of respect, even of popularity. Sometimes they were wrong, sometimes they were right, and often they were half-right, or right in a limited way. (1)

While Minnis is a serious scholar, he is also a lively writer who knows how to introduce both a subject and a method in his opening. The issue the book investigates is the quite abstract question of how medieval writers understood their classical heritage. The answer must be complex, fluctuating variously with time, place, and author. Moreover, it must be teased out of texts, inferred and reconstructed. Minnis brings the reader into the middle of things with a carefully chosen quotation from his material. The quotation imaginatively provides the bridge to the common ground the reader and writer will share as the thesis develops because it creates a sense of life and urgency through a person speaking. Like most of the other examples of siting we have discussed, this opening siting of the reader in the world of the problem the writer is addressing is specific and lively. He could have begun by saying something to the effect that "throughout the Middle Ages the heritage of classical thought posed a dual challenge." If he had, he would have traded life and specificity for abstraction and tedium. The "remuddled" opening in the previous sentence sites the reader, too, but in a world heavy with impending boredom. In Minnis's opening a character from an eleventh-century *chanson* speaks with a boisterous absolutism that we might find in the world today, and Minnis uses that direct approach to bring the reader to the world of his material.

✎ **Writing**   In the course of your regular reading over several days, look for examples of how writers use physical siting and siting in a mental landscape to help orient the reader and to help them explain what they mean. Notice where these sitings occur in what you're reading—at the beginning or elsewhere. Think about how you respond to them and why. Try to characterize these sitings, to identify the techniques the authors used.

   After you've thought about this for a while, try the following. Place a character or an event in a physical or mental context that orients the reader to your point of view and to your subject. See how economically you can achieve the siting, so that your readers sense where you want to put them without elaborate description.

Common Social Ground

We've talked about common ground in a physical sense, in terms of time and place, and as something that exists in the world of ideas as well. In both cases, you are letting your readers know where they are, providing a place, literal or metaphorical, from which to view and hear what you have to say. The following passage shows how a writer, in this case Deborah Tannen, creates what we call a common social ground. She uses an unusual siting device, one that from the perspective of academic writing may be suspect. But we think that her technique is one that many writers will feel comfortable with, particularly if they are writing about their personal experiences:

> You know the feeling: You meet someone for the first time, and it's as if you've known each other all your lives. Everything goes smoothly. You know just what she means; she knows just what you mean. You laugh at the same time. Your sentences and hers have a perfect rhythm. You feel terrific; you're doing everything right. And you think she's terrific too.
>
> But you also know the other feeling: You meet someone, you try to be friendly, to make a good impression, but everything goes wrong. There are uncomfortable silences. You fish for topics. You bump into each other as you both start at once and then both stop. You start to say something interesting but he cuts you off. He starts saying something and never seems to finish. You try to lighten the mood and he looks as if you punched him in the stomach. He says what may be intended as a joke but is more rude than funny. Whatever you do to make things better makes them worse.
>
> (*That's Not What I Meant!* 3–4)

Tannen establishes common ground by her tone and her mode of direct address, by her simple vocabulary and phrasing, and by her reference to shared experience. We feel that we are immediately in conversation with her, almost as if we were in her living room. Tannen's first two words are perhaps more revolutionary than you would think: "You know." Most writers, particularly experts, want to say, *you* don't know; *I do*. Tannen, however, attributes knowledge to you and "sites" her opening in the readers' experience. To do that, she had to think of an opening topic that would allow her to do so. (Her subject, people's conversational habits, leads her in that direction.) But you can begin simply by imagining yourself in conversation with a friend or by writing an imaginary letter to a friend. Such an approach may change other things in your style and will subtly make your writing seem more accessible. Tannen creates a style in which she has not so much reached out to us as invited us in, made us feel that the world of her essay is a comfortable and welcoming place to be. Such a feeling suits her subject, the ways in which different conversational styles do or don't work. Tannen is an expert in her field of psycholinguistics and has at her disposal the specialized vocabulary of her field. Hers is, then, a conscious choice, designed for her particular purpose of writing about conversational styles in an accessible book.

In some cases, this mode would present an inappropriate common ground and would be received as false intimacy or a breach of professional etiquette. We will, in fact, in subsequent chapters, be discussing issues raised by passages like this in terms of both the presentation of the author in a text and the different expectations that specialized discourse raise. We will be arguing simply that a greater range of style is available than many writers think. At the moment, our point is that you can provide common ground for your reader not only by establishing a physical setting or indicating a reference point in the landscape of ideas but also by modifying your tone and mode of address.

✎ **Writing**   See how it feels to you as a writer to break the usual conventions and write directly, conversationally, to the reader about any subject of your choice—politics, social issues, or life as you have seen it lately. In your writing, try to use both *I* and *you*. (You'll notice that while Tannen doesn't use the pronoun *I*, it's clear that her personal opinion and experiences form the basis of everything she asserts.)

3   DEFINING PERSPECTIVES

As the writer has located the readers in the world of the text and established connections with them, he or she will also be letting readers know what the view will be—where their attention will be focused or how the subject will be presented. We refer to this process as framing, that is, the writer's signaling of what will be included and what will be excluded in the text. In siting we are interested in bringing the reader into the writer's world. In framing we are interested in the writer's definition of and approach to the topic. Whenever we write we commit ourselves—and invite our readers—to consider a carefully defined and relatively small issue, often part of a much larger topic.

Writers usually frame their ideas at the beginning of their texts, often at the time that they site the reader, so that they can help the reader understand the context in which they are writing. Good framing helps readers because they feel that the verbal space they are moving into is well defined and has recognizable limits; this in turn helps to reduce the amount of work the writer has to do by way of explanation. In other words, you will not feel obliged to consider the whole picture, nor can your readers accuse you of failing to consider x, y, and z when you have proclaimed by your framing that you will be considering only a, b, and c.

Some writers present their topics in such a way that their opening paragraphs function very much as a physical picture frame does. You may have had the experience of choosing a frame for a work of art you've just bought or one you want to have reframed. If you have ever done this, you know that in addition to defining what's included or excluded, the frame's relationship to the picture is really central to how the picture will look and how the whole thing will strike the viewer. The passage below is taken from William Howarth's *John McPhee Reader*. In it Howarth leads the reader through a series of views of McPhee in order to present McPhee as a certain kind of writer and to encourage the reader to see McPhee as he does. His beginning has framed McPhee for us by excluding much that might have been said and indicating what will be said:

> At his home in Princeton, New Jersey, John McPhee keeps a tidy collection of his books and magazine pieces. The volumes have a motley air, but they

stand as one entity, the collected works of a single author. In his office on Nassau Street is a similar gathering, not as complete but still unified. Across the street is Firestone Library, the great research center of Princeton University, McPhee's *alma mater*. Firestone does not gather McPhee's books on a single shelf. Most are in the main stacks, in sections designated by call numbers for Recreation, Historical Science, Military Science, Education, and English Literature. Others are in special areas, such as the Sporting Books Room, and in satellite libraries across the campus, like the one for Urban and Environmental Studies.

Volumes so scattered might as well be in the collection of Locked Books, since their arrangement discourages readers from seeing them as the product of one mind and craft. Yet if McPhee were a novelist, poet, or playwright, his books would all be on the same shelf, in the English Literature section. Why has this happened? Because no one has a proper name for his brand of factual writing. He writes about real people and events, but not as an everyday "journalist" or reporter. He packs an impressive bag of narrative tricks, yet everyone calls his work "non-fiction." This label is frustrating, for it says not what a book is but what it is *not*. Since "fiction" is presumably made up, imaginative, clever, and resourceful, a book of "non-fiction" must *not* be any of these things, perhaps not even a work of art. If the point seems a mere quibble over terms, try reversing the tables: are Faulkner's books on Mississippi "non-history" just because they are novels?

Since 1964 McPhee has repeatedly jarred these assumptions with his books, which have stretched the artistic dimensions of reportage. His work has a large variety of backgrounds—sports, food, drink, art, science, history, geography, education—and a strong element of narrative control. (vii)

Howarth intends the reader to view McPhee within the setting he has created, to see McPhee against a background that will highlight certain things about him. The attention Howarth devotes to the setting, to the difference between the neat and orderly arrangement of McPhee's own books and the Princeton library's scattered shelving of McPhee's writings, directs the reader's attention to the variety of McPhee's writing through the observation of how difficult it is to categorize it. Howarth's presentation of McPhee is framed by extensive discussion of one small but highly symbolic detail, the matter of how to arrange and store books in a library. He has worked this detail into a frame in which he places his fuller discussion. Moreover, his choice of this frame tells us a good deal about how he has defined and will approach his subject. Here Howarth signals that the immense topic of this writer's work will be approached by way of classification or, more precisely, the way of classifying either him or his books. The library is physical, concrete, and easily imagined. In this way it is a good metaphor for the abstract question at the heart of Howarth's writing: how does one classify McPhee, and what pigeonhole could accommodate his range of talent and subjects?

We know things not only by themselves but also in relationship to an environment. Therefore, as writers, we can give sharp definition to a topic by thinking carefully about the background and the relation of our subject to it. Instinctively you already know this; it is how you perceive. But you may need to sharpen your awareness of it by self-consciously looking at the relation between people or things and the frames within which you see them.

✎ **Writing**   Try describing someone you know well through his or her physical surroundings. In this process be careful to think about the proportional fit between your subject and your symbol. The point of this process is to realize that before you write, before you use this type of framing device, you have to do a great deal of conscious or perhaps unconscious thinking about what is necessary to your subject. This process underscores how important it is in prewriting to be analytic and observant, so that when you come to choose your words they will reflect what you understand as essential to your subject.

Creating Perspective

We have seen that in framing the writer excludes and selects; in this process of focusing a reader's attention the writer decides on something central to the topic, subordinating other elements within the frame. The two processes are virtually simultaneous. To frame is to focus attention. Excluding some things means that what's included receives special attention. Some writers, however, are so skilled at framing and focusing that they are quickly able to shift both, creating a series of contexts in which to understand the central point. Henry Louis Gates does this in the letter below by comparing a contemporary event to a famous historical event. This kind of comparison becomes a double image. Readers see and understand several main points framed in several different ways. It is as if they were seeing from several angles of vision at once. Gates uses this approach in a letter to the editor of the *New York Times* about the 2 Live Crew rock lyrics trial of 1990:

To the Editor:
    At the trial occasioned by the paperback publication of "Lady Chatterley's Lover" in Britain, the counsel for the crown posed a simple question to the jury: "Is this the sort of book you would wish your maidservants to read?"
    It's usually not expressed so boldly, but the notion that the "lower orders" are particularly susceptible to obscenity's baleful effects has proved remarkably persistent. And it's shared by most commentators on the 2 Live Crew controversy. Black youth are seen as dry kindling, ready to burst into fire with any stray spark. We saw the same assumption in last year's hand wringing over the Spike Lee movie "Do the Right Thing." It's the potent image of a mass of unthinking, animal-like black youth waiting to erupt into a frenzy of wilding or rioting, depending on the provocation.

That's presumably why there has not been such concern over hit songs like Madonna's "Hanky Panky" ("don't have to thank me/just spank me"). We trust her (mostly white) audience not to get any ideas. Is it any wonder, when the airwaves are saturated with sexist, even misogynistic songs, that we have singled out an album that has received virtually no air time at all?

Lyrics by 1930s blues singers like Lucille Bogan are as raunchy as anything in 2 Live Crew, certainly no more sexually enlightened. Then, as now, middle-class blacks and intellectuals were mortified. Today, some black stalwarts say if something is obscene, it isn't part of black culture. Conversely (this thinking goes), the claim that it is part of black culture is somehow exculpatory. Both implications have to be resisted. The sexism in street culture only reaffirms the need for forceful feminist critique.

Yet we should resist the temptation to imagine (as many commentators do) a causal relation between dirty rap and the enormous social ills affecting the black community. By this logic, we could solve the problems of the underclass by having home boys at the projects play Johnny Mathis on their ghetto blasters instead of Bel Biv Devoe. If only it were so.

There is no point in trying to whitewash a multifarious cultural heritage, casting it as a monolith of virtue. Like all cultures, black culture consists not only of the best that has been thought and said, but the worst as well.

Henry Louis Gates, Jr.
Durham, N.C., July 8, 1990

Gates frames his argument by inviting the reader to understand his point within a historical context. He begins anecdotally, recalling the much-publicized censorship trial of *Lady Chatterley's Lover*, a book famous during most of this century for its outright linking of sexual pleasure and class issues. The issue hidden within the counsel for the crown's question, he says, was not whether such a book might impel a maidservant to illicit sexual activity but that such activity as described in the book is dangerous because when upper-class women take lovers outside of their class, their action blurs class lines and threatens patriarchy. Lady Chatterley's lover is her husband's game warden and hence her social inferior. Had she chosen someone of her own class, the book might have been mildly titillating but hardly shocking by the standards of the time in England.

By opening as he does, Gates skillfully links sex and class issues and puts the discussion in 1990 of 2 Live Crew within a wider context, one that allows him to explore the class issues hidden in the attempt to censor as obscene the music of a mediocre group. Gates thus provides a moral, intellectual, and social context in which to frame and later to construct his argument. Notice how carefully he moves from period to period within twentieth-century culture to arrive at his conclusion—that all cultures, and by implication all cultural production, contain the potential for both the best and the worst that "has been thought and said."

Opening with the *cause célèbre* of *Lady Chatterley's Lover* gives Gates the springboard he needs to argue his point within a wider context than that of late twentieth-century, American popular music. The letter is very neatly framed, both at the beginning and at major points in his argument, and the frames really make a difference: they change the meaning of what he's looking at. What Gates does in the whole piece, in fact, is continually shift the reader's focus. Look at Madonna in this frame, he says; look at 2 Live Crew and Lucille Bogan from the angle of vision of middle-class blacks and intellectuals. In the final paragraph he puts the whole discussion in a framework of cultural relativism: cultures have good and bad in them. The net result is that reading the letter is an active experience for the reader; Gates has been quite careful to lead the reader through the argument and the shifting frames or contexts in which he examines his subject.

We can imagine Gates's process of thought as being something like this: "Many people are having an immediate and limited reaction to the 2 Live Crew controversy. I need a context within which this issue can be placed so that I can get my readers to see it in a different way. What case is like this? Oh, yes, the censorship case of *Lady Chatterley's Lover.* Many people will think of that case as one that not only broke down important barriers to artistic expression but also had social consequences. There are strong reasons why people cannot see 2 Live Crew in that manner, but if I let the D. H. Lawrence case serve as a kind of frame around the current one, perhaps some people will see it differently." In other words, the frame here is a kind of analogy. And we can see that it is not just a presentational device but essential to Gates's thinking because *Lady Chatterley's Lover,* far from being just a convenient frame, defines the argument Gates makes, defines the issues involved, and indicates his comparative, historical approach. Gates is successful because he has found a parallel example, a framing device that suits his argument in every particular—it's about art, it's about culture, it's about class and prejudice, and it's about sex. The fit is perfectly proportional.

Sharpen your awareness of this common technique. In the everyday writing around you, particularly on the op-ed pages of newspapers, you will find writers beginning with this sort of historical framing. An event, person, or idea is to be understood by reference to another person, event, or idea. Find several examples and analyze whether their framing devices fit their topics as well as Gates's does in the letter above. The fact is that framing devices are very powerful: they lead the reader into the text in the way the author wants. Once you're in the text, you are there on the author's terms. Be sure that the terms are both reasonable and true. Don't be lured by apparent correlations.

In framing an idea, then, you decide what to include and exclude; you define the issues you want to address. You can do this at the outset, as Howarth does, or continuously, as Gates does, constantly reexamining your topic as you define it with new frames. Learning how to frame an argument—what belongs in it, what can be dispensed with, and how to call on a contextual metaphor or analogy—is an important technique for all writers, especially for those who deal with complex and complicated issues. The right frame, the right presentation, can save extensive labor in explaining your ideas. In this case presentation is half the battle.

✎ **Writing**   Mastering Gates's technique is an important step in learning to situate an argument. It's a technique that most of you have probably used at one point or another, but it's worth practicing deliberately. Select a topic (political or historical subjects or literature might work most easily). Introduce your idea with a contextual analogy that both bears a recognizable resemblance to your topic and illustrates the point you want to make.

Impersonal and Personal Perspective

We begin the discussion of perspective with an example that you can read without being very conscious of its use as a definition. With perspective in mind, however, you will see that the passage is in fact about nothing else, though in an interestingly negative way:

> Americans transform every success and every failure in foreign affairs into a policy doctrine and a political cudgel. We refuse to rest until we possess one lens through which to view the world and one answer for all challenges. We are forever brushing off small but important lessons in the quest for great and single truths.
>
> Ours is a short and tumultuous history of taking largely unique events—the fall of Eastern Europe and China to Communism, the Korean War, the Cuban missile crisis and Vietnam—and elevating their purported lessons into policy dogmas, be they Truman Doctrines, Kennedy Corollaries or Vietnam Syndromes.
>
> Once enshrined, high priests wield these theologies like clubs to destroy their political adversaries. But at some point, they are blinded by their own convictions and commit blunders, which in turn, give rise to new dogmas and new blunders. We are the monotheists of world politics. Yet we keep abandoning one god for another with unholy frequency. Once again. . . .
>
> (Leslie Gelb, "Policy Monotheism")

What is Gelb's own point of view? We know two things about it. First, it is a critical one. He looks at the way other people—"Americans," he says rather generally—look at things and at the distortions their way of looking creates. He uses the word "ours" to suggest he is an American and must be counted among the group he's discussing, but in fact his vocabulary (notice his verbs and his modifiers: "We are forever brushing off"; "Yet we keep abandoning"; "unholy frequency") tells us that he observes and analyzes from a superior plane. Notice that his opening statement is not only declarative but also sweeping and assertive: "Americans transform every success and every failure." Here Gelb adopts the distancing perspective, the role of the analyzer of society. In fact his style in general is assertive and descriptive; he seems to be recording his observations. We know that he, like us, has lived this experience. He even makes a gesture at including himself within the group, but as we have said, it is a gesture more than a real inclusion. You may disagree with Gelb, but you will note that he is very direct about his perspective and consistent in announcing and in maintaining it. He sends no false signals to his reader. He proclaims his perspective and sustains it throughout the excerpt (and the larger editorial from which the excerpt comes).

We now want to look in some detail at a different way of establishing perspective, a way that is not necessarily better or worse, only different. Whereas Gelb's perspective was distant and impersonal, this one is personal and engaged. It comes from a speech given by Justice Clarence Thomas, presented as the commencement address at Savannah State College in Georgia:

> I grew up here in Savannah. I was born not far from here (in Pinpoint). I am a child of those marshes, a son of this soil. I am a descendant of the slaves whose labors made the dark soil of the South productive. I am the great-great-grandson of a freed slave, whose enslavement continued after my birth. I am the product of hatred and love—the hatred of the social and political structure which dominated the segregated, hate-filled city of my youth, and the love of some people—my mother, my grandparents, my neighbors and relatives—who said by their actions, "You can make it, but first you must endure."
>
> You can survive, but first you must endure. You can live, but first you must endure. You must endure the unfairness. You must endure the hatred. You must endure the bigotry. You must endure the segregation. You must endure the indignities.
>
> I stand before you as one who had the same beginning as yourselves—as one who has walked a little farther down the road, climbed a little higher up the mountain. I come back to you, who must now travel this road and climb this jagged, steep mountain that lies ahead. I return as a messenger—a front-runner, a scout. What lies ahead of you is even tougher than what is now behind you.
>
> ("Climb the Jagged Mountain")

In Thomas's powerful introduction he tells his audience not only who he is but also what that has meant to him. He uses a simple repetitive style, full of direct images. Constructions are repeated; key words—like "endure"—reappear in an almost chantlike manner. He finally identifies himself in a sharply defined role, that of front-runner or scout, someone who has gone out into potentially hostile territory and can now tell others, his audience, what he has seen. And he powerfully identifies himself with that audience "as one who had the same beginning as yourselves."

What does he see from this vantage point?

That mean, callous world out there is still very much filled with discrimination. It still holds out a different life for those who do not happen to be the right race or the right sex. It is a world in which the "haves" continue to reap more dividends than the "have-nots."

He goes on to talk in more detail about the social facts of this world that his audience of young, black college graduates will enter, but his vision is not merely a factual one. When we take account of Thomas's perspective, we also have to note his interpretation of what he sees, an interpretation that grows out of his experience:

In 1964 when I entered the seminary, I was the only black in my class and one of two in the school. A year later, I was the only one in the school. Not a day passed that I was not pricked by prejudice.

But I had an advantage over black students and kids today. I had never heard any excuses made. Nor had I seen my role models take comfort in excuses. The women who worked in those kitchens and waited on the bus knew it was prejudice which caused their plight, but that didn't stop them from working.

My grandfather knew why his business wasn't more successful, but that didn't stop him from getting up at 2 in the morning to carry ice, wood, and fuel oil.

This is the heart of his message to his young audience: "[I had not] seen my role models take comfort in excuses." Although he had a tough road to follow, he tells his young audience:

You all have a much tougher road. . . . Not only do you have to contend with the ever-present bigotry, you must do so with a recent tradition that almost requires you to wallow in excuses. You now have a popular national rhetoric which says that you can't learn because of racism, you can't raise the babies you make because of racism, you can't get up in the mornings because of racism. Unlike me, you must not only overcome the repressiveness of racism, you must also overcome the lure of excuses. You have twice the job I had.

Do not be lured by sirens and purveyors of misery who profit from constantly regurgitating all that is wrong with black Americans and blaming these problems on others. Do not succumb to this temptation of always blaming others.

Thomas, in fact, is taking what has been a rather controversial position on racial problems, opposing affirmative action programs and other "help" programs on the grounds that they lure people into blaming their problems on others rather than prompting them to work hard to overcome them. He advances his position here by carefully tracing his point of view in his own personal experience. That is the heart of his talk, and his argument and his perspective are almost identical.

Whereas Gelb establishes a perspective by stepping back and inviting us to look at an issue as at a panorama, Thomas invites us into his own world, grounds his point of view carefully in his own experience, and lets his argument emerge from within. Neither the panoramic nor the personal approach to perspective is superior; they simply have different uses and effects. You can readily imagine someone else approaching just the issues Thomas looks at from a detached, wide-angled perspective, and also being effective. What are the advantages of Thomas's approach? People's attitudes often do in fact spring from their own experiences. So, if someone carefully shows just how a particular attitude or argument emerges from something in his or her own experience, we can often appreciate seeing that connection drawn out. But note the hazard of that approach. A thin line lies between saying, "I appreciate your argument because I can see what has led to it" and dismissing your argument "because" I know that it is "merely" the product of your own experience. If someone tells us that she is against abortion because she was brought up as a Roman Catholic, we may appreciate and respect that experience but it probably won't convince us of her argument.

What Thomas has done, however, goes three steps beyond making the simple identification. First, in this case, he has looked for an area of commonality between himself and his primary auditors, the graduating class at Savannah State. (But many who do not share those experiences with Thomas and his audience will still find his argument persuasive.) Second, he has been detailed and thoughtful in illustrating how his views about self-help have evolved. He uses personal experience not as the source of an authoritative argument based on experience that he can claim as peculiarly his own but as a kind of example for his hearers: "I can trace exactly how my views evolved for you, and you can see that I have made thoughtful responses to what has happened to me." Third, he has been quite humble about his views. The position he establishes is an open one; he does not claim superiority for his experiences but creates the impression of a person who is willing to learn patiently from them.

In using this kind of personal perspective, then, you will want to devote considerable time to thinking through the way in which your experience has led to the particular view you espouse, using details, displaying your willingness to learn from your experience, and offering those experiences to your readers as a common ground. Notice that Thomas is an intelligent person who has given a great deal of thought to this particular issue; it is an issue that is central to his whole life. In short, he probably did not come to these views overnight.

✎ **Writing** Gelb's technique of establishing the writer as a distant, removed observer and commentator is one that you are undoubtedly familiar with from the pages of newspapers, news magazines, and a good deal of academic writing; so also is Thomas's of using his own experiences and person as a bridge to the reader. Find other examples of these techniques and examine them, asking whether they maintain a consistent perspective throughout. In short, how well do they work in telling the reader the writer's approach to the topic? After you've identified and analyzed several examples of both sorts, try writing a short paper on some political topic in which you establish, communicate, and maintain a distant perspective. Then rewrite the essay, using yourself and your experience to connect with the reader. As you write about the origin of your position, use the tools Thomas so clearly draws on and that we talked of in our first chapter—details, metaphors, and anecdotes. Does one of these approaches work better for you? Is one particularly well suited to the topic on which you are writing?

CHAPTER 3

Creating a Common World of Feeling

We have been talking about structural ways of establishing common ground between you and your readers, about establishing sites and points of view to give your readers a sense of where you are and how you are seeing things as you begin a text. Often, however, at least in our daily lives, our sense of connecting with other people occurs at the level of feeling. Writers know this: they use feeling to connect with readers, sometimes powerfully, sometimes subtly. At other times, the misplaced injection of feeling will have the opposite effect; it will scare off the reader. The reader will say, I don't want your feelings about the subject; I want your thoughts, your research, some facts. Building connections through feeling is, like most other tools of writing, not something a writer will always use or always use in the same way. Like certain spices in cooking, however, it can, if used properly, make all the difference. Sometimes, in fact, it lies at the very heart of the matter.

1   USING HUMOR

We begin with humor, which may not seem like a feeling at all. Oddly, however, medieval psychology attributed what we call feelings or emotions to bodily fluids and used the word *humor(s)*—which originally meant fluid, as in our current word *humid*—to describe the emotions. Our subject here is not what makes things funny or how you can become a humorist. Instead we will assume that, like pretty much everyone else in the world, you have your own sense of humor, your own sense of the ridiculous or laughable. (When we say that someone lacks a sense of humor, we usually mean that they lack *our* sense of humor.) We notice two somewhat paradoxical qualities of humor. First, it is communal. Someone has to "get" the joke. Second, it is rather highly individualized. There are distinctive national, regional, and ethnic forms of humor, and that is part of what makes it communal. There are also forms of humor that seem distinctive to particular people.

When it works well, humor is an ideal way of keeping the reader with you. It helps to site both reader and writer, it opens up a path for the reader to follow, it creates a mutual vantage point (there's nothing more uniting than a shared joke), and it opens a way into and smooths the way through a text. This said, though, we must also add that it's really difficult to tell you exactly how to use humor in your writing, for many obvious reasons. First, humor is the most perishable form of shared experience, coming in and out of fashion very quickly. Second, humor, or the perception of humor, is highly individual and idiosyncratic. What one person finds humorous another might find dry or decidedly unfunny. Third, humor can fall flat—who has not experienced hearing, or worse, telling, the joke that no one laughed at? Why expose yourself and your writing to such problems? Many perfectly fine writers never attempt humor and live very happily. Nevertheless, because humor is an enduring form of verbal expression that serves several purposes at once and is supremely concerned with reaching out to the reader, we want to discuss it as one answer to the question of how to build connections between yourself and the reader.

Here is a sample of comic satire from a columnist who is commenting on a change in public policy by which government regulations of airlines were eased or lifted (with the result of a number of traffic delays and long waits at airports). The writer is Russell Baker, and the piece is called "Flying with a Heavy Heart." The title suggests a sentimentalized mournfulness, like an Everly brothers song—perhaps the author is flying to a funeral or just lost his beloved. But no, the subject in fact turns out to be nothing more tragic than a change in airline regulations:

> Economists say airline regulation is the best thing to happen to customers since the invention of the electric salami slicer, and they have figures to prove it. Economists always have figures to prove what they say, and figures don't lie, so three cheers for free marketing in the sky, say I.

Of course, economists *don't* just say that. Already, quite subtly, we're in a slightly Chaplinesque world of exaggeration and incongruity, carried forward by a "speaker" or "persona" who is at once a floundering, slightly befuddled man caught in a crazy, crowded airport scene that is about to become crazier as the regulations disappear:

> Yet, why does my heart grow heavy when I arrive at the airport?
> Is it because there are twenty-nine customers ahead of me in line, and the flight for which I need a ticket is scheduled to leave in thirty-five minutes, and the man at the head of the line has already spent fifteen minutes to search his luggage for his checkbook, and there isn't another ticket seller on duty because having two working on the same day would run up labor costs?
> No, that is not why my heart grows heavy, for I know I can leave this line and race with my suitcases to the faraway gate where the airplane awaits and, there, find other authorities who will put me aboard before it leaves.
> Then maybe my heart grows heavy because I realize I am not so young as I used to be and, therefore, while racing through the airport with my suit-

cases will probably trip over one of the family groups, college sorority chapters or sleeping (possibly dead) individuals who camp on airport floors because flying is so cheap they can't afford to go by bus.

No, that is not what makes my heart grow heavy, for I know that even if I trip on several such people and fracture them, they will not become cross because they realize that to benefit from the low cost of flying they must be willing to put up with a lot of inconvenience. (33–34)

Like a stand-up comic, Baker is at once a wit and a caricature of a certain kind of person. The wit shows in the language: odd rhymes ("sky"/"I"), amusing metaphors ("since the invention of the electric salami slicer"), unexpected conclusions ("individuals who camp on airport floors because flying is so cheap they can't afford to go by bus"), reliance on a repetitive sentence and paragraph structure ("Why does my heart grow heavy?" "Is it," "No," "Then maybe my heart," "No"), and his tendency to exaggerate his points as well as his language (the passage is a composite of every flyer's worst nightmares). At the same time he gives us a picture of a muddled sad sack, almost defeated by the scene before him, who sees all we see except that he sees it through magnifying glasses as he lives through it. At the heart of his humor is the contrast of the language of sentiment ("my heart grows heavy") to describe his dealings with the highly mechanized, bureaucratic world of airlines. Having introduced this stylistic device, he plays on it, exaggerating it, and returning to it repeatedly, to structure his argument. In so doing he delineates his persona as befuddled, sensitive, and put upon.

At the same time that Baker's anxieties are exaggerated, the reader can identify them as his own. Probably all of us have been in some such situation. That's an important element in Baker's appeal: he has something to criticize; he identifies it clearly; and he creates a persona who is both Russell Baker and every person who flies—and yet one of those sad characters we somehow find funny, a kind of weeping clown. He has engaged us in a fictional world of his persona's experience and has at the same time allowed us, through that persona, to feel critical superiority to the problem. By exaggerating his list of causes for his "heavy-heartedness," Baker increases his chances of touching most readers' experiences. Even if all his readers have not shared all his fictional experiences, all who have flown recently must surely have shared some. Thus this humorist builds a bridge of shared experience and a shared vantage point through his own experience. The mere fact of this sharing means that reader and writer stand on common ground in opposition to the bureaucrats who thought deregulation might be a good idea.

✎ **Writing** Start with a real or imagined situation that could have been quite serious. See if you can convert it to humor by describing in exaggerated terms your failure to cope with it. See if you can describe your inability to cope with the world while in fact suggesting indirectly that it's the world's fault, with you as the humorously innocent victim.

Baker's technique can be described as that of the split screen. He gives the reader two subjects to laugh at—the social issue he is criticizing and himself as an "average" person who experiences the problem. In the following excerpt from a column entitled "Getting Tired of High-culture Humility," the technique is again grounded in exaggeration, but exaggeration that works in two directions. Baker makes himself out to be more ignorant and naive than he is, and he attributes more "culture" and knowledge to establishment critics than they have. The reader is introduced to the absurdity of the situation because of the exaggeration, which, as in the airline passage above, acts like a magnifying glass. Here he ridicules the cultural one-upmanship of the New York writing establishment while proclaiming his envious distance from the group he is clearly a part of. We laugh at the follies of the establishment and at Baker's putting himself on the "outside" of that establishment. Again, as above, Baker focuses on a wider cultural issue—just what gives some people the right to set, proclaim, and uphold standards of taste and/or cultural knowledge—through a specific instance, his own experience as a mere writer of the "Observer" column:

> I have long intended to become as knowledgeable about the arts as that critic who reviews them for wise-guy weekly publications issued from New York.
>
> Surely you have read his reviews. If he goes to a Rembrandt exhibition, he spends most of the review talking about Rembrandt's debt to Masaccio or Vlaminck or some other painter I have never heard of. . . .
>
> I suspect the reviewer cited above is less interested in telling me the cultural news than in reminding me that I don't know Vlaminck from Minsky; that I still haven't got around to reading Pushkin or Celine; that I am physically incapable of reading James Fenimore Cooper without lapsing into a coma; that I can distinguish a Brahms quartet from Beethoven's Ninth Symphony only because the Beethoven is noisier, that—
>
> But never mind. You see his game. Like the comedian on "Saturday Night Live," who used to say, "I'm Chevy Chase, and you're not," he is saying, "I am conversant with all art, and you are a pathetically undereducated numbskull."

Notice that this split-screen technique works here partly because Baker keeps his paragraphs short and varies his style. Short paragraphs indicate the immediacy of a thinking voice, a stream of consciousness that's valuable in setting up the sort of persona Baker uses in his humor—the quick-thinking, quick-talking responder to insult and injury. Varying sentence style also allows him to capitalize on the energy of short sentences; look at the paragraph that begins "I suspect the reviewer." It's one long sentence that, in its heaping up of clauses, represents Baker's persona, one who feels heaped upon by "culture." The next paragraph begins with two crisp sentences that allow the persona to reclaim the field, the center stage, and then reestablish things on his level, "Saturday Night Live." Thus he keeps the persona alive through style as well as through subject.

Baker doesn't always use the split persona in his writing. Often he will pick up on a statement that seems to him, as it comes to seem to us after reading his column, patently ridiculous. In cases like these he mimics the official style of modern American journalism, but by always mixing conventional form with unexpected diction, undercutting the form. Look at the opening of "So Happy in Omaha":

> Campaigning in Omaha the other day, President Bush ecstatically told a room full of people, "How nice it is to be out where the real people are—outside of Washington, D.C.!"
>
> It is true that Omaha is jam-packed with real people. The latest study shows that real people make up 79 percent of the population. Still, the city has no reason to be smug. Five years ago 85 percent of Omaha's people were real, and ten years ago the figure was 91 percent.
>
> People who study these things find the same downward trend in almost all cities in the 300,000–400,000-people class. Real people in Albuquerque, N.M., for example, have declined from 68 percent to 53 percent. Charlotte, N.C., has had a drop from 71 to 60 percent.
>
> What is happening? Some experts believe that as a city reaches the 300,000 level, it just naturally attracts a faker class of people. Others think real people are being driven out by pressures to which real people, being sensitive, are peculiarly vulnerable.

Words like "jam-packed" and "a faker class of people" reveal the humorist's touch here, as does the dogged literalness of taking a cliché like "real people" as a serious phrase. Once again, much of the humorist's appeal comes from Baker's ability to exaggerate, a tendency to overstate and to understate things. Here, Baker exaggerates by dwelling on a small detail, one thing among many that George Bush said. In effect he places that statement under a magnifying glass and invites the reader to join him in contemplating all of its implications. Baker's work here also demonstrates the effect of intentional misuse of a word or a form of a word ("a faker class of people") in order to engage the reader in saying with the writer, "Isn't this ludicrous?"

A close look at Baker's writing offers, as we have noticed in passing, a lot of tips on how to structure your writing to give the comic effect a chance. Baker shows us the value of focusing on a single individual to discuss larger issues; the value of exaggeration; the importance of structure, repetition of phrasing, and variety in sentence type and structure; and in the case of the "real people" column, the value of recognizing the humorous potential of a phrase. But most of all, he shows how important it is that humor have a writing personality to give a center to all this activity.

✎ **Writing**   One way to sharpen your appreciation of how humorists focus to exaggerate and reveal latent absurdities is to learn about your own sense of humor. Look at the nationally syndicated cartoon strips that appear in most daily papers—*Peanuts*, *Garfield*, and *Doonesbury*, for example—or books of earlier cartoons like *The Far Side* and *Calvin and*

Hobbes. After you've read the same strip for several days, try to explain for yourself and others where the humor comes from and how it works. Looking closely for the sources of humor in your own thinking and that of others can provide valuable training in analyzing diction and the structure of ideas.

Making Fun of What You Know Well, Even Yourself

If you want to use humor in your writing, in addition to sharpening your stylistic skills you need to hone your receptive skills—to look about and identify what seems ridiculous. Often the best rule is to think about what you know well and to extrapolate from the real to the not-too-distant ridiculous. Consider a typical situation, identify the attitudes you think are very much part of the situation but are usually hidden, and then rewrite the scene making the implicit explicit and exaggerating it.

John Kenneth Galbraith is not a humorist by profession but an economist, just the kind of person Baker was poking fun at in the first passage above. Galbraith's writing, however, is full of wit, lively awareness of the absurdity in human affairs, and free use of language to locate that awareness in his writing. Galbraith seems to have a natural gift for treating a serious subject with a show of so much seriousness that he parodies his own topic. Look at this example from *Economics in Perspective:*

> [John Maynard Keynes] was selected to serve with the British delegation to the Paris Peace Conference in 1919, an assignment of no slight interest and distinction.
>
> The behavior of a young specialist—Keynes was not yet thirty-six— brought into such awe-inspiring company as that at the Paris Conference— David Lloyd George, Georges Clemenceau, Woodrow Wilson—and to such an awe-inspiring task as ensuring the peace of the world ought to be wholly predictable. One so chosen and favored should enjoy the resulting self-gratification and the envy of others not so fortunate; he should offer advice with all appropriate deference; and he should accept and even defend the result, however unwelcome, unwise or bizarre, as the best that could be done. To behave otherwise would be to deny the wisdom that led to his selection and to impair his own self-esteem. Keynes, in no need of any enhancement of self-esteem, left Paris in June 1919 in a mood of deep contempt for the proceedings. He returned to England to write *The Economic Consequences of the Peace* over the period of the next two months. It was published in England later that year, sold eighty-four thousand copies in the British edition, was widely translated and still stands as the most important *economic* document relating to World War I and its aftermath. (229)

Humor could easily explode this subject. Here it enlivens it. Galbraith gives little sign that he knows he's being funny; he merely exaggerates a few details, understates others, and allows us to see the incongruities that result. Essentially he adopts the verbal equivalent of dead-panning. He develops incongruous statements that both he and the reader know are funny, but he refuses to laugh, to bring the joke to a conclusion. In contrast to Baker's style, which is largely one of brief, emphatic sentences, each focused on a humorous phrase or idea, Galbraith's style is one of long, complex sentences that spin out the humor, drawing it through the paragraph. If we enjoy this sort of thing, we feel that we and he are in league together, witty people who see not only the things that duller people cannot see but also the pretensions and delusions of the wise; we feel that a favorite aunt is winking at us while recounting the vicar's sermon in a way that will impress grandfather but sharing her amusement with us. Take this sentence of Galbraith's: "To behave otherwise [than with extreme gratitude] would be to deny the wisdom that led to his selection and to impair his own self-esteem." Galbraith is giving us a little parody of the kind of thinking people engage in who choose a bright, young person and expect him to be extremely grateful. Galbraith may be said, as an author, to take the pose of putting his arm around the reader's shoulder and saying, "Look at how it seems to me." That he is part of the very world he chides here makes it even more fun.

Drawing on Humor in the World Around You

Not all humorous writing is the product of the writer's invention. Often wit and a lively receptivity to the humor around you can allow you to write humorously without a great deal of invention of phrase. What's required for this type of humor is a good ear and an ability to see the humorous in the everyday. Here are some excerpts from an "Our Towns" column in the *New York Times* by Michael Winerip. Winerip's subject is a thorny issue, the evident need for recycling packaging and paper. At the same time, he is aware that a desirable social goal is not always easy to achieve or to balance with other desirable social goals. He chooses to convey his message by recounting and quoting the efforts of a third-grade class in Great Neck, Long Island, to make an impression on the adults in their immediate community and within the general area of Manhattan. It's interesting to speculate which came first, the idea of the column or of listening to the children talk. What's clear is that in the column Winerip lets the children speak for themselves. As adults we read their language and see absolute gut-level commitment to the issue and a comparatively unformed sense of tone and voice. Winerip invites us to smile at the children's earnestness, thereby creating the bond between reader and writer that effective humor often employs to make its point. By the end of the column, though, he manages to bring the issue full circle and to show how even these totally committed children, under the pressure of circumstance in their classroom, learn about the hard choices we all have to make about how to live within our culture and also within the earth's environment.

In September, Annette Berson told her third graders at Kennedy Elementary School about a recycling program run by Kroger, a supermarket chain in the

Middle West. If you bring back your paper bags and use them for your next bag of groceries, you get a 3-cent refund for each re-used bag.

The third-graders got very excited about all the trees they could save and decided each of them would ask a store to create a bag-refund plan. Aaron Israel's letter to A&S stores began: "I am writing to you because our world is not doing too well." Jessica Moussazadeh wrote Children's Warehouse: "All of the people in Room 258 of John F. Kennedy School are concerned about the earth."

While they waited for answers, Mrs. Berson taught them to be good recyclers. They got a box to recycle white paper. Every day they'd learn a scary environmental fact. (*The average American will need 465 trees to provide him with a lifetime of paper.*) "All the houses being built, all the paper being used," said Alex Safian, "it's just going nuts around here."

They became rabid recyclers, hunting for violations. Jessica hung out while her baby brother drank milk. "As soon as he finished, I recycled the carton." They tacked non-biodegradables on the board. "Here's an outlaw juice container," Mrs. Berson said.

They tried doing something about their parents. "My Mom goes to the supermarket, brings home brown bags and does nothing with them," said Jason Amirian. "Oh my God!" said Jessica. Zach Rechler caught his parents throwing out cans.

At home, parents were routinely harassed and made to feel inadequate. "We come home from the supermarket, Carey starts in about saving trees," said Elayne Greenberg. "I use computer paper. He says I use too much, I could be more efficient. Whenever we go by a supermarket, he wants to talk to the manager. He keeps showing me figures about the trees."

No one was safe. The other day, during recess, Mrs. Berson had her head in a wastebasket. "I threw white paper in here by mistake," she said. "Have to fish it out and put it in the recycling box before they find it. They yell at me."

By mid-October, only two stores had responded to the letters. They sent a second batch. "I'm surprised at you!" Danielle Broomes wrote Associated Food Stores. "I hope you know I am giving you a piece of my mind." Sarah Levitt wrote Bloomingdale's: "Dear Mr. Marvin Traub, I would like you to take this matter seriously. This is our world, Mr. Traub."

By the third letter they were in an environmental fever. "Now I am telling you, not asking you, write back. Please Mr. Traub do something about our environment. . . . I am going to be very strict with you now." Mrs. Berson suggested she tone it down a mite. "Some of them are very intense," Mrs. Berson said.

Sarah agreed to revisions. "I was sort of angry, you know. Mrs. Berson said it wasn't appropriate to say I'm going to be strict—I'm not his mother. I was just angry."

Eight of the 14 have now responded. It was surprising how many adults had illegible signatures. "Kind of messy," said Alex. "I can usually read cursive writing." Most stores said they would consider the idea. A few were testing other measures. Glen Rosengarten of Sigmund's wrote Alex that he was using biodegradable plastic bags to save trees, but wasn't happy about it. "Jobs will be lost," he wrote. "Customers won't have the security of paper bags to protect their purchases. I think it's a shame." The owner tried to put Alex on the defensive: "I apologize for not responding to your request of 10 days ago, but I had a death in my family, which I'm sure you can find in your heart to understand."

Alex said, "I felt sorry for the person who died but I still didn't like this letter."

He wrote another letter. "Since you did not respond immediately, I have been wasting paper," Alex wrote. (At this rate Alex will use up his 465 trees in a week.)

The other day in art, Mrs. Berson had them do pastels in the style of Van Gogh. "I brought in acrylic spray to lacquer them so the color wouldn't rub off," she said. Immediately Jessica shouted, "Bad for the environment!" Mrs. Berson agreed, but explained at times you must balance environmental concerns with other factors. Jessica stood firm. But most wanted to be sprayed. Alex said it would actually be better for the environment to spray because if the pictures smudged, he'd have to make another, which would waste trees. And Diana Sanchez said: "I wasn't going to do it. But I said just one more spray and that's it. I'll never ever spray again. Because I really did a lot of work on it."

Winerip uses other people's language almost exclusively. His one overtly humorous line—"At this rate Alex will use up his 465 trees in a week"—builds directly out of what his "characters" have said and done. Note that he, too, uses short paragraphs, often ending with quotations. He is also fond of the short, direct sentence whose crispness underlines the children's initial black-and-white attitude toward recycling ("Jessica stood firm"). The effect of this style is to suggest what it must be like to be with a class of smart and active third-graders for several hours—ideas all the time from everywhere. But more to the point that we are making, Winerip's style and his humor gently ask the reader to consider the points the children are making about the environment, the way adults respond to them, and the children's growing awareness, through the art project, that choices are sometimes difficult. Using children to make this point, Winerip enlists the reader as part of the "superior" group of adults who through his writing "watch" the proceedings with an indulgent smile. Like many true social critics who use humor, however, he leaves the reader at the end wondering about just where she "fits"—with the children, the parents, or the store owners. We are amused by their earnestness ("At home, parents were routinely harassed") and also engaged by it. The principle of incongruity is again at work: a sentence like "no one was safe" sounds as if it belongs to a different kind of reporting altogether. Yet our amusement doesn't diminish our sympathy with the children. Their adult seriousness may even lead us to change our behavior.

You don't have to be a humorist to use humor in your writing. Just listen to and look at the world around you. Trust yourself. If something strikes you as incongruous or ridiculous, try to capture its essence in words. Winerip's technique is one you can use, too. Quote the conversation, speech, or presentation, adding your own comments at various strategic intervals where you feel you can or want to make a comment.

✎ **Writing**   Observe some children who are busy at a task they take seriously, who are not trying to be funny but are amusing because of the incongruity of their attempts at adultlike seriousness. If possible, record some of their words. Now describe in a straightforward way what you've observed, trying for comic effect by taking their seriousness seriously and letting them speak for themselves.

Humorous Beginnings and Endings

While we may be able to imitate Winerip's model and learn to listen to the world, trying to identify the humor it offers us, most of us will use humor infrequently and then probably only as a way into or out of a topic. We have seen from the passages above that one of the chief benefits of humor is that it draws the reader and the writer together in a shared joke. This effect can also be achieved through the careful use of humor in the beginning of an essay to suggest to the reader your point of view and your concern that the reader be "with you" in spirit. Humor is a handy way of siting yourself and your reader. Here are some humorous openings by Anna Quindlen. In the first she uses humor, particularly in the last line of the first paragraph, to indicate her own sense that things are "out of hand" in Washington and to suggest that this feeling is not uniquely hers but is shared by many others, particularly the reader:

> Not since the tall ships has there been national esprit as great as that inspired by the budget negotiations. In bank lines, drugstores, supermarkets and parking lots, Americans have gathered in a spirit of grand unanimity to discuss the possibility that the people who run the Government are completely out to lunch.
>
> ("At the Circus")

Obviously the humor here arises from the contrast of styles she uses. Everything up to "are completely" is typically middle-style journalistic writing. The phrase "out to lunch" stands in sharp contrast to the controlled, moderate formality of the dominant style and suggests that the subject—"the people who run the Government"—doesn't deserve the moderate style.

Quindlen creates humor through the contrast of styles in a similar way in a later column about the 2 Live Crew case:

> Stupid prosecutor's trick of the month—and the competition is fierce for this one—goes to the assistant state attorney in the 2 Live Crew case who said one of the jurors, a 76-year-old retired professor, was trouble from Day One. "She was a sociologist, and I don't like sociologists," Pedro Dijols said. "They try to reason things out too much."
>
> Now there's an indictment if I ever heard one. You let people go reasoning things out, next thing you know they'll be using logic. And before you

know it the place will be overrun with common sense and then where will we be?

("Grand Juries")

The wise-guy irreverence of the opening words immediately catches our attention, with its fanciful creation of a competition among stupid prosecutors. Then Quindlen adopts the common tactic of adapting someone else's style as her own, trying it on to show how, when it's separated from the person, it sounds rather foolish. Within the context of being one of the prosecutors, the assistant district attorney can make his point about not liking people who "reason things out too much." In effect his position provides a frame for understanding "what he really meant." But Quindlen's ear is alert to the fundamental absurdity of what's being said within the frame, and she uses the original quotation as a springboard from which to write her column "Grand Juries." To create the necessary bond with the reader, she adapts the style in the second paragraph, and reaches out explicitly to the reader with such phrases as "And before you know it the place will be overrun with common sense and then where will we be?" The reader shakes her head over the folly of the world and proceeds to follow Quindlen, whose next paragraph, a one-line paragraph, is "In the jury room, that's where." Quindlen thus skillfully leads the reader along the path she lays out to get to the main point of the column, the surprising and heartening fact that American juries seem able to bring in verdicts upholding constitutional principles rather than reflecting popular, media influence. The humor at the beginning of the column gives Quindlen the room to move herself and the reader into the main matter, on the same level.

Along this line, let's look again at Russell Baker, who is expert at bringing the reader into the text through funny openings. Look at his column called "The Bad Bugs," where he picks up on his column about having been stung by a bee:

People keep writing to ask if I survived the bee sting reported here on Aug. 29. The answer is yes, but these letters are troubling. Do my published columns since Aug. 29 read like something written by a deceased person?

I have just reread them all and admit, yes, there is a certain lifelessness in them. Still, practically all newspaper columns seem to be issuing from the grave, don't they? Have mine since Aug. 29 been deader than the national average?

Here the humor is closely tied to the series of questions designed to draw the reader into the column. Note the way he draws out the topic. Each sentence is a separate whole, but all could easily be combined into one. The humor here derives from style and from diction: "canned" phrases like "a deceased person" or "national average." Of course, he is also playing out an old joke: he couldn't be dead if he were still writing; nonetheless he asks the reader to continue asking if he is.

Humor at the end of a piece can help you wrap up your writing with a flourish and also help you avoid those deadly last-paragraph problems. To illustrate this point, let's look at *The Economist*'s style. It frequently depends on snappy exit lines that sum up the story ironically or that introduce a humorous edge. Such conclusions contribute greatly toward the style of the magazine—that slightly bemused, world-weary, human-nature-is-so-predictably-silly tone that suggests superiority of understanding on the part of the writer and reader both. Here's the conclusion of an *Economist* article of July 7, 1990, about Imelda Marcos's trial on charges of stealing from the Philippine people:

> Mrs. Aquino believes that Marcos money was behind a coup attempt against her last December.
>
> Mrs. Marcos's friends dismiss such suggestions. Mr. Francisco Tatad, who was a spokesman for her husband, says she is "a woman transformed by suffering, in quality and substance. God in his infinite mercy has blessed her." He has certainly moved in a mysterious way.
>
> ("Imelda Marcos Not Guilty")

The last line, the writer's editorial comment on the story he has been writing, provides a note of humor and a strong exit. Part of the humor here is from incongruity, using a religious phrase to conclude a column about political corruption and greed. It's the "wrong" phrase here, so it lends a note of parodic exaggeration to the scope of the topic. In short, it works. Whatever we might think about the fairness or the truth of this story, we have to admit that the ending is lively and provocative.

The same issue of *The Economist* carries a story about the Zebra mussel's invasion of "North America's huge fresh-water lakes." Apparently the mussels are a new introduction into the ecosystem of the Americas. At the moment they appear to have few natural predators. As a result, they seem to be breeding out of control, fouling the water intake systems of a number of midwestern cities. Here's the last paragraph of the story:

> Fishermen worry that Zebra mussels will compete for food with algae-eating fish. The creatures cannot be eaten by humans and have few natural predators. And though an enterprising Ohio man has turned some of them into jewelry, supply greatly exceeds demand.
>
> ("Nasty Little Stowaways")

The dry turn of the last sentence provides a note of humor as it summarizes the point of the article: the Zebra mussel is out of control. The humor here comes from the allusion to the law of supply and demand that is supposed to keep production and consumption in balance; its application within a biological context is witty as well as ironic. Clearly Zebra mussels have never heard of the law, but the joke bets that the reader has. The comic effect of the last sentence derives from the fact that the writer offers the allusion as a bridge to the reader, whom the writer counts on to recognize the reference. Once again humor is the bond between reader and writer, the point at which they both stand apart from the subject and contemplate it with detachment. Standing on that mental bridge, the reader and the writer part company, the reader satisfied with herself and the "view"—recognizing the reference to classical economic theory.

2 DRAWING ON EMOTION

In speech we use our bodies, our facial expressions, our tone of voice, and our gestures, and we adjust to our listeners, depending on their responses. Emotions live in our bodies, in our physical beings; writing can produce or refer to emotion, but in itself the act of reading is a very "unbodily," unconcrete act. Our eyes are involved but primarily in decoding marks and passing them on to the brain. Sometimes we read under rushed circumstances, skimming the printed text and looking for the end. Both writing and the process of reading can act as deterrents to conveying emotions. But it's odd that this should be so because poetry, for example, is so successful in conveying and in evoking emotion. The success of poetry in recollecting and conveying the sense of strongly felt experience suggests that emotional filters woven into other kinds of writing are deliberately created and are not a function of language or of the nature of writing. It's harder to factor emotion out of writing than to include it, and given a chance, many people will find writing a natural place to explore and share emotions.

It may be hard to incorporate emotion into your writing and hard to evoke an equivalent emotional response in your reader if as a writer you find yourself facing writing as a purely intellectual exercise. Our culture tends to separate intellectual and emotional responses from each other, as if one could live without the other. But almost every response that we term either "intellectual" or "emotional" is a mixture of the two. No strongly held opinion is merely an idea: it's almost always a feeling—a gut feeling, we frequently say, existing powerfully in the body as well as in the brain.

Even if we admit that the conventions of writing in our culture require us to present and to evoke emotion indirectly, at times we still want to persuade and to argue on the basis of emotion as well as, or instead of, logical intellectual arguments. The writers we cite in the following pages write out of emotion. In doing so they try to re-create the energy—anger, despair, sorrow—that impelled them to write in the first place. They concentrate on reaching the reader, riveting her attention, persuading her to share their convictions and feel their emotion. By and large they do so out of the rhythms and patterns of the language they construct—out of diction and sentence structure. Their writing offers useful

models of how to use and convey strong emotion and how to keep the
reader with you.

Anger

James Baldwin was a master of the language of indignation. His book
The Fire Next Time stands as a powerful expression of one kind of social
rage. Written in 1962, it has three parts: an introductory "letter to my
nephew on the one hundredth anniversary of the emancipation"; a memoir of the author's conversion that led him to a brief career as a child
preacher; and an interview with Elijah Muhammad, leader of the Nation
of Islam. After describing his interview with Elijah, which left him both
impressed and ultimately at odds with Elijah's vision of separate black
and white nations, Baldwin reflects on the relations between blacks and
whites in America.

Notice that Baldwin uses diction—word choice—as a tool to express
deep emotion, drawing on "ordinary" language of intense meaning and
layering it to achieve the moral equivalent of the extraordinary:

> This past, the Negro's past, of rope, fire, torture, castration, infanticide, rape;
> death and humiliation; fear by day and night, fear as deep as the marrow of
> the bone; doubt that he was worthy of life, since everyone around him de-
> nied it; sorrow for his women, for his kinfolk, for his children, who needed
> his protection, and whom he could not protect; rage, hatred, and murder, ha-
> tred for white men so deep that it often turned against him and his own, and
> made all love, all trust, all joy impossible—this past, this endless struggle to
> achieve and reveal and confirm a human identity, human authority, yet con-
> tains, for all its horror, something very beautiful. (132)

Baldwin conveys intense emotion here within a carefully controlled
grammatical form. This is all one sentence, one long and carefully constructed periodic sentence. One can talk about the kinds of verbal devices
here—repetitions, lists, and the redirection of the sentence at the end.
But what really counts is that Baldwin uses the sentence, its sheer length
and its sheer weight, to express and to symbolize his anger.

The sentence is 115 words long. It starts simply, "This past." That
phrase is its grammatical subject. But then 88 words tell you about
"this past" in a series of modifying phrases and clauses that show it as a
collection of horrors and injustices. Finally, Baldwin repeats the phrase
that has been modified at such length that it needs restatement in order
to lead into the predicate, which will say what "this past" is or does.
"This past," he says again and immediately gives it a new modification,
as not only a tale of horror and injustice but also an "endless struggle,"
a struggle "for a human identity." And finally, 8 words from the end,
comes the verb, "contains," and its completely surprising object,

"something very beautiful." The structure is somewhat like a chemical reaction: this past + struggle = something beautiful. The sentence is equivalent to holding your breath and controlling your anger while cataloging a litany of grievances. We've all done that, although perhaps not so skillfully as Baldwin.

Baldwin is a resourceful writer whose diction, like his sentence structure, is full of strength and energy. Look at how he goes on to answer the question "What is that 'something very beautiful' that this terrible past contains?" "I do not mean," he says, "to be sentimental about suffering—enough is certainly as good as a feast—but people who cannot suffer can never grow up, can never discover who they are." He explains:

> That man who is forced each day to snatch his manhood, his identity, out of the fire of human cruelty that rages to destroy it knows, if he survives his effort, and even if he does not survive it, something about himself and human life that no school on earth—and, indeed, no church—can teach. He achieves his own authority, and that is unshakable. This is because, in order to save his life, he is forced to look beneath appearances, to take nothing for granted, to hear the meaning behind the words. If one is continually surviving the worst that life can bring, one eventually ceases to be controlled by a fear of what life can bring; whatever it brings must be borne. And at this level of experience one's bitterness begins to be palatable, and hatred becomes too heavy a sack to carry. (133)

Notice how much energy there is in this writing, in verbs suggesting strong action and in vivid images—"suffer," "forced," "snatch," "rages," "survives," and "the fire of human cruelty." Notice also how richly mixed Baldwin's emotional language is; how fear, joy, love, the appreciation of beauty, and rage are mixed together; how many emotions are extended to the reader; how he changes and modulates emotion throughout. Notice how Baldwin often uses a very complex sentence structure, full of qualifications and interruptions, to define a problem and then a simple or compound structure—such as "He achieves his own authority, and that is unshakeable"—not so much to solve the problem as to define a powerful stance toward it. His writing epitomizes the use of rhetoric to convey and to control intense feeling.

In the passages above, Baldwin creates two simultaneous emotional fields. One is defined by the long litany of abuse and hatred; it arises out of the sentence structure as well as Baldwin's diction. The other is the affirmation out of suffering, the assertion that his people will triumph even over such injustice; it arises from the grammatical construction, the very simple frame of the first very long sentence. The sentence is very simple but very emotional—all the more so, we would say, because it carries two intense messages to the reader. What Baldwin has done here is a result of his skill as a writer and a result of his peculiarly painful subject, race relations in America.

✎ **Writing** Baldwin's style may not be at all like yours, but after reading his writing you may be able to experiment with the effect of structure and diction in conveying strong emotion and in eliciting it. Notice that his sentences are full of specific illustrations, full of active verbs, and full of images based on living. He has learned (or knew instinctively) that to be effective, anger in writing must be tied to images that will stir the reader's imagination. Try this technique. Choose a subject that you feel strongly about. Your goal will be to write movingly about it in a statement of what is wrong, why, and what the likely outcome will be. First, identify your topic; it can be an abstraction, or a generality—for example, "careless logging of the national forests." Then identify your verb, your action—for example, "wastes valuable resources." Then jot down particular reasons why and how "valuable resources" disappear with careless logging. Work in the particulars in a series of parallel phrases between the subject and the verb. This is called a periodic sentence structure: the verb is withheld until the end of the sentence to create suspense and perhaps surprise. Keep working at just this sentence to see if you can re-create emotion for your reader out of the images and sentence structure themselves rather than by "describing" your emotion. See if you can create something like Baldwin's sense of controlled rage.

Anger and the Plain Style

Baldwin's use of rich structure and diction is not the only way of communicating emotion. A writer can rely on spare, direct sentence structure and direct, intense communication with the reader. Look at the passage below from a column by Anna Quindlen about a rape. Quindlen uses a rhetoric of emotion, too, but one quite different from Baldwin's:

> It is difficult to find the right words to talk about rape. I don't have to. Someone else found them for me on her way to the car after studying late at a campus building at the University of Nebraska more than a year ago. Listen:
>
> "I only sensed fear in him for a moment. His face then turned into an expression of satisfaction. It was the most sickening sight that I have ever seen. It was also the most humiliating and degrading moment of the entire ordeal, even more repulsive than the physical act itself. He was very obviously pleased with himself, with what he had just done to me. It was this look of self-gratification that the police could not have seen through my words the way in which I saw it through my own eyes. I believe that he will do to someone else the very thing he did to me. I wish I could stop that from happening. I know the hell that his next victim will go through on her way back from the place that a person like him takes you to."
>
> ("A Bias Crime")

The heart of this excerpt was written by the victim of the crime. As Quindlen explains in the column, the account was written for an English course and sent to her by the instructor, with the author's permission. Both the instructor for whom it was written and Quindlen recognized in it an extraordinary quality. Its plain style is exactly suited to its subject. Short, declarative sentences begin variously with "I," "it," and "he." The writer's attention, and the reader's, are focused on the fact of the rape. She uses strong language, but sparingly. Words like "sickening" and "humiliating," and "degrading" fill out the sentences. In most cases the writer attaches one powerful word to each idea. The rapist was the most "sickening sight" she had ever seen. The rapist was "very obviously pleased" with himself. The victim recalls her perception of her attacker's "satisfaction" as a "humiliating and degrading moment."

She concludes with a series of almost chilling sentences, simply written. "I believe that he will do to someone else the thing he did to me. I wish I could stop that from happening. I know the hell that his next victim will go through on her way back from the place that a person like him takes you to." Notice the number of monosyllabic words in these sentences. They help the text flow with simple conviction. The writer does not seem overwhelmed by her encounter with brutality but through her writing suggests her control of the experience, the memory, and the emotion that has led her to record them all in words. This passage shows that it is possible to convey intense feeling in a very simple rhetoric. In large part it works through understatement; the writer plays the role of observer. She observes herself as the victim of a horrible crime. In this detachment it's almost as if she lets the rape happen again for the reader, so totally does she involve the reader in her point of view. Above all this passage illustrates the principle that control of language is the foundation of any attempt to share deeply felt experience.

Quindlen uses simmering anger to make her own point, which is a somewhat complicated one, because two much-publicized New York rapes at the time had been written of as racially motivated. Hence her title, "A Bias Crime." "Let's get it straight," she says, "Sexual assault is mainly about gender. It is about how some men feel about some women."

> The Nebraska woman's case is typical: one woman, one assailant, same race: "He was talking to me, saying such revolting things, things that he said I had to do to him and what he would do to me. He was forcing me to touch him and he was ripping my blouse."
>
> Can't bear to read it? Let's stop it.
>
> That's another infuriating part of this discussion. Deterrence centers on the victim. Take self-defense classes. Get good locks. Strike out with your keys in a clenched fist. "I started to want to own a gun," writes the Nebraska woman.
>
> No. Change the rapists.

Perhaps the crucial sentences in Quindlen's writing are the two short ones in the middle of the last quotation: "Can't bear to read it? Let's stop it"—that is, let's stop things that bring about rape. Quindlen uses simplicity, direct address, and short, stinging sentences to assault the reader. The last two sentences are moving in their strong assertion that the system of our culture has misplaced its attention: "No. Change the rapists."

We want to make a difficult point here. Unlike Baldwin, neither writer in this piece lets language stand on the page as a symbol or representation of emotion. We are not dealing here with writing that in its diction or complicated structure signals a shift from the ordinary to the extraordinary and in so doing signals a subject of importance, a center of emotional energy. No, this writing is different; it is transparent. It reaches out to the reader in its simplicity. "I started to want to own a gun." It's a simple sentence but in many readers it raises a host of thoughts and feelings about why and under what circumstances someone would want, would own, and would use a gun. This effect is the deliberate result of the style both women have chosen. It is plain talk, straight talk. It goes straight to the reader's heart and mind. Moreover, the writing, like the column, insists that feelings need to be recognized, not submerged. We see this in Quindlen's use of the reader's natural desire not to hear the details about rape, not to experience the emotions, as a lever to argue for a new way of treating rapists. She begins by listening and making us listen to someone who has been raped. She makes us acknowledge those feelings as the starting point for her discussion. However intelligent her proposed solution, the power of the argument comes from the way she recognizes and channels emotions. Emotions are literally what move us here, not words. That's only because she has found ways of using words that make emotion present

✎ **Writing**   Often our deepest feelings can be shared only through verbal simplicity. (If you've ever had to shop in a card store for a sympathy card you will know what we mean. Where emotion is strong, too many words too artfully—or clumsily—arranged seem all wrong.) Try the plain style. Again, choose a topic you feel strongly about—something in politics, the environment, the state of education in the United States, for example, perhaps the same one as in the last exercise. As you write, try to re-create your anger and indignation in your words. Listen to how your sentences sound. Strive for the brief, emphatic assertion like Quindlen's "No. Change the rapists." Think of your sentences not as descriptions but as actions.

Emotion and Indirection

We've been looking at writing in which the writer and the emotion are clearly the subject at hand. It's the most direct and the most obvious way to convey emotion—from self to reader directly through language that in turn directly addresses the topic. But there are other ways of expressing emotion. One of the most useful and the most adaptable is indirection. Often writers can displace their subject, using a metaphor, that is, constructing a metaphorical situation, to comment on one topic through another.

One good example of this approach comes from Lewis Thomas's essay, "Late Night Thoughts on Mahler's Ninth Symphony."

> I cannot listen to Mahler's Ninth Symphony with anything like the old melancholy mixed with high pleasure I used to take from this music. There was a time, not long ago, when what I heard, especially in the final movement, was an open acknowledgement of death and at the same time a quiet celebration of the tranquility connected to the process. I took this music as a metaphor for reassurance, confirming my own strong hunch that the dying of every living creature, the most natural of all experiences, has to be a peaceful experience. I rely on nature. The long passages on all the strings at the end, as close as music can come to expressing silence itself, I used to hear as Mahler's idea of leave-taking at its best. But always, I have heard this music as a solitary, private listener, thinking about death. (164)

Thomas puts us in a complex emotional world where melancholy mixes with high pleasure and where the author is at ease with death. Note how he contrasts complex sentences with simple ones. His language is simple, too, and direct. Apparently he is writing about the symphony, but as we will see below, he is primarily concerned with the danger and horror of nuclear war. Mahler's Ninth Symphony is the metaphor, the means of talking indirectly about the subject he is really writing about. Note that the emotion he feels about his subject, the horror of such a war, is always channeled through a reference to music, nature, geography, or culture. This is not surprising since no one knows how awful such a war might be, and it's not surprising because we can feel emotion only in terms of what we know, what we love, hate, desire, or fear. "Now," Thomas continues,

> I hear it differently. I cannot listen to the last movement of the Mahler Ninth without the door-smashing intrusion of a huge new thought: death everywhere, the dying of everything, the end of humanity. . . . All through the last notes my mind swarms with images of a world in which the thermonuclear bombs have begun to explode. In New York and San Francisco, in Moscow and Leningrad, in Paris, in Paris, in Paris. In Oxford and Cambridge, in Edinburgh. I cannot push away the thought of a cloud of radioactivity drifting along the Engadin, from the Moloja Pass to Ftan, killing off the part of the earth I love more than any other part. (164–165)

"Door-smashing" carries considerable power. A new thought comes smashing into the chambers of Thomas's mind just as a new kind of emotion smashes into the essay. Note how "door-smashing" contrasts with the quiet atmosphere that has been established and the picture of an older man sitting quietly alone at night, listening sadly but peacefully to a favorite piece of music, a piece that, as he puts it, is "as close as music can come to expressing silence itself." Note also how well he uses simple details like the names of places: two American cities poised against two Russian cities; the great university towns of England, for which Thomas might be expected to have special affection; Paris repeated three times, as if to say, how could anyone let a city as beautiful as Paris be destroyed; and finally the names of places uniquely special to Thomas personally.

Thomas uses a technique of displacement throughout the essay. He discusses everything in terms of music, in which he finds a concrete way of talking about an emotionally complicated issue. Thomas has found a metaphor through which to channel his emotion. It helps if the reader knows Mahler's Ninth Symphony, but it is not necessary because in the essay Thomas creates the Ninth as a haven of calm and peace through his style.

We can see an even more radical example of displacement as a way of describing and sharing deep emotion in the passage below from *The Education of Henry Adams*, the autobiography of the grandson and great-grandson of the Adams presidents, in his own right a great writer and historian. Adams here refers to himself in the third person (as he does throughout the book), describing his beloved sister's death from tetanus in Rome in 1870.

> The last lesson—the sum and term of education—began then. He had passed through thirty years of rather varied experience without having once felt the shell of custom broken. He had never seen Nature—only her surface—the sugar-coating that she shows to youth. Flung suddenly on his face, with the harsh brutality of chance, the terror of the blow stayed by him thenceforth for life, until repetition made it more than the will could struggle with; more than he could call on himself to bear. He found his sister, a woman of forty, as gay and brilliant in the terrors of lockjaw as she had been in the careless fall of 1859, lying in bed in consequence of a miserable cab-accident that had bruised her foot. Hour by hour the muscles grew rigid, while the mind remained bright, until after ten days of fiendish torture she died in convulsions. (287)

The distancing Adams achieves by speaking of himself in the third person, as either "he" or "one," actually seems to increase the emotional impact: we perhaps feel him trying to shield himself from an emotion too powerful to absorb and yet unable to avoid. Note that Adams is still dealing with the issue Thomas has accepted at the beginning of his essay, death as a natural occurrence:

> One had heard a great deal about death, and even seen a little of it, and knew by heart the thousand commonplaces of religion and poetry which seemed to deaden one's senses and veil the horror. . . . Death took features altogether new to him, in these rich and sensuous surroundings. Nature enjoyed it, played with it, the horror added to her charm, she liked the torture, and smothered her victim with caresses. Never had one seen her so winning. The hot Italian summer brooded outside, over the market-place and the picturesque peasants, and, in the singular color of the Tuscan atmosphere, the

hills and vineyards of the Apennines seemed bursting with midsummer blood. The sickroom itself glowed with the Italian joy of life; friends filled it; no harsh northern lights pierced the soft shadows; even the dying woman shared the sense of the Italian summer, the soft, velvet air, the humor, the courage, the sensual fullness of Nature and man. She faced death, as women mostly do, bravely and even gaily, racked slowly to unconsciousness, but yielding only to violence, as a soldier sabred in battle. For many thousands of years, on these hills and plains, Nature had gone on sabring men and women with the same air of sensual pleasure. (287–288)

A comparison with the magnificent art of Greek vase painting will illustrate Adams's technique here. At first, figures were painted on the red clay of the vases with black paint, the details on the figures depicted by letting the red of the clay show through. Later, it was discovered that if you painted the whole vase, except the figure, black you could then use a few strokes at crucial points on the figure, which was merely red clay that hadn't been covered by paint, to give the most subtle and expressive details. Adams, in effect, devotes much of his attention to the surroundings, to the country in the midst of life, saving only a few strokes for the central figures of this particular scene, his sister and his feelings. What creates the emotion is the contrast of the scene depicted with the horror we know is there.

✎ **Writing**   Once more, find a topic that you care deeply about. First think of an analogy that matches it. Now write a few paragraphs, drawing out the analogy as fully as possible. Reread the paragraph, being particularly careful to note how the fact of making the comparison has shaped the structure of your sentences and has influenced your diction. Now rewrite the paragraph, concentrating on two points: use the analogy as your focus, and write about your original subject by dealing largely (if not exclusively) with the analogy. Write into the discussion of the analogy the emotion that prompted you to write in the first place. This will probably be difficult for you, especially because the length of a paragraph does not allow for development. At each step of this exercise you will likely "feel" the transitions as you shift from topic to analogy, trying to maintain the same focus. At the end of this experiment we think you will see that writing indirectly about one subject through another, an analogy, is somewhat of an art; it looks easy but is actually a matter of control. Equally important, you will see that this method succeeds only insofar as the analogy is a good one to begin with. By "good" we mean an analogy that is proportional to the subject. Mahler's Ninth Symphony fits nuclear war; it is strong, deep, brooding, and difficult to understand or comprehend. A popular rock song would not fit in its place; the proportions would be wrong.

CHAPTER 4

Leading Your Reader Through That World

We've all experienced the unsettling process of losing our way while reading something, suddenly realizing that we were heading in one direction and the writing somewhere else. "I sometimes think," C. S. Lewis said, "that writing is like driving sheep down a road. If there is any gate to the left or right, the readers will most certainly go into it" (Barzun, *Simple and Direct*, xi). As readers we may not appreciate being compared to sheep, but as writers it is useful to recognize the inborn tendency of our consciousness to stray, to pick up false leads and follow them, to follow whatever most commands attention. A clear path through a text will help a reader find the way. A driving, nagging shepherd may make us feel literally like sheep. How are we able to create the one while avoiding being the other?

1   BLAZING VERBAL PATHS

Consider the following passage from a memoir by former President Richard Nixon.

> In 1973, illness put me out of action for the first time as President. While I was recovering from a debilitating case of viral pneumonia, the existence of the White House taping system was made known. I was faced with a difficult decision. Some of my advisers urged me to destroy the tapes, while others urged me to keep them, because they felt the courts would support our contention that confidential conversations should not be made public. Most of my friends and even some of my critics agree that I made the wrong decision. If I had been up to par physically, there is certainly a chance that I would have stepped up to the issue and ordered the tapes destroyed.
>
> *(In the Arena*, 168)

Nixon is careful, even methodical, in keeping the connections between sentences clear. The principle is generally the simple one of overlap, wherein an element from one sentence appears in the next. Look at the sentences which are now listed with the connectives in each sentence in italics.

1. In 1973, *illness* put me out of action for the first time as President.
2. While I was recovering from *a debilitating case of viral pneumonia,* the existence of a White House *taping system* was made known.
3. I was faced with *a difficult decision.*
4. Some of my advisers urged me *to destroy the tapes,* while others urged me to keep *them,* because they felt the courts would support our contention that confidential conversations should not be made public.
5. Most of my friends and even some of my critics agree that I made *the wrong decision.*
6. If I had been *up to par physically,* there is certainly a chance that I would have stepped up to the issue and ordered *the tapes destroyed.*

Sometimes, the connection is made by the simple repetition of a key word, such as "tape" or "illness" (and it is surprising to see that even in complicated and sophisticated writing, that device still prevails). Sometimes the connection is made by using a different phrasing of the same idea. Nixon moves from the first to the second sentence by moving from a general category, "illness," to a specific member of that category, "viral pneumonia." If he had reversed the order of the third and fourth sentences, the system of links would be clearer:

> discovery of tapes ⟶
>   two kinds of advice ⟶
>   difficult decision

But we're used to small jumps like these, and the short third sentence serves the function of connecting the second and fourth sentences, so that the logic of the sequence is this: because the existence of the taping system was made known, I had to make a difficult decision, which was framed by the kind of advice I received from my advisers.

Notice that Nixon doesn't explicitly say what he decided. He probably assumes that he doesn't need to tell the reader that he decided not to destroy the tapes. Perhaps the whole matter was still a sore spot with him. As a writer, he faced a less dramatic decision than that of whether to destroy the tapes: whether to make the links explicit or implicit. Most of the time he makes them explicit and gives the reader's attention relatively little chance to stray.

We call Nixon's approach here the *shingle style.* He makes sure that there is overlap from one sentence to the next. (The extreme example of the shingle style is the kind of book that is read in first grade: "Yolanda has a brother. Yolanda's brother is Junius. Junius likes to play with dolls.")

It is a methodical style, and we may find it useful when we want guidance. If we went back again and looked at the italics in the Nixon paragraph, we would see that he is guiding us through a series of steps to illustrate the connection between illness and certain kinds of decisions, so that the line we follow is a series of connections. The shepherding here may seem rather forceful, and, using Lewis's metaphor of open gates alongside the road, we may even have a sense that Nixon is both tempting us to look down certain paths (that there was "certainly a chance" that he would have ordered the tapes to be destroyed) and trying to keep us from looking down certain others (all our questions about what was on the tapes). He guides us through the counsel of his advisors and toward the tantalizing suggestion with which he concludes, that he might have had the tapes—whose existence finally led to his forced resignation—destroyed.

But there are inevitably going to be spaces between each of our points, and how we establish the connections will do a good deal to establish our connection with our readers. Different readers will have different needs. It seems safe to say that you can think of times when someone was patronizing in giving more directions than you needed, as well as times when you were frustrated because someone failed to give adequately detailed instructions. There's no formula for just how overt the directing should be. The subject at hand and the reader's familiarity with it are your two best guides.

Trailblazing

Annie Dillard, whose work we will be looking at in detail in a moment, begins her book *The Writing Life* this way:

> When you write, you lay out a line of words. The line of words is a miner's pick, a wood-carver's gouge, a surgeon's probe. You wield it, and it digs a path you follow. Soon you find yourself deep in new territory. Is it a dead end, or have you located the real subject? You will know tomorrow, or this time next year. (3)

The line of words becomes a path. The path is at first the one the writer follows, trying to find out where she is going. In the final product, it is the path the writer marks out for the reader to follow; the writer blazes the trail, clears it, and puts out markers so that the reader can follow it. The most obvious kind of trailblazing and perhaps the most useful occurs when writers are aware of readers' presence and so refer directly to the course their argument will take, with phrases like "my next point" and "as you can see."

Regard the successive stages in your argument as turnings in a road. At crucial intersections you need to be extra careful of the reader, to make sure she can follow your path. Much work goes into finding your own way before you can mark it for readers. As you look at finished products, remember, that is just what they are. They didn't become finished products easily, and even to the extent that they did, it was only because the writers were experienced and could do the chore more quickly than relative beginners can.

Notice the markers in this passage from a book by Cynthia Russett:

> Scientific interest in women's nature had, then, a lengthy history. Yet the sexual science that arose in the late nineteenth century was something more than simply another chapter in that history. It was distinctive in a number of ways. In the first place, it attempted to be far more precise and empirical than anything that had gone before. In addition it was able to draw on new developments in the life sciences as well as on the new social sciences of anthropology, psychology, and sociology. And, finally, it spoke with the imperious tone of a discipline newly claiming, and in large measure being granted, decisive authority in matters social as well as strictly scientific.
>
> (*Sexual Science: The Victorian Construction of Womanhood*, 3–4)

"Then" in the first sentence; "yet" in the second; and "in the first place," "in addition," and "finally" in subsequent sentences all guide the reader, letting us know where we are. Deciding how many, if any, of these to use will not be easy; it all depends on your sense of what your reader needs.

✎ **Writing** Write a paper and deliberately incorporate signposts. Don't be afraid to tell the reader what's coming, how many points you will be making. Look closely at the beginning of your sentences, be sure that you take advantage of their importance by using them to employ clear and directive transitions.

Subtler Guidance

Follow the line of development clearly laid out in the following passage by Shelby Steele. You'll see immediately that he does not use explicit signposts of the sort you were using if you tried the exercise above:

> In the past few years, we have witnessed what the National Institute Against Prejudice and Violence calls a "proliferation" of racial incidents on college campuses around the country. Incidents of on-campus "intergroup conflict" have occurred at more than 160 colleges in the last two years, according to the Institute. The nature of these incidents has ranged from open racial violence—most notoriously, the October 1986 beating of a black student at the University of Massachusetts at Amherst after an argument about the World Series turned into a racial bashing, with a crowd of up to three thousand whites chasing twenty blacks—to the harassment of minority students and acts of racial or ethnic insensitivity, with by far the greatest number of episodes falling in these last two categories. At Yale last year, a swastika and the words "white power" were painted on the university's Afro-American

cultural center. Racist jokes were aired not long ago on a campus radio station at the University of Michigan. At the University of Wisconsin at Madison, members of the Zeta Beta Tau fraternity held a mock slave auction in which pledges painted their faces black and wore Afro wigs. Two weeks after the president of Stanford University informed the incoming freshman class last fall that "bigotry is out, and I mean it," two freshmen defaced a poster of Beethoven—gave the image thick lips—and hung it on a black student's door.

(The Content of Our Character, 127–128)

After siting the discussion with phrases like "in the past few years," "we have witnessed," "what the Institute calls," the first sentence announces the central subject—racial incidents. The next sentence enlarges that subject by indicating the number of incidents. The third sentence—the long one—defines the nature of "these incidents." And the rest of the paragraph gives a series of easily recognized examples of such incidents. By the time we get to the series, the phrase "racial incidents" is well established in our minds, and it is clear that precise examples of such incidents will follow. Steele here has not reached out explicitly to readers by offering apparent and deliberate signposts, but he has constructed the essay in such a way that although he never refers directly to readers, he nevertheless leads them along his path with certainty and clarity. We never wonder where all this is going; we never question the relevance and the illustrative usefulness of his examples.

✎ **Writing** Following Steele's example and keeping the readers' needs in mind, construct a paragraph that leads them directly through an idea but does not obviously acknowledge their presence by using overt signposts.

Loops in the Trail

Now let's see how a writer can lay a trail through an even more discursively written text, that is, a text that is apparently reflective and admittedly digressive. The following long passage by Annie Dillard develops in two ways: it tells of her intention to take a spring walk in order to catch "the edge of the season" and of her discovery on that walk of a peculiarly knotted snakeskin. After describing the snakeskin, she continues:

The point I want to make about the snakeskin is that, when I found it, it was whole and tied in a knot. Now there have been stories told, even by reputable scientists, of snakes that have deliberately tied themselves in a knot in order to prevent larger snakes from trying to swallow them—but I couldn't imagine any way that throwing itself into a half hitch would help a snake trying to escape its skin. Still, ever cautious, I figured that one of the neighborhood boys could possibly have tied it in a knot in the fall, for some whimsical boyish reason, and left it there, where it dried and gathered dust. So I carried the skin along thoughtlessly as I walked, snagging it sure enough on a low branch and ripping it in two for the first of many times. I saw that thick ice still lay on the quarry pond and that the skunk cabbage was already out in the clearings, and then I came home and looked at the skin and its knot.

The knot had no beginning. Idly I turned it around in my hand, searching for a place to untie; I came to with a start when I realized I must have turned the thing around fully ten times. Intently, then, I traced the knot's lump around with a finger: it was continuous. I couldn't untie it any more than I could untie a doughnut; it was a loop without beginning or end. These snakes *are* magic, I thought for a second, and then of course I realized what must have happened. The skin had been pulled inside-out like a peeled sock for several inches; then an inch or so of the inside-out part—a piece whose length was coincidentally equal to the diameter of the skin—had somehow been turned right-side out again, making a thick lump whose edges were lost in wrinkles, looking exactly like a knot.

So I have been thinking about the change of seasons. I don't want to miss spring this year. I want to distinguish the last winter frost from the out-of-season one, the frost of spring. I want to be there on the spot the moment the grass turns green. I always miss this radical revolution; I see it the next day from a window, the yard so suddenly green and lush I could envy Nebuchadnezzar down on all fours eating grass. This year I want to stick a net into time and say "now," as men plant flags on the ice and snow and say, "here." But it occurred to me that I could no more catch spring by the tip of the tail than I could untie the apparent knot in the snakeskin; there are no edges to grasp. Both are continuous loops.

(Pilgrim at Tinker Creek, 72, 73–74)

Her point is a tricky one that you may need to reread to grasp. *Our* point is simpler: to describe her discovery, she marks her path very clearly, as we can see by looking just at the beginnings of her sentences and major clauses in the first paragraph quoted:

> The point I want to make
> Now there have been stories
>> but
>
> Still
> So
>> and then I came home.

It may be useful to give a general description of the movement through these sentences. The first describes the main point that she wants to make, that the snakeskin was whole and tied in a knot. The second shifts you a little to one side: "Now," the first word, signals something like "hold what I just said in your mind for a moment while I say something related but not advancing the argument." She next introduces the fabulous stories about snakes tying themselves in knots, but uses "but"—as we just did—to reject any such suggestion. She then settles temporarily on another hypothesis: neighborhood boys. And then she moves on ("So" means something like, "in the way I just indicated"). The next sentence talks about the ice on the pond and the skunk cabbage visible in clear-ings, and "then," indicating merely sequence, she came home.

The path is quite easy to follow, even though it is intentionally somewhat meandering. The next paragraph is equally well knit but moves in a very different manner. It describes the stages of discovery. It begins with the knot that has no beginning. A series of repeated con-structions describes the process of how she came to her conclusion:

> I turned it
> I came to a start
> I traced
> I couldn't untie
> I thought
> I reasoned.

Then she describes what this process reveals, as well as in the next sen-tences: "I have been thinking," "I don't want to miss," "I want to distin-guish," "I want to be there," and so on, again leading to the conclusion: both snakeskins and seasons are continuous loops.

Think for a minute about what the outlines of these conversational but clear paragraphs suggest. They tell us that each paragraph has a skele-tal structure. Within each structure Dillard has moved in sequences: from general to specific or specific to general. She has given examples; she has connected similar and dissimilar things; she has introduced two ways of understanding what she's looking at—the abstract idea that time has no edge and the concrete symbol of time and change caught in the snakeskin. All the way through, though, she has guided us along by mak-ing sure that the structure—the flow and the development of the ideas she is dealing with—is absolutely clear and that the ideas are promi-nently positioned. Notice how the repetition of "I" as the subject linked to various verbs provides the structure in the paragraph that starts "The knot had no beginning." We might expect that paragraph to focus on the knot or the snakeskin. Dillard prefers to center herself in the paragraph, to make herself and her response to the snake central. In doing so she or-ganizes the subject and helps the reader follow her thinking.

Writers often do something like that as they guide you along. Often, the guidance is by pointers: *then, therefore, so, on the other hand, how-ever,* and other words or phrases. These pointers help us to find the path between sentences, to see directions. Sometimes, the pointing is often done by structure or reference. The most obvious technique is repetition: we repeat a crucial phrase or, as in the case of Dillard, a pattern of syntax. We ordinarily expect progression; the repeated patterns of phrasing, along with the continuity of contact, accomplish for Dillard's second and third paragraphs what the more overt pointers do in the first.

As we will say later in a section on sentences, reading and writing and listening are multidimensional activities. Sentences succeed one another; they also (as in this sentence) refer to points made earlier (or perhaps less often, to points ahead, as when we use a phrase like "as we shall see" or "more of this later"). You can think of Dillard's style as a combination of the shingle style and the signpost styles we looked at above. It's a closely structured style with an overlay of conversation and reflection, just enough to give it the quality of a speaking voice. Look for other examples of such discursive styles. Isolate the structure, the paths laid out for the reader. Identify the signposts and where they point.

✎ **Writing**   Write a two- or three-page essay explaining how you came to realize or to understand something. Give full play to the complexity of the process but use signposts and structure to keep your reader with you.

2   MOVING THROUGH THE TEXT

As you consider the overall organization of essays and other pieces of writing, we suggest that you think not simply about the order of the text but also about the movement of readers through it, about the text that will be re-created in the reader's mind. This order is not static, like the order of objects in space, but dynamic, active, sequential, and also simultaneous. You organize your words on the page in certain sequences, and your purpose in doing so is to bring your readers through the sequence so that they will end up agreeing with you, seeing what you see, or understanding your vantage point.

Planning Movement

Probably the most familiar way of organizing large blocks of material is to outline them first. Outlines can indeed help you put your thoughts into sequence, but they can also mislead you if they let you forget that your writing needs to lead and move readers. An outline can be effective if you have thought your topic through and put your ideas in order; it cannot, by and large, make that order. From this angle, you might better think about your essay in terms of the kind of flowcharts computer programmers make to tell computers precisely what steps to take to do what the programmer wants them to do.

Flowcharts need to be precise to an extraordinary degree (which some of us find very frustrating, in that we think a computer should have known what we wanted it to do). Programming instructors like to say that computers are very stupid; they will only do what you tell them, a little like Lewis's sheep. In that sense, the comparison may begin to break down. Readers—we should assume—aren't stupid in the sense that either sheep or computers are; the enterprise of writing is more collaborative than programming or shepherding; readers join you in making meaning out of their experience as well as from the directions you've given them. But the comparison is useful at the outset. Your readers generally know nothing about what *you're* going to say, except for what you tell them. That is how a certain familiar kind of misreading occurs. Readers see that a piece of writing is about a subject they have some knowledge or opinion of, and they think *their* thoughts about it, or the thoughts they *expect*, rather than the writer's intended thoughts. From the writer's point of view the same problem exists: you allow readers to take their own paths rather than yours.

At the outset, then, it is important to remember that order takes place ultimately in your readers' minds, unfolding through time; and that your text is a set of clues and signals and directions for your readers, to direct them to think this thought, understand that point, and move from one to the other through certain kinds of connections. You are in control of those signals and clues. To change the metaphor, you might think of yourself as the mythological Ariadne, whose father, King Minos of Crete, built a huge maze, occupied by the Minotaur, half bull and half human, to whom Athenian youths were sacrificed each year, caught by the Minotaur as they struggled to find an exit. The Athenian hero Theseus volunteered to stand in the youths' place; Ariadne fell in love with him and gave him a string that allowed him to keep track of his turnings and trace his way out, the man–bull in hot but futile pursuit. As a writer, one of your jobs is to provide your readers with threads that will allow them to trace their way through the maze that your own ideas can sometimes be to baffled readers.

You can begin working on movement in the large sense by inventing something like a flowchart, adapted to your own ways of thinking and visualizing; this is simply a projection onto a larger scale of what was said in the previous section. Some people begin by writing down ideas, in shorthand of some sort, on a large piece of paper. They include all the things they think might go into their essay; it's good to start inclusively—an idea at this stage is innocent of being a bad one until proven irrelevant. Then, as they mull it over, they try to see how the ideas connect, which really have meaning for them, and in what order they want their readers to proceed from one to another. This technique asks you to identify and trace all the paths, all the steps that are part of your idea. Once you identify them and understand what each requires by way of explanation or elaboration, you can concentrate on how to unite them. Such an approach has the advantage of letting you ask, "Where do I want my reader to end up?" Then, "Where is a good starting point, given my goal and my sense of my potential readers?" And then, as you actually write, "How can I show them the way?"

Another approach is to begin by freewriting, rapidly writing down your thoughts, skipping and jumping when appropriate so that you can get your ideas down as your mind races ahead. Then you can go back and mine what you've written, underscoring the most important points. Take them out, now, and draw lines, adding material where you think the jumps are too far; begin to flesh out ideas, culling material from your freewriting but probably in the end throwing quite a bit of it out. Some people can do this best in their minds and don't need freewriting to get the ideas flowing. Word-processing programs make this kind of cutting and pasting quite easy, at least in comparison to rewriting, retyping, or literal cutting and pasting. You can assemble material, move large blocks from place to place, cut, add, and print as you go along. This allows you to think about your material as something that can be reassembled in a great variety of different orders and, in effect, to play with different possibilities before you construct a paragraph.

Paragraphs and Thinking

Paragraphs are unlike some other parts of writing in that they are not natural parts of speech. We speak in sentences and we use words, metaphors, and images in our speech; but we only say that people speak in paragraphs when we mean that they sound bookish or perhaps just very well organized. In that sense, paragraphs are like weeks; unlike days and years (and lunar months), they are human constructions.

What this means is that paragraphs are something that you construct for purposes of writing, partly helped along by visual clues of indenting or spacing. The conventions of paragraphing vary from nation to nation, even within subgroups in one culture (newspaper paragraphs, for example, tend to be much shorter than those in many books or scholarly pieces). What does a paragraph correspond to? The answer cannot be too precise but, roughly, to a single point of some substance, along with some explanation, definition, or other discussion. It usually is a grouping of related material under a heading of some sort, which may be very explicitly stated (as in a topic sentence) or may not be. Perhaps more important is what happens between paragraphs: a paragraph is in some sense a turn, a break, a move, a next step.

✎ **Writing**   Try freewriting or the flowchart method as a way of discussing a complex subject. You might start by thinking about something physical, for example, what you need to do to get ready to go away on vacation. List everything that has to be done. Then arrange the items on the list in sequential order. What must be done first, before anything else? What must or can be last? Don't try to start at point A or number 1, but identify all the topics that you want to include. Find a governing idea. Now try organizing these parts into a whole composed of several paragraphs.

Narrative Movement

Sharp distinction is often made between narrative writing and expository writing, the kind of writing you do when you systematically present a set of ideas. Although we recognize the distinction, we think it overdrawn. Our English word *narrative* has its origin in a Latin word meaning "to know" and is connected with a great body of words having to do with knowledge and recognition. *Narrative* means that someone who knows is helping someone else to know. We think of it primarily in connection with stories, whether true or fictional, and as the presentation of a series of incidents that unfolds in a time sequence. But it is useful to think of the presentation of ideas and arguments as a species of narration, in which the ideas are incidents and the logic of the argument takes the place of the time sequence. Narrative flows whether you are telling a story or presenting an idea.

Here is an extended passage of narration from *The Broken Cord*, by Michael Dorris. In the book Dorris describes his tragic discovery that his adopted son is seriously ill as a result of fetal alcohol poisoning. In the passage below he is assembling the background knowledge he needs to understand his son's history. Look at the passage as an example of how to present a complex idea in a flowing narrative style:

> The Sioux, or Lakota ("the people," in their own language), lived before contact with Europeans in sedentary agricultural villages in the area west of the Great Lakes. They made fired clay pottery, hunted small game, enjoyed a social system in which men and women shared power and authority in all sectors of their societies. The Lakota got along with some of their neighbors, feuded with others, practiced a complicated religion, made music with flutes and rattles and drums, and prized oratory and story-telling above all other arts. They traded with culturally dissimilar peoples from many parts of North America and believed that the creative force, or *Wakan*, had formed their ancestors in what are today called the Black Hills (*paha sapa*), those strange, evocative, dark protrusions in the otherwise glacier-flattened landscape of western South Dakota.
>
> When Spanish horses finally reached their lands via a trade route that extended from Mexico through the Pueblos to the Great Plains, the Lakota for the most part elected to forsake their stable communities for the excitement and challenge of constant movement. The horse for them was an agent of revolution, as the wheel or the automobile has been for other peoples in other times. It set them free on the long, mostly uninhabited corridor of open

land between the eastern prairies and the Rocky Mountains. This was a country stocked with buffalo, the ultimate one-stop-shop animal whose harvest could feed, clothe, and shelter a society that didn't demand too much in the way of material possessions; the tribe, to the horror of latter-day Western anthropologists who don't think such things should logically happen, "abandoned the pot" and embraced a lifestyle at once more risky and more thrilling than horticulture.

The plateau west of the Missouri River, while starkly beautiful, a sage-scented expanse of yellow grass cut with deep gullies, was a precarious abode, a land of poisonous snakes and scrub weed, of wolves and coyotes, where eagles and hawks dominate and prey at will upon earthbound creatures. The climate is measured by extremes of cold and heat, drought and flood. The high plain has no ocean coast; rather, its boundary of reference and mythological inspiration has always been the changing sky, the source of light by day, of star-pointed direction by night. The hues of dawn and dusk are the palette in an otherwise monochrome universe. In a territory circumscribed by the luxury of far vistas, the birds of the air are most at home.

Scouring winds rise unpredictably, in dry summers lifting dust into cyclone devils or igniting the live match of lightning wherever it touches down, in winter whipping snow to such gray frenzy that to stray a foot beyond one's door without a secure tether is to lose all bearings. In traditional times, for human beings to survive at all in such an environment was a measure of ingenuity and invention. It required fast reactions, a constant fluidity, an unshackled, parrying response to whatever surprise nature might spring. Life was chance, and death was immobility.

For a few glorious generations, the Lakota shared all the earth that mattered to them with other Indians—Cheyenne, Arapaho, Crow, Pawnee, and Assiniboine—groups whose basic attitudes and values the Lakota could appreciate, even when intertribal relations were not friendly. As might be expected from a people who opted for bareback itinerancy rather than for plowed fields, the Lakota prized independence and individuality; even the issue of whether or not to go to war, even the gender role an adult might play, were matters of personal responsibility.

The Lakota had a live and let live attitude toward the first trickle of Europeans and Americans who penetrated their territory, in search of trading partners in the late eighteenth and early nineteenth centuries. When gold was "discovered" in the Black Hills, wagon loads of unruly white entrepreneurs, prospectors, and bandits invaded and tore at the sacred earth, slaughtered buffalo by the thousands, and left the carcasses to rot in the sun. It was widely known that other tribes had tried to live in peace with these newcomers and had still been massacred or deported, so the Lakota mounted a fierce, now legendary resistance. With the defeat at the Little Big Horn of General George Custer, a man who had been murdering unarmed Indians for a decade, the Lakota and their allies shocked the nation at the very moment of its Centennial. Their victory, which by any contemporary standard must be understood as temporary self-defense, earned them a stereotype for being "warlike" and became the excuse for the federal government to partition their aboriginal territory, supposedly protected forever by Senate treaty.

To a nomadic people, the imposition of tight restrictions on movement was in and of itself devastating. Confined by martial law to restricted reservations poorly suited to farming, devoid of buffalo, and administered by an overabundance of corrupt government appointees, the Great Sioux Nation, as it was once called, was politically and spiritually crushed. In light of their history and cultural values, the Lakota who survived the ensuing waves of disease and military attacks, like Wounded Knee, to which they were vulnerable, were especially susceptible to feelings of despondency, embittered dependence, and demoralization. (80–82)

A flowchart of this passage might look something like this, lining up the way things are in the middle, events to the left, and effects to the right:

(Dorris decides to find out his son's background)

Lakota way of life before Europeans came: sedentary, agricultural

The Spanish bring horses

the Lakota take up hunting

nature of the environment they now operate in as a result of the horses

effects of living in this new environment

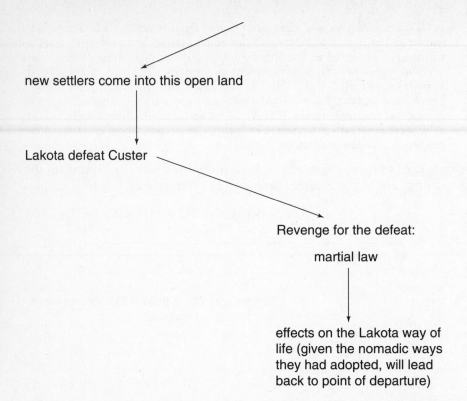

new settlers come into this open land

Lakota defeat Custer

Revenge for the defeat:

martial law

effects on the Lakota way of
life (given the nomadic ways
they had adopted, will lead
back to point of departure)

All this, we recall, is a part of the story of Dorris's son (or vice versa), a
loop in Dorris's primary narrative. It reads quite simply; we can imagine
someone calling it a straightforward narrative. And yet, looking at the
flowchart, we realize that it is quite a complicated story, with a variety of
influences affecting a line of action: the Lakota way of life, the introduction of horses, the environment of the Great Plains, the new settlers, the
defeat of Custer, and more than anything else the changes in the way of
life of a people over several centuries. The reason it seems simple when
we read it is that Dorris has paid a lot of attention to the movement of
our minds through the story.

The first paragraph situates you, tells you where and when and then
how the Lakota lived: before the coming of horses brought by Spain, they
were a settled, agricultural people. The second moves us in time: the crucial event is the coming of horses; the settled people became nomadic,
using horses to roam far across the plains while hunting buffalo. Note
some of the ways in which Dorris moves you along, keeping in contact
with phrases like "the ultimate one-stop-shop animal" and comparing
the horse to the wheel and the automobile. The next paragraph talks
about the new locale of the Lakota, mentioned in the second, and the
fourth continues that description, moving toward the point that this environment required certain survival skills. The next paragraph moves us

ahead in the time sequence once again, until the time at which this wide-open space was taken over, the treaty broken, and the Lakota's movements curtailed. The last paragraph moves us to the consequences of this curtailment, ending the sad story with their "despondency, embittered dependency, and demoralization."

Narrative is a natural mode of movement, probably the most widely used, and can be relied on for many uses, not just when there appears to be a story. For example, this particular narrative is embedded within a larger one, wherein Dorris is telling what he found about his son's illness. As he says just before this passage, "I needed to find out who Adam was in order to discover who he could be, yet I was faced with little evidence, with precious few clues, and with court-sealed medical records that would take me fifteen years to crack open. I knew Adam's tribe. From there, his story of the Lakota begins. But Dorris is also telling the story of how he discovered what he came to know about Adam and is presenting that knowledge in narrative, the story of how the Lakota came to the dependency and despondency that made them vulnerable to the introduction of alcohol into their culture.

You won't always be able to present your material as a narrative, nor want to. But it is well worth your time to look for a story when presenting material, and if one is available, to use it as a means of ordering, of moving your reader from point to point. In this case, the signal points are clearly demarcated by events and consequences. The Lakota lived in such and such a place; Spanish horses arrived, and their farming culture was transformed; Europeans came into their open country, and after the defeat of Custer, the Lakota territory was taken over; the restrictions destroyed a people whose culture was based on wide-ranging nomadic existence. All the rest is details and observations; readers follow the movement through time easily.

Notice how Dorris feels free to move in any of several directions—straight forward in sequence; to the side, so to speak, to describe or compare; and so on. Zigzagging is okay, sometimes necessary, as long as you let your readers know where they should go and then you bring them back. We are reminded of a story about the Wright brothers, who were, before they got into aeronautics, bicycle manufacturers. When they arrived on the scene, it is said, everyone was trying to make airplanes that were strong by virtue of their solid construction. What the Wrights' bicycle manufacturing had taught them was that strength came from flexibility, particularly strength that combined the ability to move on three different axes. The same is true of writing. Order in writing is a matter of flexibility, of dimensionality, and of movement of several sorts. There are a number of useful-looking schemes for ordering your essays (like the keyhole structure or the three- or five-paragraph theme) that, though they embody useful principles of order, can become straitjackets for your thinking and can force you into patterns that are too rigid to fly.

✎ **Writing** Choose something in your life that has an element of history, a story larger than your own. Extract the essential moments that lead to the impact of these historical events on your life. Make a flowchart that marks the major stages of the events. Then put it into an essay, thinking of an audience as you tell the story and of what the reader needs to know.

Interlocked Style

As we have said, material that is not generally thought of as a story unfolds in much the same manner and can be thought of as a kind of narrative of ideas. Here is a ten-paragraph editorial column by Anna Quindlen, paragraphed by newspaper conventions. As you read it, watch for the movements from paragraph to paragraph; try to imagine it as a flowchart, instructing you about directions to take, mental operations to carry out.

First, look for starting points and end points—not necessarily in terms of first and last sentences but in terms of where the writer assumes the reader to be at the beginning and where the writer wants to get the reader to at the end. Second, look for the writer's signals for when to move; look for marked turnings or jumps, places where the writer turns you in a different direction, and for those where the writer asks you to advance by means of illustration, contrast, definition, and the like. As you do so, remember that these systems of order are deeply connected with the subject matter and are not something that you can easily impose on your material from the outside—although there are certainly some standard moves and standard signals that you can employ (see the earlier section on paths). Underscore what looks to you like the important turning points, remembering that not every paragraph will have one and that they won't always be in the first sentence. Third, draw a picture of some sort of the movement—a flowchart or map or something of your own invention—or, if you are more comfortable with it, an outline.

> [1] Almost everyone has known a grandfather who was a bootstrapper. The stories of hard work and personal achievement have a certain sameness: how he delivered newspapers to buy school shoes, how he worked his way through college driving an ice truck, how he started a business even though no one wanted to rent to someone of his ilk. (Pick an ilk. Many ilks. I have heard this story from grandfathers Irish, Polish, German, Italian.)

> [2] These are inspiring stories that reinforce the notion that the United States is a place where perseverance and hard work can turn a poor person into a rich one. But there is sometimes something mean-spirited at the core of these simple parables. They do not allow for lucky breaks or for the differences between the past and the present. They assume that ad-

versity is somehow ennobling. The stories contain an accusatory moral, a rhetorical question. If I did it, why can't you?

[3] At this moment America's best known bootstrapper is Clarence Thomas, a man who has moved from the abject poverty of Pinpoint, Ga., to a nomination to the Supreme Court. His public statements on his past have been deeply moving and extraordinarily contradictory; this is a man who once said "any race-conscious remedy is no good," but also said of affirmative action measures, "But for them, God only knows where I would be today." His policies as chairman of the Equal Employment Opportunity Commission and his politics as a black conservative are classic bootstrapper, sure that individual initiative is key and that government aid—affirmative action, quotas, welfare—is demeaning and ineffective.

[4] "Employment is typically based on skills," he said in 1982, when he became chairman of the E.E.O.C. "To become a news reporter, you must be able to write. Simple as that."

[5] Oh, that it were so simple. This is a bootstrapper's belief, that merit is everything: in college admissions, in the job search. But it is human nature that when a hiring partner, a senior editor or a construction foreman looks across the desk at an applicant, one of many things that may play a part is a sense of seeing himself in the other person. That is one reason law firms, newspapers, construction sites are still mainly occupied by white men.

[6] Affirmative action has changed some of that. In every job I have gotten in the last 15 years, my gender has played some part. I was hired and promoted during a period when the corporate world was feeling the heat about diversity, just as Clarence Thomas was hired and promoted when the governmental world was feeling that heat.

[7] Why should we deny or decry that? The fallacy is that there is some inherent conflict between self-sufficiency and programs that encourage or require participation by competent members of minority groups. The latter open the door; once inside, the challenge is to give value for money, to do the job competently. The risk is that a white man who fails is considered incompetent, while a black man who fails is seen as evidence that blacks cannot do the job.

[8] Several weeks ago, the President stood at Clarence Thomas's side and said that race had played no part in his selection for the Court. Everyone knew that was not true. The question is, does it matter?

[9] It matters to the bootstrappers, who embrace the fiction of color-blindness and who persist in saying that Judge Thomas's race is irrelevant, although he himself once said, "There is nothing you can do to get past black skin." It matters to liberal opponents, who are uncomfortable opposing a black man but cannot support a conservative. And it matters to some supporters, too. "Given the choice between two conservatives, I'll take the one who's been called 'nigger,'" the columnist William Raspberry quoted a friend as saying.

[10] I don't believe that it matters how you get in the door, only how you perform once you're inside. Thurgood Marshall was chosen by Lyndon Johnson in no small measure because he was African-American. He will always be known as the first black Supreme Court Justice. He will also be known as a great one. Putting those two adjectives in the same place at the same time moves this country forward in its national perceptions. Bootstrappers move it back, to a time when our grandfathers pretended that hard work alone could surmount prejudice for anyone. ("Getting in the Door")

The first paragraph begins with a useful device: "Almost everyone has known"—in this case, a grandfather who claims to have pulled himself up by the bootstraps. The next paragraph takes a turn in its second sentence, upon "But." Nice as these stories are, Quindlen says, "there is sometimes something mean-spirited" at their core. Quindlen has not yet really let us know what her real subject is, her real purpose in writing; that comes in the first sentence of the third paragraph, with reference to Clarence Thomas, having at the time of publication just been nominated for the Supreme Court. The rest of this paragraph simply illustrates this point, with examples of his "deeply moving and extraordinarily contradictory" statements about his past. The fourth paragraph moves ahead simply by being another example, one that Quindlen uses the brief paragraph format to highlight, something that probably works better in newspaper columns than elsewhere; and it introduces the crucial word "simple."

The next paragraph, the fifth—coming just about halfway through the whole piece—focuses on a general statement of her major point: "Oh, that it were so simple." She changes the form of her statement, to the exclamatory, thus signaling that this is the heart of her argument. She immediately gives details as to why it isn't as simple as Judge Thomas's statements make it appear—because "like hires like." The sixth paragraph contrasts those practices with the statement of what affirmative action has done; Quindlen turns to her own experience to illustrate the benefits, almost in a confessional manner. In the seventh paragraph, she comments on that program, this time underscoring her turn with a question: "Why should we deny or decry" opening doors to people to whom doors have been shut merely because they are different? The next move, in the eighth paragraph, is to apply her experience, and the interpretation she gives of it, to Judge Thomas's own career, disputing the president's claim that race had played no role in his decision to nominate Thomas. "Everyone knows that was not true." Immediately comes a new question: "Does it matter?"

In the last two paragraphs Quindlen gives two answers, first that of the bootstrappers, liberal opponents, and some supporters; then hers: "I don't believe that it matters how you get in the door, only how you perform once you're inside." She uses the example of Thurgood Marshall, whose retirement opened the vacancy Thomas was nominated to fill, as an example (in her view) of a great justice whose appointment also had something to do with his race.

Quindlen has covered a great deal of ground in this brief article of about 750 words; we, as readers, have also covered a great deal of ground. At the end, we can see that the subjects of the column, the Thomas nomination and affirmative action, have been approached rather slowly, as befits—especially in the latter case—touchy issues on which many readers will have their own opinions. Leaving that tactic aside, however, we are most concerned with the flowchart Quindlen has constructed for us, moving us from subsidiary point to subsidiary point in a clear and coherent but not totally predictable way. The method of movement is a flexible one—she is able to move sideways as well as forward in order, for example, to bring in her own experience as a reference point against which to measure Judge Thomas's—and it is also tight. In the first sentence she talks about grandfathers who "pulled themselves up by the bootstraps"; in the last she talks about "a time when our grandfathers pretended that hard work alone could surmount prejudice for anyone," with "pretended" being the keyword. She has come a long way, but she is nearly back to where she began.

✎ **Writing**   To try this charting for yourself, choose a topic. Begin by assessing where your readers are likely to be at the outset and where you want them to be at the end. Now, map their journey. This is the hard and creative part of the work of organizing. You can think of it as devising a strategy, a kind of game plan for this particular piece of writing. Start with simple steps. You may find it useful to write out your plan roughly in the form we used to describe what we imagine Quindlen's plan to be— to write a kind of precis of your case, in which you try to describe what you want your reader to see. Sometimes it is very useful to let this evolve as you make drafts. Write a draft, and then write a note that answers such questions as, "Who are my readers?" "What do I assume them to know or believe about this subject?" "What am I trying to get them to do?" Then reread to see if you have really done that. Sometimes, such an exercise reveals major holes in your argument, tangents, or improperly sequenced orders. Especially in the drafting stage, take advantage of artificial aids—phrases like "my first point is," "you all agree," "now let's look at," "on the other hand," "it follows," "another example is," and so on.

CHAPTER 5

❧ ◯ ❧

Moving Through Words and Sentences

Every written text, we have argued, is a partnership between reader and writer. The writer's goal in this partnership is to communicate ideas, experiences, and feelings; the reader's, to understand them. Each of us understands language individually, yet at the same time we share a common language and we are able to communicate. Simply put, all texts have "rights," meanings the author intends; all readers have "rights," the unique ability to say that a text means something more in the reading, makes "sense" to them in a certain way that the writer may or may not have anticipated or consciously intended. Both reader and writer bring experience of life and language to every text. The challenge is to align the writer's intention and the reader's interpretation, respecting the rights of both the text and the reader.

This is not a simple matter. All of us have had the experience of writing a piece and of finding that our reader doesn't quite get the point or perhaps sees something that we never intended. This is not necessarily the fault of poor writing or of poor reading. The issue is more fundamental. Miscommunication and partial communication come about partly because of the nature of language. Because most words have multiple meanings, connotations and denotations, we can never be sure that the meaning we intend to be primary is the one that our reader thinks of. We all know what the color red means, but each of us in imagining it would probably imagine a particular hue or associate the color with a particular item, person, or experience. For some it may have political overtones; to others it will suggest embarrassment. When we combine words into texts, we multiply the potential variations.

In this book we have been discussing how writers, aware of the independence of the web of words they create, need to be aware of what happens in the reception of language. To know how your words reach your reader's mind, what sort of words invite open interpretation, and what sort of words forestall a reader from being "on your wavelength" is to be able to control the appeal and to some extent the interpretation of your writing. The writer's job, as we see it, is to calculate how meaning is to be retraced by readers. An illustration might help.

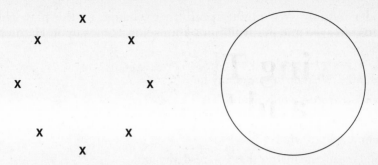

If asked what figures one sees here, one answer is probably going to be "two circles," though some might say, "a continuous line and a pattern of x's, both approximating a circle." In the one on the right, however, a line seems to trace the complete figure, whereas the viewer creates the one on the left in the mind's eye. (In fact, both are re-created in the mind's eye, but that fact is much less clear in the right-hand drawing.) If the writer's equivalents of the x's fall too far apart, the reader may re-create the wrong figure; if they are too close, if the writer explains too much, the reader may feel that the partnership is one-sided, dictatorial, and boring. The trick is to achieve balance—enough x's in the right order so that the reader can draw the line.

Once we get away from circles traced with x's or lines and into words, we find that the gradations and variations are almost infinite and that there are no sure-fire rules for getting the right balance in the partnership between close guidance and free rein. The more you write, the more you learn to vary the relationship according to the demands of the particular piece of writing. But there are tools that can be used to create and fine-tune that balance.

1 WORDS, WORDS, WORDS

Here we want to discuss the ability of words to go off in several directions, the tendency toward multiplicity of meaning and implication. We call it multivalency. Take this sentence:

He's mad.

It's about as simple as you can get, yet it could mean several things. It could refer to a person's anger; it could refer to a certain impulsiveness (as in "It's a mad mad world"); it could assert insanity. The statement could be used ironically about the most obviously sane, placid, staid person in the world, and thus could mean just the opposite of what it seems to say.

Words, in short, have a capacity to convey different meanings. Indeed, they have a tendency to do so, as we all know from instances of misunderstanding. We might recall an exchange in the play *Hamlet*. Polonius, an aged and platitudinous counselor, comes upon Hamlet reading a book:

> **Polonius.** What do you read, my lord?
>
> **Hamlet.** Words, words, words.
>
> **Pol.** What is the matter, my lord?
>
> **Ham.** Between who?
>
> **Pol.** I mean, the matter that you read, my lord.
>
> (II, ii, 191–195)

Of course, "words" is not the answer to the question Polonius is asking, nor by "What is the matter" did he mean "What's wrong with you?" Words, even simple ones, have multiple possibilities; and it is worth considering how much either of poetry or of humor would exist if words did not have that capacity. Hamlet has tuned Polonius's inquiry into a kind of knock-.knock joke, but the point beneath the banter is a central paradox that a writer confronts.

This multivalent quality of language both gives words enormous power and ultimately limits that power. Words can mean different things, they can imply different things, and they can connect with each other in different ways. That's what we mean when we say that words are multivalent. Sometimes—in the case of poetry, for example—we glory in the multivalence. In other kinds of writing, we often move in the opposite direction. We move toward a condition of univalence, toward restricting their meanings so that the words can be understood as precisely as possible in the way that the writer intended. Even poets can be frustrated by the resistance of words to being completely controlled. T. S. Eliot puts it this way:

> Words strain,
> Crack and sometimes break, under the burden,
> Under the tension, slip, slide, perish,
> Decay with imprecision, will not stay in place,
> Will not stay still.
>
> (T. S. Eliot, "Burnt Norton," ll. 149–153)

How far we move in the direction of making words univalent, trying to prevent them from cracking and slipping, depends a lot on circumstances and expectations. To give you directions, I may sacrifice some of the richness of language to ensure a kind of clarity that allows for no mistakes; in all probability I don't want you to take a wrong turn. If, however, I am proposing marriage or a trip to the zoo, I may want to draw more heavily on the capacity of language to create a rich and powerful statement. To propose marriage in the language of street direction may, in fact, give an entirely false impression of my feelings and purposes in proposing.

Perhaps the extreme case of language being used univalently—denotatively, we might say—is that beautiful abstract set of nonverbal symbols called mathematics, if, indeed, it is appropriate to call mathematics a language. For example:

$$2 + 2 = 4$$

means something like this: if you add two items to two other items you have a total of four items. There seems to be little margin of error; it can mean only one thing, and it seems always to be true.

Perhaps the opposite extreme is nonsense verse:

'Twas brillig, and the slithy toves
Did gyre and gimble in the wabe:
All mimsy were the borogroves,
And the mome raths outgrabe.

(Lewis Carroll, *Through the Looking-glass*)

If mathematical symbolism is pure specification, pure denotation without ambiguity or suggestiveness, these "words" come close to pure suggestiveness, pure connotation, without any clear reference. To Alice, they have some meaning: "It seems to fill my head with ideas—only I don't exactly know what they are."

Later, Humpty Dumpty offers an explanation.

'*Brillig*' means four o'clock in the afternoon—the time when you begin broiling things for dinner. . . . '*Slithy*' means 'lithe and slimy . . . '*Toves*' are something like badgers, . . . to '*gyre*' is to go round and round like a gyroscope. To '*gimble*' is to make holes like a gimblet.

And, Alice adds, "the '*wabe*' is the grass-plot around a sun-dial, I suppose." Even this seemingly nonsensical collection of words can make sense—if you know the meanings of the words.

Those aspiring to total precision want to move language as close to mathematics as possible. When that is the goal, there is little room for you to invent or to amuse or to question your reader. Your reader should assent to what you say because of what lies in the statement itself, with no added persuasive props. The major tools for such writing situations are the unmistakable exactitude of your words and the control your grammar exerts over them. A student encouraged and trained to write in this manner may have difficulty when asked to invent or to negotiate a meaning with a reader, to use various rhetorical devices to underscore points, or to put herself or her own voice into the writing. On the one hand, such writing tasks challenge us to put what we have discovered into the system of accepted discovery, and that means putting it into the language that has been established for the area we are working in. Someone trained to persuade, to convince not simply by laying out "facts," on the other hand, may have difficulty in writing strictly controlled "univalent" language, in adapting ordinary language, with its richness of meaning and implication, to the highly formalized uses of legal or scientific discourse.

Writing, however, is not really at the mercy of words. Word choice—"diction," as it is sometimes called—is indeed an important way in which we gain either multiplicity or singularity of meaning. But that's not the whole story. Equally important is the tool of grammar. There's not much one can do to rid the sentence "He's mad" of its inherent ambiguities—it's about as basic a sentence as one can make. One can expand it, however, using grammar—the appositive, the relative clause, the adjective, a larger predicate—to move the sentence from the realm of 2 + 2, an open-ended, unfinished idea, into that of 2 + 2 = 4, a complete statement. In the next section we discuss grammar and syntax in greater detail. Here we want merely to make a distinction between the two terms. *Grammar*—another one of those words that has several meanings and many implications—refers, for our purposes, to the set of implicit rules that allows us to connect words in meaningful patterns. (We particularly want to distinguish this meaning from the popular sense of grammar as a series of rules of socially acceptable usage, such as not ending a sentence with a preposition.) *Syntax* is the way in which words are put together to form phrases and sentences. Those arrangements are possible because of the existence of grammar within language; and to some extent, those arrangements are limited by the rules. Literally, syntax means "arranging": grammar is the set of connections that allows those arrangements to mean . . . whatever they are arranged to mean. In the popular movie *The Return of the Jedi*, the young hero, Luke Skywalker, seeks training from an ancient master, Yoda. Yoda asks: "Look I old to young eyes?" Luke answers, somewhat haltingly: "No. Of course not." Yoda responds: "I do, yes I do. Such have I become." Then, after a pause, "When 900 years old you reach look as good you will not." The rules of grammar make it possible for us to understand this last sentence. The syntax of the sentence is not what we might expect it to be, but the screenwriter is still following the fundamental principle: say it precisely as you want your reader or listener to understand it.

2   MAKING SENTENCES MOVE

In the last section we talked about the power of words both to specify meaning and to multiply it. Some linguists say that there are two parts to meaning, the *signifier* and the *signified:* for example, the word *tree* that we hear is the *signifier;* the arboreal idea or object it refers to is the *signified.* The goal of writing could be described as making the signifier be as close as possible to the signified for a given readership. But, in the end, we suggest that such a goal cannot be accomplished by word choice alone. More particularly, we suggest that the most powerful tools for ensuring the success of our transfer of meaning lie within the realm of grammar and syntax, the management of sentences.

Without denying the complexity of syntactical possibilities and of larger organizations such as those discussed in Chapter 4, we suggest that all the different kinds of sentences and ways of organizing ideas are variations of a few very basic principles. Moreover, the principles are not foreign to the experience of even beginning writers; rather they lie at the heart of activities you have been performing since you were very young, since you began making your own sentences and since you began listening to and telling stories. The elaboration of these principles in practice can become complicated and technically somewhat esoteric, but even then the principles are extensions of the ones you've been using since childhood.

In the case of sentences, it is important to recognize that you possess expertise simply by being a language user. You may not always be exercising your capabilities fully, but when you do you are still using the same few basic principles that you use when you make sentences in conversation and informal writing.

Agency, Focus, and Energy in Sentences

The way you put your sentences together counts a good deal toward how your reader will understand what you say. It is also a highly individual matter and something you probably do by and large as a matter of habit. Everyone will have characteristic ways of shaping sentences. These are parts of a person's style. It is quite possible, however, that you are not taking full advantage of the possibilities open to you. It's as if you had grown accustomed to one way of walking to work and suddenly found that there were half a dozen other paths that exposed new views, new neighbors to meet, and new ways of getting exercise. There are choices to be made about how and where to join groups of words into sentences and how and where to join groups of sentences into paragraphs. We focus on a few basic points about how sentences work—about readers' attention and the ways in which readers experience sentences—because we think they are generally overlooked in advice to writers, probably because they are so fundamental that writers by and large pass over them as "what everyone knows." Because we cannot address your style directly, we proceed indirectly, making our points by using examples of other people's sentences. As you read, however, you must decide where and how what we say applies to you. In the long run your goal should be to think about how to shape sentences to create the writing voice you want to be yours. As you read this section keep looking at your own style to see how the principles apply.

In talking about sentences people often use the phrase "sentence structure," which suggests that a sentence is like something built, a construction. This is a useful comparison, and we will be using the language of structure in some of our discussion. But it has a danger: it may make us look at sentences statically, as things that we make by putting verbal bricks together with grammatical mortar. Such a picture leaves out the dynamic quality of sentences, the way they move and the ways in which the reader traces the path marked by the writer. This moving quality of sentences, its continual reshaping of meaning as it moves forward, is at the heart of using sentences well and connecting them so that they form effective patterns.

As we proceed we will be talking about some "rules" of grammar and some of style, but we take it for granted that you know how or can quickly find out how to make grammatically correct sentences. Grammar, of course, plays a role, or rather two roles, in sentence making. It refers to that set of connections that we make on the basis of experience and of the principles that are probably hard-wired into our nervous system, and it defines the niceties of verbal behavior that are expected in certain situations, among certain groups of people. But much of the art of sentence making is not covered by either of these sets of rules. This is what we want to concentrate on, using some of the terminology of grammar to help you understand some of these matters of style and intention.

Locating the Center of Meaning

Consider the word *girl*. Think of all the possible connotations the word raises in your mind. Now think of the same word in this sentence: The 3-year-old girl threw the ball. Immediately the meaning of the word *girl* narrows. Some of the associations we bring to the simple, free-floating noun recede. The reader is no longer free to think of *girl* as a teenage cousin nor to picture a girl running; the reader is helped by knowing more about the girl, what she is doing, and so on. The writer is both limited and helped in the same ways. By placing the word in the sentence, we limit its potential significance; but by framing it with adjective, verb, and object of action, we provide the reader with an angle of vision, a perspective from which to understand what we mean. The writer shapes the sentence to indicate how readers should construe the meaning, which of the word's myriad possibilities to focus on.

Building a sentence, then, is a way of defining and specifying meaning, of focusing a reader's attention on a few ideas and their interrelations. Consider an old, familiar issue in sentence structure, whether to use the active or the passive voice. In terms of meaning—of the limiting, defining process that occurs when you link units of language, particularly nouns and verbs—the choice between active and passive is not between the right way and the wrong way but between two ways of focusing attention:

Active: Juan hit the ball.
Passive: The ball was hit by Juan.

Both of these are grammatically correct English sentences, but they send different messages. In the active voice Juan, who is the *agent* of the action—meaning that *he* did what was done—is also the grammatical *subject*. This sentence focuses our primary attention on *him*. Our angle of vision is so framed that "Juan" is what we "look at" mentally. Juan performs the action (hits the ball) and affects the object of his action (the ball). Sequentially the sentence is classically linear: subject, verb, object. English severely limits how the parts of a sentence can be rearranged and still make sense. Other languages, so-called inflected languages, give more leeway because changes in the word forms indicate changes in grammatical function. In English, meaning depends heavily on word order. One option we do have, though, is changing the voice.

If we change the voice of this sentence, we get a different emphasis. The second sentence, the one in the passive voice, shares the same elements, "the ball," "hit," and "Juan." Our minds "transform" the surface order very quickly so that we understand that, in fact, Juan hit the ball. But, in its own small way, this manner of putting it radically alters our perspective on the action. We no longer see Juan as centrally as we did. The ball, the first substantial element in the sentence, now attracts our primary attention, and we see the action in relation to it. The ball was the thing that was hit—as it turns out, by Juan. Juan is still the agent, but he is no longer the first thing we encounter in the sentence. His agency is directed toward an object that, in our new perspective, our new angle of vision, is apparently more important. That's the message the writer signals by framing the idea in this way. The ball, coming first, focuses our attention. It becomes the center of energy, the initiator of *grammatical* activity in the sentence.

The writers of these two sentences thus create two different perspectives and two different centers of energy and attention. The choice between the two is fundamental. It comes down to these questions: How do you want to define your topic? How do you want the reader to understand it? Your style, which means the way you shape your readers' perspectives, the way readers will move through what you have written, is the sum total of all such choices that you make—not just with the passive voice but also in a hundred similarly small matters that, nonetheless, in the end make a large difference.

A number of cases have been made against the passive voice on both ethical and stylistic grounds. Perhaps the best known occurs in George Orwell's essay "Politics and the English Language," where he is particularly concerned with the ways in which vague, obscure, indefinite language can be used to mask brutality. That masking can happen because, in the passive construction, you can leave out the agent altogether: "The ball was hit." That sounds innocuous enough, until you get into sentences such as "The village was bombed" or "The villagers were moved from their homes." Who did it? The passive allows you to avoid saying who. By not naming the agent at all, you can eliminate agency from your sentence altogether, and the sentence can make it sound as if the thing "just happened." "Never use the passive voice when you can use the active" (176) becomes one of Orwell's six basic rules of writing.

Although strong, Orwell's case does not seem to us to be definitive. The overused passive voice can be dreadful in some circumstances, but sometimes the passive voice is called for because it is useful in getting your precise meaning across to your reader. What you say when you use a passive voice without an agent is that it doesn't really matter who did it. Often enough, it doesn't. Orwell's point might therefore be rephrased to say that people have for propaganda purposes learned to use the passive construction to conceal agency when in fact agency—who did it—is precisely the thing that does matter.

When we cannot quite get an idea in focus, we often have not yet found the center of agency, the center of our idea—whether the agent is politically significant or not. We write and think we have it; we reread and find the words just do not say or mean what we intended. Often a mix-up arises between the idea and the grammatical expression of it. That is, what we create as the grammatical centers of agency and energy in the sentence are not the logical centers, are not what we are really talking about nor what we really want our readers to focus on.

You might compare a sentence first to a slide show, then to a motion picture. When we see slides, we are very much aware of seeing images that are not moving; then the projector clicks, and we move on to the next slide. Movies look as if they are totally different, but in fact they differ only in degree, not in kind. A movie is a series of still shots moving so fast that we "see" things moving (which is why we call them movies). Sentences are similar. We are used to dealing with sentences in motion, and we do not, by and large, perceive the operations as a series of discreet movements. But in fact that is how sentences work: lots of small movements add up to a general sense of movement and direction.

This motion begins with something that is going to move or be moved, something that has to do with the action the verb describes. Our advice is quite simple. Think about where you want to focus your readers' initial attention and put that element early in the sentence because readers look there to get their orientation. Spoken English gives us more leeway than written English because we can use vocal inflections to indicate the relative importance of words and phrases. In writing, however, less control is available; we cannot generally signal our readers to stress a given word to create a special emphasis. Sometimes—for example, in

writing letters—we use underlining or italics or bold type or capital letters to re-create some of the control we miss. But we rely more on position, on putting words in places where the readers, as they come across
them, will recognize their importance. The rule of early position is not
infallible, but it tells you something about where your reader will look,
where you can put what you want your reader to see. Your readers will
instinctively look for the center of energy; if you don't identify it clearly,
they will create it for themselves from what you give them.

Think more generally for a minute about placement in English sentences—not about modifying words, clauses, or phrases, but about what
gets our attention. By and large, we have said, the reader focuses on the
first word of agency or the first word that is acted on in a sentence, no
matter where the verb occurs. Things then start happening to that word:
it does things; it is modified; it is connected to other things. In our next-
to-last sentence, for example, a relatively complicated series of modifiers
("By and large," "we have said," "no matter where") still does not obscure the heart of the sentence: the agent, "the reader," who does something, "focuses on," to something, "the first word of agency." Notice that
the word "reader," at the beginning of the main clause, directs or brings
into focus everything that follows.

An apparent exception to our principle is the sentence in which the
subject and the predicate appear after their modifiers. It is only apparently an exception, as the following example illustrates. Look again at
the first example sentence from above, the one in the active voice, and
expand it:

> Breathing heavily, with teeth clenched and hands tight, Juan hit the
> ball.

The two opening phrases serve as adjectives that modify "Juan." They
paint the background within our framing device of the active-voice sentence. We still want to get to the first major word of agency, which is
"Juan." But by the time we do, we see Juan in a framework, so that we
will think of a somewhat more complex unit, Juan–breathing–heavily–
with–teeth–clenched–and–hands–tight. That whole unit, itself internally
complicated, becomes the composite agent that does the thing the predicate describes.

What happens if we use a suspended construction with a passive
voice?

> Breathing heavily, with teeth clenched and hands tight, the ball was
> hit by Juan.

As you can see, this is the sort of sentence English teachers love to pounce
on. What's wrong with it? Technically the phrases from "breathing heavily" to "hands tight" constitute a series of dangling participial phrases and

misplaced modifiers. More prosaically, they frame not what you want them to, "Juan," but "the ball," the closest noun. (Following the basic law of English construction, meaning derives from meaning clusters; every noun is surrounded by its appropriate adjectives, every verb accompanied by its adverbs.) Obviously, the words make sense only if they describe Juan, but he is inaccessible to them—they cannot get at him. We read English sentences sequentially and look to join component elements by rules and conventions, and so we naturally try to unite the modifiers and "ball." The result is a moment of confusion. What has the writer of such a sentence communicated to the reader? Unintentionally the writer has communicated confusion, and has generated it for the reader.

All this comes back to the fact that English sentences have centers of energy and that you need to be aware of where you locate them. The way you frame the sentence, what you designate as the subject, the voice you use for the verb, how you construct the modifiers—these locate the energy. Rules of grammar exist to help you control that energy and to channel it where it will serve the meaning you intend to create. There's no difference between the active and the passive voices except that they redefine the center of energy in a statement of action. Your choice is free; make it a deliberate choice.

✎ **Writing**   Sentences and our comprehension of them exist in time, as well as on the space of the printed page. What comes first and is acting or is acted on is what our mind wants to use as the subject. To get used to reformulating your sentences and to calculating their effect on readers, write a series of ten sentences on any topic. Next, recast them into the opposite voice; if a sentence is in the active voice, make it passive, and vice versa. Then read the two sets of sentences. What difference does voice make in expressing your ideas?

Nature and Artifice in Sentence Making

How does one make these choices about sentences? To begin with, it is useful to recognize that sentences are both natural and artificial. They reflect the way you speak and think and write in unpremeditated circumstances, but you can also arrange, rearrange, or prearrange them to suit particular purposes. You have probably been creating new, unheard-of sentences since you were 2 or 3 years old, without instructions on how to make sentences. Sentence-making instructions seem somehow to be hard-wired into our brains and nervous systems. That means that you intuitively know how subjects and predicates and modifiers and coordinators and subordinators work, even though you probably did not learn these terms until much later. You are, then, by nature a grammatical creature and have natural skills that you should not underestimate or allow to be taken from you.

Just as there are arts of weaving and fly-fishing and dancing, so there are arts of sentence making. But since sentence making goes on in our heads and conversations all the time, keeping its natural and artificial aspects straight can be difficult. The arts of sentence making, developed and practiced over the centuries in literature and rhetoric and advertising and journalism and the discourses of disciplines and so on, give us extraordinary resources with which to refine our even more extraordinary, natural sentence-making abilities. Books on grammar, rhetoric, or style may seem to imply that we build sentences and paragraphs and essays in the way that seamstresses make clothes, cutting parts (words) out of material external to us (language) and stitching them together according to the patterns of grammar. The analogy may have some merit, but only, we think, if you remember that sentence making occurs as an internal process, as well as an external one, and that the implicit rules in your mind have their own validity.

Oddly, it is only within the last fifteen years or so that teachers of writing have widely recognized the power of internal generative and transformative capabilities and some of the dangers of ignoring them. We have long assumed, quite reasonably, that the way to teach grammar and style is to emphasize their artificiality—in the best sense of that word—and to give students the rules by which to refine these arts. Considerable success has come from these traditional approaches.

Unfortunately, however, these rules sometimes become obstacles, obstacles not only to improving one's writing but sometimes also to writing at all. If you think about rules all the time, you may (1) stop thinking about what you are saying (you may indeed stop thinking altogether) and (2) fail to draw on your mind's amazing power to generate sentences on its own. All those rules may make writers feel stupid and inept and make them want to distrust their innate powers. Recently, teachers of writing have been discovering useful ways of redressing the imbalance between natural sentence making and idea generating, on the one hand, and artificial refining of style and argument, on the other.

In doing so they have awakened interest not just in the finished products of writing but also in the whole process by which these products are created. One particularly useful distinction concerns the different approaches that writers take to *composing* and to *revising*—approaches that seem to draw on quite different faculties and mental habits. For present purposes this distinction leads us to suggest that you think about the fine points of arrangement we discuss here and elsewhere *not* while you are putting essays together but only when you are revising.

Therefore, compose expansively, verbosely (or if it is your natural way, in shorthand), tangentially, conversationally, using your innate powers freely and as fully as you can. Doing so will probably free you for your first and most important work, incubating ideas, and you may find that some of what you generate will have freshness and power that can be transferred to the finished product with only a little tidying and with great benefit.

But in the process of revising, think about arrangement for the purpose of getting your ideas across to your readers. Over time, as you think about the choices available to you, your natural style will probably begin to change and reflect the self-conscious choices you have been making. You will also sometimes discover that your "natural" style is full of artificially induced habits from which you may or may not want to free yourself. You may find that you have become so involved in not splitting infinitives or in getting *who* and *whom* straight or in remembering that the word *data* is a plural noun and *phenomenon* singular that temporarily you need, first, to stop thinking about them so that your ideas can flow and, then, to deal with such details, and the more important matters of arrangement, in the process of revising.

✎ **Writing** Look at something you have written fairly recently. Try to locate the sources of energy and movement in its sentences. Read them aloud, and see what your voice wants to emphasize. Some sentences will have more than one such center, and over a full page you will probably find a hierarchy, a few words or phrases that get particular emphasis. Underscore them, with double lines for the most important ones. Now, ask if your sentence structures are giving your readers the clues they need to focus on the sources of energy you want to convey or if they are highlighting and drawing your readers' attention to elements that are not central to you.

Movement

You may have been urged by teachers to "find a good verb" as the start of making your style lively; if you find the right verb, it is said, you can cut out a lot of unnecessary verbiage. It is true that the correct verb can communicate volumes of meaning and save you a lot of trouble you might otherwise have to expend on explaining what you mean. That applies particularly to sentences with a form of "to be" followed by an adjective, as in "The implications of his words were serious." The point is not to save words, as if they were a scarce commodity or ink were precious, but to concentrate attention on movement. (For instance we might revise this sentence to say, "His words implied a serious threat.") Finding the right verb can focus the energy in your sentence, and eliminating "unnecessary words" can eliminate confusion about the agent, the center of energy, and the reception of energy in your sentence.

Whatever it is—often the agent—that your sentence has focused your readers' attention on, the sentence then shows *acting:* Juan *hits* a ball; an idea *dismays* someone; a flavor of ice cream *is* my favorite. The action does not need to be an act in the narrow sense. States of being or becoming or possessing are also "actions" from the point of view of sentences, so that an agent can also *be, seem, become,* or *have:* a flavor of ice cream *is* my favorite; so and so *is* a fool; I *have* three dollars; you *seem* bored; she *is becoming* restless. These are not actions in the way that walking and running are, but from the sentence's point of view, they are still actions.

Again, we can see the basis for some familiar advice: avoid relying too heavily on "state of being" verbs, on saying what things *are* rather than what they *do.* That's good advice, as well as being at times impossible to follow. So much of what we do in writing concerns what things *are* that we inevitably form many sentences around forms of "to be." But the advice still helps us see something about how sentences work. Writing means moving your reader in the path along which your thoughts have moved. "Is," used repeatedly, does not usually move you very far ("is" is a kind of static action). Verbs that state concrete actions keep readers moving more obviously than those that do not. Compare these sentences, all of which make sense and obey the basic rules of grammar:

Her actions are an indication of strength.
Her actions indicate strength.
Her actions show strength.

The more you can see the verb as a clear-cut action, the more quickly you move. When your writing moves slowly, try to trace the actual movements of your thoughts; then try to express those actions in the verbs by making them concrete and active, remembering that you will often find that you need to use a form of *to be* and will then need to find energy and movement in other places.

A terse, pithy style is not necessarily or absolutely superior to one that is lengthier and more elaborate, as long as the "wordier" one presents agency and energy clearly. This is not a matter of word rationing. Look at some more fairly simple examples. Compare

Mary angled the volleyball over the net so sharply that before anyone could return it, it hit the ground.

with

Mary spiked the volleyball.

The word "spiked" in the second sentence replaces all the modifying phrases of the first. It is the one single right word for the action that the first sentence tried to describe at such length. Now, is "Mary spiked the volleyball" a better sentence than the other? Not grammatically. The longer one is fine from the point of view of clarity. Ought we to prefer it to the second one? Not necessarily.

Again, think about the differences both in terms of the angle of vision on the action and in terms of how and what each would contribute to a writer's style. When would you want to use the shorter version? When would the longer, more drawn-out, more detailed version be better? One can see that the choices here are real. Each sentence serves a purpose all its own. If each sentence can be said to have a center of energy, the level of that energy—whether it is focused and intense or more widely dispersed—is affected by the length of the sentence. The energy of sentences moves the reader through your text and generates a style—a "Mary spiked the ball" plain style or a more extended, rhetorical style. Both have strong verbs, "angled" and "spiked." Both move.

Examining how you think is the first step toward understanding how to develop your own effective and personal style. Sometimes you need to slow your reader down, to state a point abstractly, to focus on what *is* rather than what *happens*. But sometimes habits of writing create a rhythm of thought that doesn't correspond to the way you are thinking. You are thinking, "the Soviet Union fell apart, and President Gorbachev stood aside," but you write, "President Gorbachev was passive during the disintegration of the Soviet Union." The second step is to think tactically. It is not just how you want to move; it is also how you want your readers to move, to join in your movement.

✎ **Writing**   Think about where the preference for a simple style comes from. Modern English usage tends to prefer the architecture of the shorter, more energy-compact sentences. As a way into the political as well as the grammatical reasons behind this stylistic preference, think about this passage from Orwell's essay, referred to earlier:

> In our times it is broadly true that political writing is bad writing. Where it is not true, it will generally be found that the writer is some kind of rebel, expressing his private opinions and not a "party line." The political dialects to be found in pamphlets, leading articles, manifestoes, White Papers and the speeches of undersecretaries do, of course, vary from party to party, but they are all alike in that one almost never finds in them a fresh, vivid, homemade turn of speech. . . . In our time, political speech and writing are largely the defense of the indefensible. . . .
>
> Political language has to consist largely of euphemism, question-begging and sheer cloudy vagueness. Defenseless villages are bombarded from the air, the inhabitants driven out into the countryside, the cattle machine-gunned, the huts set on fire with incendiary bullets: this is called *pacification*. . . . Such phraseology is needed if one wants to name things without calling up mental pictures of them.
>
> ("Politics and the English Language," 172–173)

Do you agree that the problem Orwell outlines here, particularly the growth of obfuscatory language in modern government prose, is a pressing issue in the current state of the English language in America? What has changed since Orwell wrote this piece in 1946? Do you agree with his ideas? Are there other areas—academic writing or advertising—that suffer in similar ways and for similar reasons? How would you challenge his argument? Can you find examples that either support or challenge his view? Collect your ideas and convey them in an essay, quoting examples.

Organizing Groups of Words

Agency, energy, and movement are the basic issues in building sentences. Virtually as basic, though, are connections of parts of sentences and ways of channeling the flow of energy through a group of sentences. Here is a string of words that may or may not be thought meaningful:

time flies like an arrow fruit flies like a banana

The addition of a few punctuation marks quickly renders the string, which many of us on first sight find baffling, quite meaningful and in fact recognizable as a quotation from Groucho Marx:

Time flies like an arrow. Fruit flies like a banana.

You could take this as an advertisement for punctuation, which gives us some, often a great deal of, help in figuring out sentence patterns. Even more, it shows the importance of pattern and expectation: we are used to "time" being a noun and "flies" being a verb, in the familiar saying "time flies." In this section we want to focus on the point that meaning doesn't just come from collections of words but also depends heavily on connections between words and groups of words.

When we read or listen, then, we are not only spotting the meanings of individual words but also processing those individual meanings (some of which may be ambiguous or difficult to discern) by trying to spot the connections they have with other words. Even fairly simple sentences involve our minds in rapid-fire, largely unconscious sorting out of parts. (Amazingly, many 2- or 3-year-olds can do this sorting, even though the most sophisticated computers can't. The skill manages to be both very simple and very complicated.) Our minds sort so rapidly that we don't notice what they're doing unless the sentences are hard to "parse," as people used to call it, and then sometimes we are irritated at the extra work the writer has caused us in making us untangle her connections.

Do particular kinds of sentence connections work better than others to build bridges to readers? Often we are too busy figuring out what we are going to say to think about the kinds of connections we are making with readers, but since getting readers to see what we mean is our ultimate goal, it is useful also to think not only about how the sentences move but also about how readers move through them. Take one memorable opening sentence:

> I had a farm in Africa, at the foot of the Ngong hills.
>
> (Isak Dinesen, *Out of Africa*, 3)

We are aware of basic simplicity here—the absence of distraction, the quick movement through the important parts, like a stone skipping across the water. The reader moves from subject to verb to object (probably the most normal pattern in English), and the prepositional phrase gives us the most important fact about the farm—it was in Africa—followed by a further refinement, that it was at the foot of the Ngong hills. The sentence embodies easy, direct, clear movement and meaning.

Although simplicity is by no means the only way of connecting with the reader, it works easily and gracefully here, leading us into the world the author wants to explain. Whether or not she planned it this way, Dinesen's first clause presents the three major terms of her whole book— "I," "farm," and "Africa"—in simple, clear relation to one another. Often, particularly when they are not used to writing frequently, people use a style that's complicated to impress their readers. Simplicity may be preferable. Simplicity is not necessarily simple-minded, nor is it necessarily easy. It is one principle of construction, one that sometimes can be used very effectively to connect with a reader. It has the advantage of concentration: since there are relatively few connections for readers to make, you can concentrate their attention on a few basic connections.

A simple style, however, will not necessarily reduce your ability to convey complex ideas. Simplicity does not just mean "Juan hit the ball" kind of writing. Here is another relatively simple sentence, declarative but with a compound predicate, from an essay by Edward Hoagland. It does not make the essential connections but leaves them for the reader to make:

> Turtles cough, burp, whistle, grunt and hiss, and produce social judgments.
>
> ("The Courage of Turtles," 23)

Its complexity comes from the six verbs that show what the subject does, from the texture of that list of actions, and its humor from the growing anthropomorphism that leads to the last item on the list: turtles seem more and more human. It may have actually taken Hoagland a long time to write that sentence, to get the list right, to pare away all the things he might have been tempted to say.

As in the sentence by Dinesen, Hoagland illustrates how, as a reader, you grasp ideas sequentially in your reading before you connect them as a whole. That very simple subject—"turtles"—establishes the topic, the focus; the sequence of verbs moves the reader on, toward the climax at the end. By the time you read through this relatively simple sentence, it has given you a great deal of information to process. You can go back to it and discover the method of its construction, its architecture: it is a simple series of verbs, culminating in an explicit anthropomorphism. After reading, you reflect on the author's creation and intention; several kinds of meaning come forward, all simultaneously present but sequentially realized in the reading. It is a simple sentence grammatically, but it presents many complex ideas. Often complexity inheres in the understanding of what is simply said, not in the complexity of the saying. Remember that writing is a partnership with the reader. Trust your reader to be able to understand the complexity of what you are able to express simply and clearly.

Organizing Larger Groups of Words

In arranging the parts of sentences, you are making the path you want your readers to retrace to find the relationships of your ideas to one another, to yourself, and to them. In one sense, that is all writing is about: to get the reader to see these relationships, to see them as you see them yourself. We have all felt the frustration of telling other people about something and having them fail to get our real point. When writing works, readers reexperience the writer's pattern of thinking. Watching this transfer of meaning occur is one of the things that makes the study of literature exciting, as we watch great poets or prose writers crystallize a perception or experience or reflection in a pattern that pulls us along through their thinking processes. It is also something that every writer can strive for.

In the previous section we discussed the simple declarative sentence and the sentence with a compound predicate. We want now to analyze in some detail how a carefully formed sentence of some complexity moves its readers through a set of experiences, tracing a pattern of lived experience. Here is a sentence from Joan Didion's essay "Goodbye to All That":

> When I first saw New York I was twenty, and it was summertime, and I got off a DC–7 at the old Idlewild temporary terminal in a new dress which had seemed very smart in Sacramento but seemed less smart already, even in the old Idlewild temporary terminal, and the warm air smelled of mildew and some instinct programmed by all the movies I had ever seen and all the songs I had ever sung and all the stories I had ever read about New York informed me that it would never be quite the same again. (225)

As a way of addressing the question of why this allegedly good writer packed so many little clauses and phrases into one sentence, we might begin by rewriting it as a series of short sentences:

> I first saw New York when I was twenty. It was summertime. I got off a DC–7 at the old Idlewild terminal. I was wearing a new dress. It had seemed very smart in Sacramento, but already seemed less so, even in Idlewild terminal. The warm air smelled of mildew.

And so on. The differences may seem fairly small, or you may prefer the rewrite, but the two versions differ in that the connections among all these various experiences are less explicit in the rewrite. A musician might say that the original is *legato*, the rewrite *staccato*, recognizing that each mode has its place and effects. Even though we may need to struggle with the original a bit to keep it all straight, that may be part of Didion's intention: to give the sense of a whole group of experiences being bound together.

Look at the structure more closely. It is a compound-complex sentence, meaning that it has both dependent and independent clauses— clauses that cannot stand alone as sentences ("When I first saw New York") and ones that can ("the warm air smelled of mildew"). We can think of a compound construction (in which independent clauses are linked by conjunctions like *and, or,* and *but* or by a semicolon) as a relatively loose one and of the complex construction (wherein the link is effected by a subordinator like *when, because,* or *if*) as relatively tight; it clearly subordinates one clause to another, defining that subordination quite specifically with a term like *when.* In the case of Didion's sentence, the opening subordinate clause frames the rest of the sentence powerfully: each of five related things, defined in the five coordinated main clauses, happened at the time the first phrase specifies:

When I first saw New York

I was twenty
[and] it was summertime
[and] I got off a DC–7 (with appropriate
descriptions of where
and of what I was wearing)
[and] the warm air smelled of mildew
[and] some instinct (with appropriate descriptions
of its origins)
informed me (of something very important).

Although we call the first clause grammatically subordinate to the ones that follow it, in the reader's experience it is probably the other way around. The moment of first seeing New York controls or at least frames the rest of this complicated sentence. But the sentence moves forward, especially through the clauses that tell you how old the writer is, where she landed, what she was wearing, what season it was, what it smelled like—until we get to the last, where "some instinct" tells her something important: that it, presumably New York or her experience of New York or "life," would never be the same again.

We would probably not like long stretches of writing like this very much (in fact, Didion immediately changes pace with her next sentence: "In fact, it never was"), but this particular sentence has the effect of a fine tracery of a series of important connections: being 20, being in a grubby air terminal, having high expectations, dressing "just right" but having it turn out to be a little wrong, being aware that the moment would fade.

One of the things that most gives a piece of writing authenticity is the feeling that the connections of experience are being retraced by the writer as relived experience. Many of the connections are simple. Readers can hold only so many connections in their mind, and if the connections become so numerous as to be confusing, the reader is likely to be alienated. Didion gives shape to these elements as she holds the conclusion off, builds suspense, and allows us to savor the subordinated material as central and independent. But the important thing is that the connections connect the important elements, the elements important to the writer's thought. When you modify, you can shoot out from a particular point and explain right then and there, as we're doing just now, what you want to emphasize about it, some additional information you want the reader to have, or the circumstances of your knowing it. Didion constantly modifies her simple narrative line because the modification is the point—nothing was quite what she expected; all her expectations were consistently modified by experience. Modification is the essence of Didion's experience.

✎ **Writing**   Try Didion's technique. Choose an experience of some importance to you—going away to school, going to a wedding or funeral, moving to a new place—something that constitutes one experience but has successive parts. Try writing this into a sequence of sentences, of which some are brief and to the point and a few resemble Didion's in bringing together some moments that are related and important, using an appropriately complex structure—not necessarily Didion's. The way to begin is with the discreet experiences, the moments, as if on slides or frames of a motion picture. Then think about which belong together and put them into a more complicated sentence structure.

Habitual Sentence Patterns

If the kinds of bonds we have been talking about in writing are not just bonds of language but also bonds of thought and memory and perception, then what goes on in our prose reflects what goes on in our minds. If that's so, it's worth looking at the patterns you habitually use in your writing and questioning whether you've gotten into habits that reduce the range of connections open to you. Very often, in the process of editing, you find a connection that has been hovering in your mind, that may even be the real point you want to make, but that has somehow gotten lost. Part of writing personally is writing about connections that are only dimly perceived, bringing them into light. Phrasing things is always a matter of making connections, and the connections are not just between words but also between the things the words stand for in your experience.

In sentences, you can do many things, just as in a car—with an accelerator, steering wheel, brakes, and perhaps a gear shift—you can go many places, by many routes, and for many distances. You can make many connections. If you look at your sentences, you may find that you've fallen into simple repetitive patterns and aren't connecting things you really want to.

To practice, start with short sentences and be aware of these basic bonds: of giving actions agents or agents actions; of completing by giving complements like objects; of changing by using modifiers; of emphasizing similarity or balance by coordinating; of emphasizing dependence or rank by subordinating.

Then, remember that any of these combinations made with two or more words can become units in new and larger combinations. A sentence resembles a mobile in this respect. Two elements combine with each other to make a balance:

Together, they may serve as a new unit, balanced in a new construction:

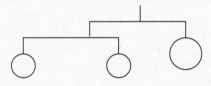

The new unit can be either unitary or a collection—as chemists might say, atomic or molecular:

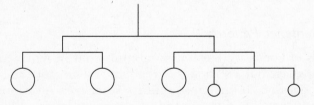

As sentences build up, the same kinds of connections operate on a larger scale: the subject of a sentence can be a single word (as in *Eating* filled me up) or a large construction that functions as a single word (*The pumpkin pie that grandfather baked before he went to Toledo* filled me up). As you make larger constructions, there's more for you and your reader to keep track of, more interesting connections to explore, and more paths down which your reader's attention can wander, either to discover or to lose her way.

It is difficult to judge practically how large the units can be before they stop being units and how complex a structure can be before it is too complex for our minds to handle. It depends partly on the reading habits of your readers. If they have been reading very complex prose, full of intricate constructions, their minds may be in good shape for putting some more together (or may appreciate a change or be surprised by bull's-eye simplicity into fresh perceptions). Newspapers and some book publishers clearly think that we perceive in small units, no more than five or six words at a time; some people tell us to read by phrases, to take one phrase in at a glance, and then move quickly to the next. Most good writers, however, are willing to take advantage of the full range of possibilities.

PART II

Professional Voices

CHAPTER 6

Reading and Writing in Professional Worlds

In this chapter we talk about how discourses create professional voices. Along the way we consider how and why discourses seem both professional and impressive, as well as a bit daunting. But first we want to define *discourse* and call your attention to the variety of meanings people attach to the term.

Some people define discourse narrowly to refer to specific professional styles—the styles, say, of law, medicine, science, or literary criticism. In each field a combination of specialized vocabulary and structure constitutes its discourse. But the word has broader senses as well. Over the centuries since its first appearance in English the word has been closely tied to reasoning, conversing, and communicating thought. *Discourse* seems to have been a word English-speaking people used to describe understanding expressed in language. That's a good definition to keep in mind, especially today when the word is so trendy and so much used, particularly in the humanities. One hears of the discourse of criticism, the discourse of feminism, the discourse of the new historicism, the discourses of power. The historical sense may be the best one to guide us through the somewhat complicated paths of modern terminology because it emphasizes the verbal expression of understanding. This kind of definition accounts for and focuses our attention on the fact that discourses, ways of speaking and writing, do reveal what we understand to be central to our subjects or even essential in our worldviews.

These older definitions, too, reveal why discourses are so important. To be able to use the discourse of a given field—the diction, the sentence structures, and the tone that dominates the discussions of that field—is a sign that you understand the field and that you intend your writing to contribute to it. It also signifies that you are willing to adapt your style and your writing personality to your audience's way of understanding the subject at hand.

1   SHORTHAND FOR THE PROFESSIONAL AUDIENCE

Once upon a time (the exact date is not known, but it is not likely to be put in issue, since the memory of man runneth not to the contrary), a little girl

111

(about whose parentage there is no issue and who will be presumed therefore to be legitimate) named Goldilocks wanted to visit her grandmother (whether paternal or maternal is immaterial) who lived on the other side of the forest (the exact location of which may be determined in metes and bounds by consulting the records of the Registry of Deeds in the county in which the said premises are located). Little Goldilocks was given permission by her parents. . . .

When little Goldilocks was perambulating the perimeter of the forest, she was attracted by a single dwelling of unusual construction set back from the highway in a manner which conformed exactly to the zoning regulations lawfully enacted and promulgated. This was not, as you will note, an attractive nuisance since the object was one with which all children are familiar and the dangers of which, if any, are obvious.

(Edward A. Hogan, Jr., "How a Law Professor
Tells His Children the Story of the Three Bears," 42–43)

This, of course, is a parody, a translation of the story of Goldilocks and the Three Bears into *legal discourse,* or an exaggerated version of it. We might ask why it is so easy to parody certain kinds of discourse. Discourse, as we have said, is the sum of all the verbal usages and conventions of a particular field or any other group that uses language in a particular way to define its practices, its interests, and its worldview. It is in legal discourse that Hogan has retold the traditional story (which, we could say, is written in fairytale discourse). Taking discourse out of context—which happens often enough in actuality—inevitably makes it sound humorous, pompous, or just plain inappropriate.

Discourse is not just a matter of words and phrases that either have specialized uses or are not to be found elsewhere; discourse can include or exclude whole categories of thought from consideration. The discourse of fairytales, for instance, is dominated by references to family relationships, stepmothers, stepsisters, mothers, fathers, children; to magic; to castles, forests, balls, and animals; to name a few. Nowhere in the discourse of fairytales is there reference to ideas such as the means of production, the material view of history, or the free market. To apply the discourse of one field—*another worldview, in effect*—to another, as in this example, often produces humor.

The words and phrases in this parody of legal thinking represent what the group with whom we associate the discourse finds important. We could say that "the discourse of fairytales" does not find exact times and places to be important, so it says "once upon a time"; the discourse of lawyers does, so that if the date is absent it needs to note the fact: "The exact date is not known, but is not likely to be put in issue." ("Put in issue" means people will argue about it; "argue about it" is exactly what lawyers do.) "Consulting the records in the Registry of Deeds" indicates that lawyers or a court find certain kinds of proof persuasive: documentary evidence, eyewitness accounts, and other kinds of verifiable accounts. The precise nature of evidence is of great importance to lawyers, and this emphasis is expressed by the discourse. Hence, we could say that to learn the discourse of a group is also to learn, in coded form, what that group finds important and what their standard procedures are by looking at the ways in which they formally talk to one another or conduct their professional business.

Because discourses are ways of expressing our understanding of what's important, or of how reality is "seen" by a particular group looking from a particular perspective, discourses can be thought of as a kind of shorthand, even though they seem long-winded to nonpractitioners. Discourses provide ways of communicating information succinctly and quickly, with a minimum of unnecessary explanation. For example, we asked a geologist for a brief passage that illustrates the discourse of his field. He sent us a passage from which the following paragraphs are taken, along with this explanatory note: "It is the description and . . . interpretation of the depositional environment of some layered sedimentary rocks in Canada. 'Bouma' refers to a regular stratification pattern in a deep water sedimentary rock type known as a turbidite. This passage is rich with both descriptive and genetic terminology."

Blueflower Formation
The Blueflower Formation is not preserved above the Sheepbed and Game-trail formations of the "typical" outcrop belt. . . . At Sekwi Brook it is 55 m thick, and consists of dark-coloured, deep-water shale and mudstone (59%), turbiditic sandstones (15%), and limestones of turbiditic and grain-flow origin (26%). It is the lower part of a shoaling-upward cycle that terminates with the peritidal dolomites of the overlying Risky Formation.
(Narbonne and Aitken, "Ediacaram fossils from the
Sekwi Brook Area, Mackenzie Mountains, Northwestern Canada," 948)

Every detail of this description is, we are told, significant to geologists; they know how to interpret each one. Every detail down to the placement of commas, which words in the title of the article are capitalized, and how references are made would be part of the discourse of this particular field. This degree of detail is not surprising because the discourse provides a conventional, common language in which geologists, its intended audience, speak and write to one another. In the discourse of geology, as in law or any other professional field that has its own pattern of language, the rules of the game are so tightly defined that if you know how to use them, you can be all but absolutely sure that your reader will understand what you say.

But a nonspecialist would want to know much more than the passage seems to communicate: Where and how was the formation "named"? What's deep-water shale as opposed to regular shale? What does "shoaling-up" mean in the discourse of geology? Does it, for example, have anything to do with shallow water shoals? The geologists who read and write this discourse know the answers to these questions, assuming the passage is properly written. For them the passage is indeed a kind of shorthand, a series of symbols that stand for the understanding of complex processes and quite precise definitions. Writing in this case is like playing chess. Your moves can vary enormously, and there are seemingly infinite chess moves that can be made; but all of them are circumscribed by a small set of rules that govern a finite number of pieces whose individual moves are tightly defined. When you are adept at using a given discourse, in one way you don't have to worry about adept readers understanding you; in another sense, you have to worry about that all the time—that's what it means to write in that discourse; by worrying about it, you get your discourse just right. To be a geologist is to learn how to handle that particular discourse, and that's why the exchange can be so compressed, and thus so efficient.

✎ **Writing**   Pick a field you're studying now or have recently studied. Read one or two professional articles or chapters from that field. Identify the characteristics of the discourse you encounter. Try to describe the diction, style, and structure of the discourse. What elements does it seem to highlight, and what elements does it pay little or no attention to?

2   THE SPECIAL CASE OF SCIENCE

Scientific discourse, such as that used in the geological passage quoted above, may seem to be the most rigid of all the scholarly discourses, largely because of the historical expectation of how language is supposed to work in communicating scientific facts, experiments, observations, and conclusions. The scientific method and discourse are designed so that one person's experience or experiment can be re-created and replicated. The conclusions science reaches, like the experiments it uses, do not depend on circumstance—human, temporal, or geographic. They obey and as a result reflect the "laws" of the universe. It doesn't matter whether you are in California or Massachusetts, the chemical equation for the production of sodium chloride, table salt, will hold true in all circumstances: $2Na + Cl_2 = 2NaCl$. Such an equation is language stripped almost bare of connotation; using its own extremely spare grammar, it is as unambiguous as it can be made to be. Like the language of mathematics, it is pure symbolism, unmediated by verbs, subjects, and modifiers. As such it is an extreme example of scientific style. Naturally not all scientists communicate this way; chemists use prose, and when they do, they, like everyone else, must open the door at least a crack to ambiguity and misunderstanding because verbal language is symbolic in a different way from mathematics and chemical formulas. Historically, scientific writing has aimed to eliminate, as far as possible, such variations in understanding. *Na* stands for *sodium* and *Cl* stands for *chloride*, elements precisely defined by atomic weight, and in chemistry those signs stand for nothing else, whereas the sign *red* can be a color of any of a number of shades, a political complexion, a sign of embarrassment, and so on. To eliminate possible misunderstandings, the sciences have developed their own conventions and rhetorical devices.

Conventional scientific discourse is modeled on this specialized use of words in which every attempt is made to use mathematical symbolism or, when that's not possible, to use language free of connotations and ambiguities. Scientific discourse aims to be as impersonal as it possibly can, and many of its conventions arise from this goal. Consider the convention of relying on the passive voice. Earlier we talked about how agency, the sense of who or what performs an action, can be essential in conveying a sense of responsibility; we usually like to know not only that skating was done or bombs were dropped but also *who* skated or bombed. Scientific writing often does not need and indeed does not want to focus on agency because the point of its communication has not been what *Jane* saw in the test tube, but what was seen *in the test tube*. Here agency is the very thing to be excluded. It shouldn't matter who saw, who did, who interpreted the results. The point is that Jane, Juan, Li, and Doreen will all see the same thing. Perspective, position, and personality do not matter; if they did, the conclusion would lack the universality science requires of its laws. For such purposes the passive voice serves well because it focuses on results and can exclude the grammatical subject when it is the agent of the action. In classic scientific discourse, agency is truly secondary to the event, the result of an experiment and the observations made. In classic scientific discourse, language is designed to be the transparent medium through which the message passes with as little distortion as possible.

We want to take time now to examine some of the assumptions behind this discourse and its influence on how we write in other fields. So important have scientific conventions been in our world that writers in many other disciplines have tried to imitate them. It's not hard to understand how this happened. The scientific style carries connotations of objectivity and disinterestedness, which is what the style is designed to do. Both within and beyond science, the style of science carries great authority, and to write in it—to imply that the results of your observing "social phenomena" or "analyzing a work of art" have the kind of validity that scientists achieve when they "analyze phenomena"—is to claim a great deal of authority for your conclusions.

But there are complications. As Francis Bacon noted nearly four hundred years ago, scientists do not merely collect observations of nature but also *vex* nature; they "put nature on the rack" and twist it to see if it will say "ouch." Nature is like a sleeping dog; scientists poke it and prod it with their long sticks to see what will happen under certain carefully controlled circumstances; then they record the results. But that means that there inevitably *is* agency even in scientific work. Once we recognize the fact of agency in science and the subordination of agency in its discourse, we can become aware that scientific impersonality is also a myth, a powerful myth that has infiltrated other disciplines.

In fields other than the sciences, to omit agency is to omit or to try to gloss over the center of the enterprise: individual, unique people have thought, felt, written, painted, or carved these works of art as lasting expressions of transitory human experience. The ideas and materials that combine to create the ceiling of the Sistine Chapel, an account of the conquest of Mexico, or an Emily Dickinson poem do not reflect any immutable laws and in fact cannot be replicated. They are products of individuals uniquely empowered and constrained by circumstances—personal, temporal, and geographic. Interpreting them, writing about them, we, too, must recognize that we are similarly created by our circumstances. No one can any longer take it for granted that the Bible, Shakespeare, the rise of Greek democracy, the spread of Christianity, or the African experience of the West can be treated objectively, separated from the circumstances of the person who is writing about them. To omit agency is perhaps to omit the very thing the reader most needs to know to understand how the events are being interpreted and what role the observer had in the creation of the data.

There are valid reasons for wanting "objectivity" and "disinterestedness," even in subjects where agency and subjectivity play a great role, and there are great branches of learning—what used to be called social studies and now are generally called social sciences—that seek knowledge somewhat like that of the natural sciences about different subjects: human beings in society, the nature of political processes, the inner workings of our psyches, and so on. Within all of these fields there are great debates about the degree to which investigation can claim objectivity, its resemblance to investigation in the natural sciences, and hence about the kind of discourse that is proper for the presentation of its results. Different practitioners in any given field feel differently about how rigorously the standards for the field's discourse are to be observed, without necessarily agreeing on what exactly those standards are.

This state of affairs can be confusing, and further confusion comes from the recognition that discourses are less stable and more historically grounded than practitioners sometimes have claimed. What looks like the most objective, fact-filled, disinterested, unemotional article on the importance of the wool trade to late medieval parliamentary development may, when examined carefully in context, betray many of the biases of its time and place and of the particular scholarly community in which the writer was working. To be well trained in a subject can often mean being adept at its discourses, but it can also mean being restricted by its discourses. Sometimes this blocks not only the understanding of nonprofessionals but also the advancement of the field itself, which can become wedded through its discourses to fixed ways of thinking about things.

Because scientific discourse has been the model for so many of the "learned" discourses in other fields, we want to look at the nature of this discourse and its influence. We want first to look at writing in which scientists are at once well acquainted with scientific discourse and aware that there are scientific matters that cannot be talked about within that discourse, at least to the nonspecialist. The writers we look at here show that it is possible to adapt the chesslike tightness of the "moves" of scientific conventions to one's own style. Like a good chess player, you have to know the rules of the game to break out of playing the obvious patterns. Success comes from understanding that creativity lies in variations on what is normal.

Discourses of Presentation and Discourses of Discovery

One of our colleagues, a biologist, distinguishes between the discourses of presentation and those of discovery. This distinction seems to offer a good place to start talking about how to break down the apparently monolithic walls of impersonal scientific discourse. The *discourse of presentation* presents fictions of orderly discovery: question q is asked, hypothesis h is formulated, experiment x is set up, method m is followed, data d are measured, results r are tabulated, conclusion c is reached. It looks good in *Nature* or the *Journal of the American Chemical Society*.

Actual scientists, however, scratch their heads, walk in moonlight, spend hundreds of hours on false leads, break equipment, make guesses, have sudden bursts of insight, jump for joy, and so on. Science isn't as scientific as scientific rhetoric and is less scientific than popular lore about science says. You sometimes hear the phrase "scientists have now proven . . ." usually completed either by a piece of common sense or something quite controversial. Actually, scientists don't by and large *prove;* they *establish* or *agree* or *demonstrate* or *argue*.

But although presentational scientific writing is strictly governed by the rules of its discourse, many scientists choose to write scientifically for other purposes. One of the most useful and professional of these alternate discourses is the *discourse of discovery*, which can use narratives of personal experience to convey the humor and joy of science, as well as arguments for ethical and political ends. In using narrative, scientists don't necessarily abandon all the conventions of the discourses of their professional fields; they often draw on them, explain them, and play with them in front of their scientific colleagues, as well as their general readers.

Much can be learned about discourses in general, we think, from reading scientific writers who for various reasons and at various times choose to use a discourse of discovery.

A good example of the differences between discourses of discovery and those of presentation comes from the different accounts of the discovery of the structure of DNA, one of the greatest scientific discoveries ever. Here is an excerpt from a scientific paper that presents the results of some experiments that later would prove crucial to the ultimate discovery:

> Sodium thymonucleate fibres give two distinct types of X-ray diagram. The first corresponds to a crystalline form, structure A, obtained at about 75 per cent relative humidity; a study of this is described in detail elsewhere [reference is given to the other description]. At higher humidities a different structure, structure B, showing a lower degree of order, appears and persists over a wide range of ambient humidity. The change from A to B is reversible. The water content of structure B fibres which undergo this reversible change may vary from 40 to 50 per cent to several hundred per cent of the dry weight. Moreover, some fibres never show structure A, and in these structures B can be obtained with an even lower water content.
>
> (R. Franklin and R. G. Gosling,
> "Molecular Configuration in Sodium Thymonucleate," 740)

The whole title reveals some of the conventions of certain discourses. The passage is full of terms that nonchemists will not understand or whose significance (like that of crystalline) many will not understand in this context; but it's clear that the writing is tight and that if we could understand the particular meaning of key words, we could probably understand the whole thing.

Here is another account of the same discovery, by the chemist James Watson, who eventually shared the Nobel Prize for his part in it:

> Then the even more important cat was let out of the bag: since the middle of the summer Rosy [Rosalind Franklin, coauthor of the first passage] had had evidence for a new three-dimensional form of DNA. It occurred when the DNA molecules were surrounded by a large amount of water. When I asked what the pattern was like, Maurice went into the adjacent room to pick up a print of the new form they called the "B" structure.
>
> The instant I saw the picture my mouth fell open and my pulse began to race. The pattern was unbelievably simpler than those obtained previously ("A" form). Moreover, the black cross of reflections which dominated the picture could arise only from helical structure.
>
> (The Double Helix, 98)

The first passage clearly uses the discourse of presentation; the second, that of discovery. Watson's account of the discovery process, published in 1968, was the source of a good deal of controversy within the scientific community because, as Watson might have put it, it let a very irreverent cat out of the bag of science, exposing personal jealousies, rivalries, and ambitions among those trying to make what some have seen as the biggest scientific discovery of the century. From our point of view, what the occasion provides is a reminder that scientific discovery is not conducted in what we think of as the discourse of science. The discourse of discovery, drawing on narrative traditions, still deals with the complex subject but places it within the personal experience of the writer.

✎ **Writing** Find an issue of *Scientific American* or other science journal. Read the first several paragraphs of each article, and categorize their discourse as that of either presentation or discovery. In what other ways do the articles differ in relationship to reader, presentation of author, and presentation of material?

Focusing on the Discerning "I"

Many scientists have wanted to say things that could not be said in the strictest and most formal presentational discourses of science without challenging the excellence of those discourses for what they are intended. Like Watson, they have wanted to use a discourse to explore the "how" and the "why" rather than the "is" conventional scientific discourse focuses on. Rather than merely wanting to popularize science, to reduce it and simplify it for the average person, each of these writers feels the need to reclaim language as a tactile, plastic medium in which to communicate the factual information of science, the emotions such information has raised in them, their own involvement in the discoveries of science, the experiences of the discoverers, or the moral and ethical consequences of scientific discovery. They do more than pass along information, more than tell you "what it is." They tell you "how it is" for them personally. To this end they create a discourse centered in first-person narrative that combines the "I" of the writer with the discerning "eye" of the scientist. Each of the writers we are considering here—all but one of whom are scientists—writes in a distinctive manner. At the same time, as you will see, the passages resemble one another. Each writer places himself as narrator centrally before the reader. The first two, Loren Eiseley and Jacob Bronowski, do so explicitly, starting their works in the first person, and by doing so drawing the reader into the narrative flow of their remarks.

Let's start by looking at a passage from a chapter called "The Slit" in Loren Eiseley's *The Immense Journey:*

> Some lands are flat and grass-covered, and smile so evenly up at the sun that they seem forever youthful, untouched by man or time. Some are torn, ravaged and convulsed like the features of profane old age. Rocks are wrenched up and exposed to view; black pits receive the sun but give back no light.
>
> It was to such a land I rode, but I rode to it across a sunlit, timeless prairie over which nothing passed but antelope or a wandering bird. On the

verge where that prairie halted before a great wall of naked sandstone and clay, I came upon the Slit. A narrow crack worn by some descending torrent had begun secretly, far back in the prairie grass, and worked itself deeper and deeper into the fine sandstone that led by devious channels into the broken waste beyond. I rode back along the crack to a spot where I could descend into it, dismounted, and left my horse to graze. (3–4)

Eiseley sites the reader in a landscape as an active agent. He does so through rich verbs that characterize nature and time as active; the verbs that describe nature's actions and those that describe Eiseley's create a kind of dialogue. His coming is not a discovery but a meeting of two powers, nature and the human, which he represents. By constructing his opening in this way, he gives the reader many of the elements of the opening of a good narrative. One senses that the two forces here will interact or at least meet dramatically. For all this, though, it is a narrative in which the "I" of Eiseley is the central recording figure.

Jacob Bronowski does something similar in the opening chapters of *Science and Human Values*, where he creates a sense of dramatic tension in his narration of how he came in November 1945 to the ruins of Nagasaki. He doesn't say it—he doesn't have to—but it's clear that he is meeting both Nagasaki and the implications of twentieth-century science. There's a dramatic opposition here, too, but it's between Bronowski the man and Bronowski the Western scientist. Once again the experience is focused through the narrator:

On a fine November day in 1945, late in the afternoon, I was landed on an airstrip in Southern Japan. From there a jeep was to take me over the mountains to join a ship which lay in Nagasaki Harbour. I knew nothing of the country or the distance before us. We drove off; dusk fell; the road rose and fell away, the pine woods came down to the road, straggled on and opened again. I did not know that we had left the open country until unexpectedly I heard the ship's loudspeakers broadcasting dance music. Then suddenly I was aware that we were already at the center of damage in Nagasaki. The shadows behind me were the skeletons of the Mitsubishi factory buildings, pushed backwards and sideways as if by a giant hand. What I had thought to be broken rocks was a concrete power house with its roof punched in. I could now make out the outline of two crumpled gasometers; there was a cold furnace festooned with service pipes; otherwise nothing but cockeyed telegraph poles and loops of wire in a bare waste of ashes. I had blundered into this desolate landscape as instantly as one might wake among the craters of the moon. The moment of recognition when I realized that I was already in Nagasaki is present to me as I write, as vividly as when I lived it. I see the warm night and the meaningless shapes; I can even remember the tune that was coming from the ship. It was a dance tune which had been popular in 1945, and it was called "Is You Is Or Is You Ain't Ma Baby?" (9–10)

Bronowski's use of the first person is critical here because his experience was almost unique in the history of humankind. His message comes from a learned scientist but a scientist who speaks here both as an expert and as a simple human, warning that unless we confront how we use science, unless we come out from behind the faceless equations, stop hiding behind the agentless calculations of thermonuclear physics, we will all find ourselves, as he did, a stranger in a chartless waste. His very humanity here is central because the horror he is trying to convey is the horror of humanity cast loose from reason, inference, and cause and effect. He sees but cannot comprehend what it is that he is looking at.

Both Eiseley and Bronowski use the self to center, focus, and anchor larger abstract issues like evolution and the nuclear age. Both use the narrative form, a form, we noted earlier, that ultimately focuses on the communication of knowledge. Listen to my story, they say, listen to the voice of human experience rather than the disembodied voice of authority.

We see an alternative pattern to the explicit first-person narrative in Vincent Dethier's opening pages of *To Know a Fly*. In the beginning of a book about the scientific method in biology, Dethier signals his presence indirectly, through the humor and the ironic tone that characterize this narrator:

> Although small children have taboos against stepping on ants because such actions are said to bring on rain, there has never seemed to be a taboo against pulling off the legs or wings of flies. Most children eventually outgrow this behavior. Those who do not either come to a bad end or become biologists.
>
> It is believed in some quarters that to become a successful modern biologist requires a college education and a substantial grant from the Federal Government. The college education not infrequently is as useful for acquiring proficiency in the game of Grantsmanship as it is for understanding biology. No self-respecting modern biologist can go to work without money for a secretary, a research associate, two laboratory assistants, permanent equipment, consumable supplies, travel, a station wagon for field collecting, photographic supplies, books, animals, animal cages, somebody to care for the animals, postage, telephone calls, reprints, and last, but by no means least, a substantial sum (called overhead) to the university to pay for all the stenographers hired to handle all the papers and money transactions that so big a grant requires. The grant, of course, must be big in the first place to allow for the overhead. Thus equipped, the biologist retires into his automated electronic laboratory. He may never see a live animal or plant. He has come a long way since the days when he pulled off the wings of flies. (2–3)

Dethier is having fun here through exaggeration and mock self-deprecation; he's playing a role. Notice, though, that while his personality dominates the passage, he adheres to one of the more obvious of the scientific conventions—he doesn't use the first-person singular pronoun at all. Nevertheless, because of the playful way he uses language we have a clear sense of the narrator as an engaging and engaged personality whose way of thinking shapes our entry into the world he is introducing. This means that he is continually in contact with his reader; a teasing, joking, self-mocking relationship is established, and it is of enormous use in helping the reader to see the more elusive or esoteric parts of scientific work. Like Eiseley and Bronowski, Dethier uses himself to give shape to his idea; everything is focused through that lens.

Dethier's style of combining wit, self-deprecation, and scientific explanations (if you read on in the book you will see that he is quite precisely scientific in his discussions but that he rarely uses the conventions of what is broadly understood as scientific discourse) may be more difficult for the ordinary writer to adopt than the first-person narrative approach of Eiseley and Bronowski. We offer it with the other two as an example of the wit and life that can characterize scientific writing when the scientist wants to break free of simple presentation, and reach out to a wider audience than conventional scientific discourse will allow, by using discourses of discovery.

✎ **Writing**   Science seems to require an alert eye, but in its ordinary professional discourse, it forbids "I." As an exercise, recall some observation, discovery, or epiphany you have had about the natural world we live in. Write about it in a short paper, keeping yourself as the observer/narrator central in the process of observation. Next, rewrite the observation in more traditional scientific discourse, eliminating all references to yourself as the discerning "I." Compare the two versions. In your class or workshop discuss with your colleagues the variations you see and the opportunities each discourse opens or closes for you as the writer and for the reader.

Mixed Discourse: Generalizations and Specifics

The passages quoted above share the kind of detail and ability to evoke atmosphere and feeling from specific events or descriptions that we explored in the first two chapters of this book. This is, after all, not very surprising because, although it is the business of science and scientific writing to convey an essentially abstract message, that abstract message must be grounded in carefully observed specifics. The writer who wants to combine personal experience and scientific observation may want to use another technique, illustrated by the passages in this section. Each of the excerpts below illustrates how writers who want to share their joy in and commitment to science with a lay audience create narratives woven of two strands: scientific method and purpose with familiar narrative details. The net effect is a combination of generalization and specification that allows the writers to address large, important issues while simultaneously keeping the nonspecialist readers with them.

Here, again, is Loren Eiseley, this time describing how, one winter day, along one of the tributaries of the Platte River he found a frozen catfish. The narrative that follows is essentially the description of a scientific experiment to see if a fish so frozen could be resuscitated, but it is presented as a narrative, a sequence of events in the life of a "cold and tired" man, a technique that allows Eiseley to interweave specifics and generalizations. Eiseley and the fish live together until one day in the spring:

> One night when no one was about, he simply jumped out of his tank. I found him dead on the floor next morning. He had made his gamble like a man— or, I should say, a fish. In the proper place it would not have been a fool's gamble. Fishes in the drying shallows of intermittent prairie streams who feel their confinement and have the impulse to leap while there is yet time may regain the main channel and survive. A million ancestral years had gone into that jump, I thought as I looked at him, a million years of climbing through prairie sunflowers and twining in and out through the pillared legs of drinking mammoth.
>
> (*The Immense Journey*, 23–24)

The fish is the concrete example that allows Eiseley to generalize; it is the implicit metaphor that opens the way to the larger conclusion. Eiseley has constructed the passage so that the generalization comes only through his own experience. *His* having "known" the fish, having rescued it and lived with it, having found it frozen and later dead, provides a witnessing quality that would be absent from any "scientific" statement of the fact that catfish can live in a state of cryogenic dormancy or that seasonally they are driven by instinct to seek the deep channels of the spring floods in order to mate. Eiseley's examples communicate these facts in a way that suggests his emotional as well as intellectual commitment to the subject.

Look now at Jeremy Campbell, who in *Winston Churchill's Afternoon Nap* explains Einstein's theory of relativity in a similar way, combining abstraction with a rudimentary narrative focused on two specific "characters":

> Suppose a man called Box is sitting in a moving train carrying a clock which works by means of light. The clock consists of a source sending pulses of light vertically up to a mirror on the ceiling, and the mirror reflects the light back down again to a photoelectric cell in the clock. The passage of the light from source to ceiling and back down again to the photoelectric cell is treated as a single unit of time, like the tick of a mechanical clock. A second man, called Cox, is standing at the side of the railroad tracks. Cox is carrying an identical light clock, which is designed to complete a cycle in exactly the same amount of time as Box's clock on the train. As the train rushes past, Cox notices a curious difference in the behavior of the light clock on the train. Since Box's clock is in motion with respect to Cox, its mirror appears to move forward a little between the moment when the light pulse leaves

the source and the moment when it strikes the mirror. The light on the train, therefore, as observed by Cox, who is standing by the tracks, has a greater distance to travel than it has in his own clock, which is at rest with respect to him. If one cycle of Box's clock on the train is to be completed in the same unit of time as one cycle of Cox's clock, we would expect that its light beam travels faster than the light beam in Cox's clock. Yet this is forbidden by the principle of the absolute speed of light. The only conclusion to draw is that if each cycle of Box's clock, as observed by Cox, takes longer to complete than each cycle of Cox's clock, then as far as Cox is concerned, time must slow down, because the light cannot increase its speed beyond a universally fixed limit. For Box, however, Cox's clock is in motion with respect to him, and his own clock is at rest, so that he observes time by the side of the tracks slowing down and his own time keeping its normal rate. Accepting the constant speed of light means throwing out the hypothesis of a uniform flow of time, the same for all observers, and that is exactly what Einstein did. (36–37)

Some immediate humor comes from Campbell's choice of names. *Cox and Box* is a nineteenth-century operetta, based on the rental of one room to two people, Box and Cox, one by day and the other by night, without either knowing of the other; it has become a term for any kind of alternation wherein two people share something generally used by one, and it carries a particularly farcical connotation, in sharp contrast to the intellectual challenge the term *relativity* presents. Campbell accomplishes two ends in this passage: first and more important, he provides an easy-to-understand explanation of a complex theory. Second, he does so in a way that playfully suggests his control of the subject and his desire to address his knowledge to the nonspecialist. He combines abstraction (perhaps the most famous abstraction of the twentieth century) with specifics drawn from the mundane and "ordinary" level of humor.

For a final example of this technique of alternating scientific generalities and familiar specifics, look at the passage below, an excerpt from R. C. Lewontin's review of *Wonderful Life: The Burgess Shale and the Nature of History* by Stephen Jay Gould:

At the heart of the philosopher's preference for physics over biology is the question of uncertainty. Science is supposed to be a study of what is true everywhere and for all times. The phenomena of science are taken to be reliably repeatable rather than historically contingent. After all, if something happens only on occasional Tuesdays and Thursdays, popping up when one least expects it like a letter from the IRS, it is not Science but History. So, philosophers of science have been fascinated with the fact that elephants and mice would fall at the same rate if dropped from the Tower of Pisa, but not much interested in how elephants and mice got to be such different sizes in the first place. In terms of the formal calculus of propositions, the statements of science are supposed to be so-called 'universally quantified' statements of the form—

For all x, if x is A then x is B

—rather than historical statements, which are only existentially quantified—

There exists an x such that x is B

The point, Popper [a philosopher of science] tells us, is that the first kind of statement can always be falsified, by finding a single example that does not obey the rule, while we can never disprove the second kind because we may have accidentally missed the cases that agree with it. So the first kind of statement is what characterizes a science, while the second kind is just story-telling. (3)

While many things are worth noticing in this passage (the way Lewontin opposes science and "just storytelling," for example), for our purposes its main importance lies in the way in which he moves in and out of the technicalities of his topic. He is writing for an intellectual audience but not one particularly learned in either physics or biology. To make his point he does not abandon the discourse of science altogether but alternates it with examples drawn humorously from life, examples most of his readers would be familiar with. For the average reader the letter from the IRS represents the height of unpredictability, if not the depth of despair, because of the amount of work such letters often require in formulating a reply. To use it as the example of a random chance is to draw on an example the reader will recognize not only intellectually but also emotionally. He doesn't belabor the analogy, but passes on to the mice/elephant/Tower of Pisa example, again a lively choice because it focuses the reader's imagination on a humorous instance while recalling what for many people is a puzzling "law" of physics, the universal gravitation that causes all objects in a vacuum to fall toward the earth at an equal rate. Lewontin's examples are lively and imagistic. But more to the point, they serve as counterpoint to the spare scientific language of the two equations that follow, equations in which symbolism is highly concentrated and whose language is the exact opposite of the language of the two examples. "For all x, if x is A then x is B" is not a statement that evokes much association, unless it is a sinking feeling recalled from high school algebra class. It is scientific language; it abstracts and summarizes the point the two examples make. It is the generalization toward which the whole paragraph moves. Thus Lewontin takes into account his audience and writes to them, inviting them into the text, but does so in order to converse with them the more readily in "scientific" prose.

All three writers discussed above use a technique that you can readily adopt. The writers state their ideas in two complementary forms, the abstract and the close-to-home specific. Think of Eiseley and the fish, Campbell's Cox and Box, and Lewontin's IRS. They mix the world of science, which seems in its discourse so distant from most readers, with the world that most readers live in. In doing so they bring science to the readers, inviting them to think about large, complex issues by focusing their attention on discrete specifics.

✎ **Writing** Choose one of the subjects below and write an explanation of the principles involved for a reader who is not particularly knowledgeable in the field (if you feel unsure of your knowledge, imagine that you are writing to an intelligent 9-year-old). Following the lead of the writers here, try alternating or mixing the scientific facts of your essay with examples drawn from daily life.

Eutrophication	Barometric pressure
How airplanes fly	What waves are
Automobile engines	Hummingbird flight

CHAPTER 7

Working with a Range
of Discourses

It's not surprising that academic and professional discourses pose a special challenge to the writer who would prefer to discuss a subject without having to use certain kinds of specialized verbal patterns to signify expertise in the subject. Professions, learned and otherwise, assert the authority of expertise, and a major way in which they do so is by using discourses that have been developed for that particular field. When you turn to your own experience or use your own writing style, if it differs markedly from the discourse of the field, you may be perceived at best as challenging the value of that expertise or at worst as having no expertise or knowledge. That's because one way discourse works is to give special emphasis to knowledge that has been codified, categorized, tested, and finally presented verbally by "experts in the field."

It would be foolish to try to say when it is and when it is not appropriate to invoke a discourse to signify your expertise or even to gloss over your incomplete understanding of the field. You alone must answer such questions as these: How do I sound like an economist or chemist or historian? Do I have any right to talk about money if I don't know how to sound like an economist, or about the past if I'm not an historian? Has learning the discourse presented to me as the proper way to write like an economist or historian committed me to some assumptions and biases that I don't really hold? Our purpose here is to recognize the claims discourses are making and to try to provide answers to this kind of question: If I am an economist but want to make clear my personal stake in what I'm writing, are there ways for me to modify—or even altogether to leave—that discourse and still be "heard"?

1 CHANGING THE RULES OF DISCOURSE

Our examples of how to modify professional discourses in this section are taken from essays in literary criticism, but their techniques are not limited to that discipline. In the first the author begins somewhat casually and unconventionally by giving her readers a strong sense of her personal investment in her scholarly work, an investment she invites us to share:

Once, during a difficult period of my life, I lived in the basement of a house on Forest Street in Hartford, Connecticut, which had belonged to Isabella Beecher Hooker—Harriet Beecher Stowe's half-sister. . . . I made a reverential visit to the Mark Twain house a few blocks away, took photographs of his study, and completely ignored Stowe's own house—also open to the public—which stood across the lawn. Why should I go? Neither I nor anyone I knew regarded Stowe as a serious writer. At the time, I was giving my first lecture course in the American Renaissance—concentrating exclusively on Hawthorne, Melville, Poe, Emerson, Thoreau, and Whitman—and although *Uncle Tom's Cabin* was written in exactly the same period, and although it is probably the most influential book ever written by an American, I would never have dreamed of including it on my reading list.

(Jane P. Tompkins, "Sentimental Power:
Uncle Tom's Cabin and the Politics of Literary History," 81)

The essay begins almost like a novel, in a variation of the familiar "once upon a time." Tompkins establishes her own presence, and her own relationship with her reader, by situating the reader clearly in both a geographical place and in intellectual space. She makes a confession: she had ignored *Uncle Tom's Cabin*, even when living within a few blocks of the author's house. Even though Tompkins is ultimately going to be concerned with a rather abstract question, the dismissal of "sentimental" novels written by nineteenth-century women lacking high literary merit, she poses that question by situating us in a visible place and by telling a personal anecdote, in ways we discussed in chapters 1 and 2.

But Tompkins is not being unscholarly (though some of her academic readers may have said to themselves when they first read it, "This *sounds* most unscholarly"). From this opening she moves easily from rather personal tones to those of the scholar. After summarizing the "male-dominated scholarly tradition that controls both the canon of American literature . . . and the critical perspective that interprets the canon for society" (82), she presents her own argument:

The thesis I will argue in this chapter . . . holds that the popular domestic novel of the nineteenth century represents a monumental effort to reorganize culture from the woman's point of view; that this body of work is remarkable for its intellectual complexity, ambition, and resourcefulness; and that, in certain cases, it offers a critique of American society far more devastating than any delivered by better-known critics such as Hawthorne and Melville. Finally, it suggests that the enormous popularity of these novels, which has been cause for suspicion bordering on disgust, is a reason for paying close attention to them. *Uncle Tom's Cabin* was, in almost any terms one can think of, the most important book of the century. (83)

"The thesis I will argue in this essay" is a standard opening of a scholarly essay. Using this phrase she signals the reader that she is also comfortable with a scholarly discourse. "The popular domestic novel of the nineteenth century" is a recognizable scholarly category (albeit one that many of her scholarly readers will not—as she herself originally did not—hold in high esteem); even using the categorical singular ("the domestic novel") is a bit of scholarly discourse; nonscholars would talk about "domestic *novels*." Anyone who reads criticism of this sort regularly will quickly pass by the standard phrases—"it offers a critique," "it suggests that," "better known critics such as," and so on—almost without noticing them as anything special and yet probably with a comfortable sense that "this person speaks my language."

But even as Tompkins works through the scholarly terminology, there are traces of passion in her words. She has said, in effect, that the expected discourse of literary criticism is not enough to carry the burden of her meaning. If you were to read further in the essay it would be clear that Tompkins has a solid argument that is well supported in the way that literary critics support their arguments, and yet it would also be clear that she is challenging a standard idea: that works like *The Scarlet Letter* and *Moby-Dick* are much better—"more monumental"—than *Uncle Tom's Cabin*. This has been the judgment of the establishment, dominated by white, American, male values. By beginning as she does with a personal anecdote, she challenges both the establishment's values and the adequacy of its discourse to recognize or to explain what is happening in a novel like *Uncle Tom's Cabin*, a novel focusing on the abstract question of the nature of evil embodied in slavery through a lens of family ties created, broken, and mended. What Tompkins shows is that the ordinary discourse of literary scholarship and criticism, having no language for domesticity, has failed to recognize the importance of domesticity in the history of American literature.

To do what Tompkins has done—introduce an argument in the discourse of a field by a personal narrative—is to expand the potential audience for the piece and to challenge the discipline and its authority, and yet not totally to reject it. It's a move toward freedom and individual assertion. To use the discourse is to play the game by the rules, to conform to the audience's expectations of the conventions. To mix or to discard discourses may be perceived as breaking the rules, but mixing discourses is also a way of setting new rules, creating a new game with new umpires.

Writers often face circumstances wherein the degree to which they must adopt a given discourse is not clear or wherein adopting the discourse creates difficulty. For someone who is *not* adept in a given field, reading prose that uses the field's conventions—much less writing it—can be baffling and frustrating. When facing these situations it might help to think of discourse as the way in which the playing field and rules of a game are defined by the people who got there first, and then redefined by those who have come into the game later. Coming onto a field where you are interested in the subject but haven't been playing the game, you may feel both baffled and excluded by the boundaries and rules that have been established.

✎ **Writing**   Notice that by opening with a brief narrative, Tompkins invites the reader, both specialist and nonspecialist, into the world of her text. As an experiment with this technique, find a piece of academic writing you have done or have to do in which you plan to use the expected, conventional discourse of your field. Rewrite the opening paragraphs to include a brief narrative of how you came to this field or to the opinion you will be developing in the paper. Try to construct that narrative as a way of helping your reader understand the material. Think of this as a matter of tactics, of providing your reader with a path into and out of the material.

Reader-conscious Discourse

Writers modify the prevailing discourse of their fields in other, less direct ways than bringing their experience into the text. Looking at another piece of literary criticism, Samuel Hynes's essay "The Whole Contention Between Mr. Bennett and Mrs. Woolf," we hear the voice of a critic, very much part of the establishment, but one who modifies the discourse of his field by creating a personal relationship with his readers and a series of clear and conscious verbal signals to help them follow the argument.

Hynes begins in the middle of the subject with a strong, simple, declarative sentence that tells the reader that the writer is at home with the subject and with the audience, whom he identifies from the outset as a group: "For most of the readers of this journal, Arnold Bennett's literary criticism probably exists—if at all—only as a reflection in his enemy's eye" (34). From the beginning Hynes marks himself as a writer/expert and his audience as readers/experts, part of a special group within the larger reading public. You know where and who you are. Intuitively, or perhaps over a career as a scholar and writer, Hynes has grasped a central principle of lively scholarly writing, that to define himself as a writing personality he must also, simultaneously, define his audience as knowledgeable readers. Making scholarly writing interesting almost always requires creating the fiction of the writer and reader as personalities moving together through an idea. The traditional stress put on constructing the scholarly essay presupposes a reader who must be led surely and carefully, closely guided through the broad paths or labyrinthine turnings of an essay. Hynes has gone one step further and regarded the reader as a colleague. As a result, his essay comes alive in a way that a merely well-crafted and well-organized piece cannot:

> Mrs. Woolf's essay has come loose from its context, and is read as though it were a complete, objective statement of the differences between two writing generations. But in fact it is neither complete nor objective: it is simply one blow struck in a quarrel that ran for more than ten years, and was far more

personal than generational. Reading "Mr. Bennett and Mrs. Brown" as a separate critical document is like watching the third round of a fifteen-round
fight. We will understand both the essay and the combatants better if we understand the whole of their quarrel. (34)

Hynes's argument takes a familiar form—it's good not to extract docu-
ments from their contexts—but he advances it with a refreshing
metaphor: the essay is a blow struck in a quarrel that has turned into a
real boxing match. By the simple use of the pronoun "we," Hynes has
aligned himself with his readers, defining them as the kind of people
who, like him, know and care something about Virginia Woolf, Arnold
Bennett, and literary criticism. For this audience he is willing to make
things clear through anecdote, humor, and analogy.

As he goes on, Hynes simultaneously advances his idea and considers
the reader's position in relation to it. He keeps the "we" relationship central, making sure that he and the reader advance through the argument
together. He makes sure that his readers have the basic information they
need to follow the argument: "In 1919, when the quarrel began, Bennett
was 52, successful, and astonishingly prolific"; "In 1919 Mrs. Woolf was
younger, less known, and less productive than Bennett." By paying attention to such details he provides a steady foundation of shared knowledge
on which to build his argument. In a crucial sentence, after quoting Bennett—a place where many student writers fail to reclaim the text as their
own by neglecting to discuss the citation they have just included—Hynes
proceeds, "here Bennett is testifying to his belief . . . "; citing Bennett
again, he resumes his discussion with a conversational opening that signals his control of the quoted material and his reliability as a guide: "The
striking thing about this passage. . . . " On the following page, developing
his argument, he maintains this sense of control, introducing new material with "Clearly" and "The first document." Hynes thus controls his
idea and the way the reader receives it.

It's worth pausing here to emphasize that following up on quoted material by providing a clear and full discussion of its relevance to your argument is an important but often neglected element of reaching out to
your reader, of marking the text as your own, and of breaking through the
discourse of your field. The lines that follow cited material are central to
the development of every argument; they are the natural place where the
writer reaches out to the reader. Hynes's essay provides an example of
how a fine scholar and writer handles this technique subtly but surely,
with ease as well as with control.

Making his personal experience and his literary insight into a public
statement, one that others will accept and share with a degree of enthusiasm proportional to his own, Hynes controls the unfolding, the pace,
and the direction of the article at recurring stages in its development. As
the article progresses, Hynes constructs his own persona and voice as
those of the impartial judge or referee. Once again one sees this most

clearly in the "signposts" sited near quotations: "This," he notes after a quotation from Woolf, "is a fairly accurate account of the origins of controversy" (41). He thus becomes both guide and arbiter. By this point the reader trusts the narrator because he has taken such pains to incorporate the reader into the forward movement of the argument.

This is possible in part because of the way in which Hynes defines himself in relation to his topic. He is primarily trying to set the record straight. (It is generally thought by literary scholars that the argument between Woolf and Bennett was about aesthetic principles and that Woolf got the better of it.) Hynes shows that the argument was primarily a clash of personalities, not principles. He suggests that Woolf's "victory" was not completely deserved and that Bennett and Woolf, in fact, agreed about many of the principles in question.

Through these techniques Hynes both establishes his expert knowledge of the subject and engages the reader's respect—not through pompous or pedantic argument but an argument framed within a continuous awareness of the presence of a reader who becomes a traveling companion for the duration of the essay. These techniques—signposts, language suggesting control of the pace and movement of the idea, indications of genuine knowledge of the subject—work together to earn him the right to his conclusion. In addition, they provide a model easily adaptable to any sort of writing, a model that actually takes into account the existence of the reader as more than audience.

✎ **Writing** Find two examples of scholarly prose from any field—one that shows the author reaching out to the reader and one that's flat. Think about why and how each succeeds or fails in respect to structure, tone, the construction of signposts for the reader, and the dramatic creation of an authorial presence as a teacherly guide. Edit all or part of the less successful example, using Hynes's technique of being sure that the reader can follow closely every step of his argument.

Lecturing and Conversing

Hynes's essay illustrates a major issue in scholarly discourse, that of where and how the writer "pays attention" to the reader. This issue is wider than merely providing signposts and being sure that the reader is with the writer. It lies at the heart of the expectations of discourses: that the writer and reader are jointly engaged in the text for the purpose of shared information or shared ideas. Some texts approach the reader as a vessel to be "filled" with knowledge, facts, and ideas. Disciplinary discourse can be very useful in such a case. Yet other texts give the strong sense that the author is writing to highly sophisticated experts in the field and doesn't much care whether anyone else understands what he is saying. Such texts seem untroubled by doubt or speculation. We are all familiar with this kind of scholarly discourse, the printed equivalent of a private conversation between two scholars or of a teacher who seems to be talking to the blackboard or to some absent audience other than the class assembled. In such cases we might have learned a valuable and instructive lesson, but we have come away thinking that the real point of the lesson or the printed material was more for the author to lay out the idea for other experts than to persuade or engage the nonexpert. Much excellent scholarly writing shares elements of the "professor talking to the blackboard." It is clear, concise, direct, and focused on the smooth presentation of a topic.

The following passage, from Victor Ehrenberg's *From Solon to Socrates* (subtitled, in academic fashion, "Greek History and Civilization During the Fifth and Sixth Centuries B.C."), exemplifies clear academic prose of this traditional sort. Notice the structure of the argument in respect to the opening of his sentences, and note, too, how Ehrenberg supports various points along the way with references to appropriate primary sources:

> The greatest number of laws likely to be Solonian is concerned with family law. This may be partly due to the fact that most of the cases dealt with by the orators belonged to this sphere. It is, however, probably quite true that Solon regarded as one of his most urgent tasks the establishment or reestablishment of what was the very foundation of Athenian society, the permanence of the family. It is typical of him that he gave various rules to bind both parents and children, thus, as in politics, taking the middle line. Of great importance was his law on heiresses (*epikleroi*), who, especially when orphaned, were protected in order to continue the existence of the family (AP 9,2,56,6.Plut.20). Therefore the heiress did not enter her husband's family but was to produce the legitimate male heir to her father's family. A similar purpose was served by Solon's law on adoption, allowing under certain conditions a man without legitimate male offspring to adopt a man and thus make him his heir. This law chiefly concerned the upper class; it was to prevent a family from dying out, as is said in one speech (Dem.43, 11.76) "that the *oikos* be not made destitute (of heirs)". The law was at the same time a first small step towards freeing the individual property from the clan. It was still far from being private property especially as the adopted son could only leave the estate to his actual son, not again to an adopted man. Marriage, naturally most important in this context, was generally to be protected, adultery and unchastity of women were severely punished; so were, though less severely, violation, procuring, and the prostitution of boys. (72)

Ehrenberg's style here is a model of one kind of scholarly discourse. He seems aware of the reader (notice how he guides you with phrases like "Of great importance," "Therefore," and "A similar . . . "). Yet it's clear that he sees his job to be the presentation of his argument as a relatively seamless statement of how modern, informed scholarship understands the family legislation of the Athenian city-state. Why, for instance is marriage "naturally" of great importance in willing and inheriting property? Such potential questions are submerged in the discourse of this text, never really brought forward. There is a great deal of technically valuable information here, and Ehrenberg is thorough and careful in giving you sources and references. But you may feel that he is excluding you from a monologue that is primarily directed at other scholars. More important, he doesn't seem to be evaluating the topic, by raising questions and issues. It seems to be a presentation before a board of directors or a paper at an academic conference, designed to persuade the listener both that what's said is true and that it constitutes all the truth needed. That's fine, but this discourse may exclude all but the most scholarly readers.

As a contrast, look at another book on this topic, women and family law in Athens, *Goddesses, Whores, Wives and Slaves* by Sarah B. Pomeroy:

> If respectable Athenian women were secluded and silent, how are we to account for the forceful heroines of tragedy and comedy? And why does the theme of strife between woman and man pervade Classical drama? Before proceeding to complex explanations which are directly concerned with women, it is necessary to repeat the truism that the dramatists examined multiple aspects of man's relationship to the universe and to society; accordingly, their examination of another basic relationship—that between man and woman—is not extraordinary. It is rather the apparent discrepancy between women in the actual society and the heroines on the stage that demands investigation. Several hypotheses have been formulated in an attempt to explain the conflict between fact and fiction. (93)

Pomeroy, in contrast to Ehrenberg, structures her discussion around questions, siting herself and the reader in the midst of a scholarly tradition ("the truism that . . . ") but signaling a different approach. This paragraph begins with questions and ends with an introduction to conflicting opinion ("several hypotheses"). In between, even in making statements, Pomeroy subtly disrupts the usual academic smoothness of printed arguments by seeing what Ehrenberg takes for granted—marriage—as just one more formulation of the basic relationship between humans and the world each individual inhabits. By opening her topic and her presentation to questions and pointing to its "holes," Pomeroy has engaged the reader as a partner in the discussion.

We present these two passages not to say that one is superior to the other but to alert you to the kinds of scholarly discourse available to you and, most important, to the different ways you can use them. The examples above represent two different kinds of discourse, each fully controlled in a "professional" manner. Their main difference lies in the relationship they establish with the reader. One presents a completed idea; the other traces the formation of a "new" idea, one that challenges previously held conceptions. Each is a useful model, depending on the situation. As a writer you can determine how you appear in relation to your topic and to your reader and what kind of style you want to adopt. Naturally in some cases the more traditional Ehrenberg style will be the sort of thing you feel the occasion calls for. In other cases the questioning, redefining style that Pomeroy exemplifies may more nearly fit your needs.

Think about where you would use each style and which is more useful for your situation and needs.

Questions and Contact

Perhaps the most significant element of the Pomeroy passage is that it frames its discussion as a series of questions as much as answers. Regardless of field or discourse, thinking of the text as an attempt either to formulate questions or to answer them offers advantages to the writer. Think for a minute about how different an answer you would write to this topic phrased as a statement, "Name five causes of the American Civil War," and as a question, "What in your opinion were the five essential factors leading up to the American Civil War?" The second topic invites you to a conversation with yourself and the reader; it asks you to sift among potential causes, to select some and reject others. In college, instructors often remind students to think of their subjects as questions. We would urge you to go one step further and conceive of all your writing as a question to be defined or an answer to be suggested. Writing to define the question opens up discussion, invites pros and cons, and gives you rhetorical room to maneuver. Questions breach the monolithic wall of discourse, revealing the topic at hand as faceted and multidimensional. Questions invite the writer to analysis, evaluation, and comparison in a way that description or the more typical expository answer doesn't. Virtually anything you write can take on the same life if it is shaped by the same assumption that you are writing to answer a question or to pose one.

Very often writers of professional discourse, particularly academic discourse, forget how important it is for the writer to convey a sense of being actively working through the issue at hand, of being in contact with the idea, the words that convey the idea, and the reader. In a recent essay entitled "Reflections on Academic Discourse," Peter Elbow talks about a "certain rubber-glove quality to the voice and register of most academic discourses . . . a kind of reluctance to touch one's meanings with one's naked fingers" (145). What we sense in most of the writers whose works we have discussed as alternatives to conventional discourses is a willingness to display their own bare-handed contact with their ideas and a sense that they can use that contact to make their ideas real to their readers. Tompkins, Pomeroy, and Hynes all show how a serious writer can still bring the reader into the text and the text to the reader.

2 USING ORDINARY LANGUAGE

"Discourse" may still sound forbidding. You may associate it with language that does not work as language should, that is, to communicate ideas and feelings from one person to another. In this respect some uses of discourse *are* dysfunctional. They do not advance understanding, and they do not help the reader to share the writer's feelings. Instead they make the reader feel manipulated, sometimes confused and angry.

Sometimes valid discourses are misused in that they appear to be aimed not at communicating with fellow practitioners in time-saving shorthand but at convincing readers that the authors are learned people, that their conclusions are very "scientific," that only a flat-earther would dispute them—aimed even at excluding people who aren't in the know, in a kind of replay of games children play to exclude an unwary outsider. It is the case in almost every field of learning, for example, that discourse is used to establish the authority of particular points of view—and to do so in ways that aren't really necessary to the process of communicating.

For example, Bruno Bettelheim has demonstrated that Sigmund Freud's English translators transformed Freud's idiomatic, beautifully written, and generally accessible German into a pseudoscientific vocabulary. What Freud described as the *Ich* and the *Es*—"I" and "It"—were translated "ego" and "id," the Latin pronouns, with the result, whatever the intention, of making them sound more specialized and less accessible to the ordinary reader, something only an expert could understand. It's easy to see this kind of translation—Bettelheim gives many examples of it—as part of an attempt to convince readers that the new field of psychoanalysis, challenging and threatening to many established religious and social views, was in fact a scientifically valid one. It may even have been part of an attempt to retain control over psychoanalysis for the medical community.

On occasion you'll find it tempting to robe yourself and your ideas in highly specialized discourse. The sound of long sentences made up of Latinate polysyllables or of terms so modish that they do not yet appear in the dictionary is alluring, particularly for the writer who is anxious to be taken seriously. But be aware of what you're doing; do it consciously. To prepare it's a good idea to study with a sharp eye the discourse of the fields you encounter. Read introductions to textbooks; look at the modes of presentation; and try to decide what is encoded within them, what assumptions are there implicitly. Most of all ask yourself whether the discourse is really necessary—whether, as in the geology examples above, it is a convenient, efficient shorthand or, instead, a magician's cape designed to conceal and confuse.

It's also a good discipline to see regularly if you can explain a complex idea in simple language. Part of James Watson's scientific genius must have resided in his ability to see science in rather down-to-earth terms, to bring metaphors from life into science. (He suggests that his active romantic life led him to hypothesize a double rather than a triple helical structure for DNA: nature, he said, likes to work in pairs.) You may discover that you need less in the way of technical vocabulary than you think. We are sometimes tempted by sophisticated surgery when hot towels and stretching exercises will do the trick. This is certainly true in writing, wherein considerable practical benefits derive from appearing to be master of a field that few other people can understand. Don't be ashamed of your specialized vocabulary. Know what it means, and use it when you need it to make that meaning clear. But don't use it merely to impress people (especially if you don't have command of it); worry about your readers' understanding of the technical terms you use. Give examples, consider using metaphors and anecdotes, and think about who you and your reader are when you write. Seek the joy that comes from putting complex arguments into clear, comprehensible language that still respects the complexity of the ideas.

Discourse and Ordinary Language

To explore some of the complex issues involved in our point about the comparative usefulness of technical discourse and ordinary language, we want to look at a passage from *The Rhetoric of Economics*. In this excerpt Donald McCloskey prints, in parallel columns, the crucial sentences from an important article in economics, "Rational Expectations and the Theory of Price Movements," by John Muth, and his own translation of Muth's prose into what he believes is a more accessible, conversational mode. McCloskey's subheading for this exercise reveals his point of view about Muth's prose: "Muth's Main Points Can Be Expressed in English." Without trying to capture the whole of Muth's argument or of McCloskey's argument about Muth, we can take one excerpt of "original" and one of "translation" to see how the game works.

Original	*Translation*
[A] The objective of this paper is to outline a theory of expectations and to show that implications are—as a first approximation—consistent with the relevant data.	The paper asks how people guess about what the future will bring. The answer is tested against some of the facts in agricultural markets. (92)

McCloskey's point is not that Muth is writing "badly" or "obscurely" but that his writing is governed by a particular kind of discourse, the rhetoric of what McCloskey calls "scientism" (which, in different terms, is exactly what Bettelheim faults Freud's translators for). Readers will see McCloskey's point clearly enough even from this short example. The article, he says, "is composed in a foreign language, but the language is a sacred one, like Old Church Slavonic. Its style is the key to its rhetorical appeal, because it is the style of scientism" (96). That means that there is a kind of secondary argument being pursued at the same time as the primary one, an argument about ways of knowing:

> The theory of knowledge put forward by the objective, data-respecting, sober style of modernism in Muth's paper is that the privileged form of knowing is knowing by the lone person himself, *solus ipse*. That is, real knowing is said to be individual and solipsistic, not social. (99)

In other words, behind the style there lies a claim to special knowledge (like the one McCloskey makes by using the Latin phrase *solus ipse*). Although it is not the full story of specialized discourses, a major strain comes from those that have been developed as a rhetoric that makes special claims to be the repository of highly privileged knowledge—knowledge detached from the observer, from the circumstances, and usually from the reader.

But you can also see a problem with "ordinary language" here. (By "ordinary language" we mean well-written standard English, free of specialized diction and tropes.) Note that McCloskey has lost something in the translation, the emphasis on theory (with which, of course, the language of theory goes). Muth wants "to outline a theory of expectations," while McCloskey wants to ask "how people guess about what the future will bring." Some people and situations call for one of these approaches, some for the other.

When so-called ordinary language appears in a text where professional discourse might be expected, its presence is hardly neutral. We might go so far as to say that there is no neutral language, that language is always ideological in that it symbolizes who the writer is, how the writer looks at the world, and how the writer wants the world to respond to him or to her. All language offered in a text is to some extent manipulative. Ordinary language in the place of discourse, however, proclaims a rebellion from the verbal conventions of the discipline in question and from the unspoken assumptions of that discipline's worldview. It may say, "Look at me, I'm accessible to the ordinary person, I'm not one of those stuffed-up specialists who is trying to snow you; I'm talking straight." Ordinary language is a powerful tool, one that can have powerful results. But it can also tend to obscure important distinctions. In the translation above, ordinary language may seem more user-friendly than the original, but it is loaded with implications: we don't need technical terms to understand complex issues; anybody can understand this; to use technical terms and structure is to be obfuscatory and professorial; real people talk like this. The truth is real people talk both ways. More to the point, though, as in this passage, ordinary language is comprehensible but often not sufficiently nuanced to explain the technical complexities of a subject. The questions the writer has to ask are "What do I gain by using either discourse or plain language? What does my audience expect? What will I lose if I try to explain complex issues in ordinary language?"

Some writers in highly specialized fields solve the problem of inaccessible discourse and accessible but simple language by falling back on the interwoven style, alternating technical discourse and ordinary language. Here's a brief example by Lester Thurow from his book *The Zero-sum Society:*

> Our political and economic structure simply isn't able to cope with an economy that has a substantial zero-sum element. A zero-sum game is any game where the losses exactly equal the winnings. All sporting events are zero-sum games. For every winner there is a loser, and winners can only exist if losers exist. What the winning gambler wins, the losing gambler must lose. (11)

Thurow has achieved a real integration of the technical and the conversational. The organizing feature of the passage is also the central organizing feature of his whole book, Thurow's whole theory of economics: a zero-sum game. A game of a certain sort is what economic activity is like, Thurow says; probably, to Thurow, that's also what it *is*. He explains the idea clearly in the paragraph quoted above: "What the winning gambler wins, the losing gambler must lose." Now look at the first sentence of that paragraph, and notice how it weaves together the spunky gamesman style of "zero-sum" with political and economic language—so smoothly that we don't really notice it.

Interweaving ordinary language into a specific discourse can be a helpful way to understand your material, as well as to transmit your ideas to other people, especially an audience that may be suspicious of purely professional discourse. We don't want to say that technical terms are completely out of place in writing or that a student won't sometime need to use elements from the specialized discourses of particular fields. But the exercise of moving back and forth from specialized discourse to ordinary language may bring some powerful results, especially increased clarity for both the writer and the reader. More important, we urge you, when appropriate, to experiment with translations and mixtures of the sort we have seen in the writings of the three economists.

3 PLAYING AND WORKING WITH LANGUAGE

We've been talking so far in this chapter about discourses, the individual's participation in a group's conventional language, which uses set patterns, often quite definite and quite prescriptive, to communicate. To use discourse, we have said, is to announce yourself publicly to be part of and speaking to the group whose discourse you share. But that's not the whole story. We have discussed when discourse is useful and not useful and how to modify or to adapt its limitations. We've looked at ordinary language—what it is, what's gained by it, and what's lost by it. Now we want to look at rhetoric, language used exuberantly and individually, language crafted by artistry attentive to sound and rhythm, to achieve some of the results of discourse—shared understanding and common ground.

The term *rhetoric* is an ancient one, of classical origin. For centuries, rhetoric was one of the central subjects of education. It meant training in oratory and, later, in certain kinds of writing as well, but it never lost its essential identity as an art tied to the sound of language. To study rhetoric meant to learn how to convince people of something, especially in public forums like law courts and political assemblies. Scholars of rhetoric cataloged the means by which successful speakers persuaded their audiences to agree with them or to act in certain ways, and students learned to name as well as to practice their devices—and how to imitate the masters. After print technology allowed the written word to replace the spoken in many arenas of persuasion, the devices and tactics continued to be studied and used.

Our dictionary tells us that we in the late twentieth century have several distinct notions of what the word *rhetoric* means. *Rhetoric* can mean the study of the elements of literature and public speaking, content, structure, cadence, and style. This is how the word is used in many college introductory rhetoric courses. These are courses that introduce students to, or continue their study of, the elements of how to use our language. *Rhetoric* also means the art of prose and the art of oratory, particularly the art of influencing people to accept your point of view. On the negative side, *rhetoric* is a word some of us use to refer to exaggerated or affected language or to unsupported or inflated discourse. No matter which of these definitions we use as a basic definition of *rhetoric*, notice that we all assume that rhetoric is the use of art in language to persuade an audience to see things your way. This is where rhetoric and discourse intersect. Discourse is a pattern of language, a subset of the larger category, rhetoric.

Discourse can, as we saw above, be rhetorical; it can sway by an appeal to something other than pure intellect; it can sway by a focus on language itself rather than the information language is meant to convey. Paying attention to patterns of sound, repetition, or how to join elements of language for maximum emotional or persuasive effect is not by and large the purpose of discourse. Discourse aims to convey information or to suggest that information is being conveyed, whether or not the reader is wise enough to know it. Discourse may be thought of as an attempt to control the natural complexity and ambiguities of language so that there can be no mistakes and no wasted time; properly used, discourse aims for control and precision, perhaps at the cost of flexibility and openness. Rhetoric tends to mine the rich complexity of language and take advantage of its profuseness, but we may sometimes emerge from a rhetorical performance feeling that we don't know how we have been convinced; we may have assented but not know why. Those who use the terms *rhetoric* and *discourse* interchangeably, especially using *rhetoric* where we might expect to find *discourse*, probably are saying that there are subtle persuasions and appeals being conveyed through the discourse, that discourse is being used in a rhetorical manner.

Rhetoric, Power, and Art

In the broad sense of studying persuasion in all its means, rhetoric continues to be an interesting and useful subject because it focuses on the relation
of the speaker or writer to the listener or reader, particularly on the ways in
which the writer can persuade the reader. Most people would say that the
following is an example of rhetoric (and indeed of very skilled rhetoric):

> Death and sorrow will be the companions of our journey; hardship our gar-
> ment; constancy and valour our only shield. We must be united, we must be
> undaunted, we must be inflexible.
>   (Winston Churchill, Official Report of the House of Commons, 303)

Part of Churchill's appeal here is emotional; he's trying to persuade people to remain steadfast, to give their military support, and he uses a variety of verbal devices to do so. We can call his *style* rhetorical; the *means*
he uses to persuade are also part of rhetoric.

One of the chief rhetorical means Churchill adopts is parallelism; the
two sentences are full of parallel constructions, which act on the ear, the
mind, and the emotions of the audience. In these sentences, as in so
many of his wartime speeches, Churchill calls on rhetoric to give his
ideas, unattractive by themselves (he is, after all, calling on English people to suffer and perhaps die), greater allure. Churchill's ability to use
words, which was considerable, gave him great political power to unite a
nation behind him in a time of crisis.

To explore a few of the ways rhetoric works further, we want to take a
detailed look at what, in the old-fashioned sense of the term, almost everyone would call a highly rhetorical style, wielded by a widely respected
rhetorician who happened also to be the commissioner of major league baseball, Bart Giamatti. Giamatti was originally a professor of literature, who
well knew the ancient practices of rhetoric as a scholar of Renaissance epics;
later he was president of Yale University. We might expect to find a good
deal of rhetorical flourish in his public addresses and official speeches and
perhaps even in his scholarly writing—and we do. But among his most dash-
ing rhetorical performances are his writings about baseball. In *Take Time for
Paradise: Americans and Their Games*, for example, he writes as follows:

> When we watch a contest or sport, and internalize the deep fact that this is
> an activity that has no ultimate consequence, no later outcome, no real ef-
> fect beyond itself, we invest it with tremendous significance because in this
> world of history and work and endless, tangled consequence, to have no
> "real" consequence or sequel is such a rare event. (34–35)

In some ways, the sentence's meaning is relatively straightforward
(games are significant because, unlike most of the rest of the things we
do or watch, they don't have any consequences beyond themselves), but
when we realize that it *is* just one sentence we may begin to see some of
its rhetorical artistry. Rhetoric does not simply mean making long sentences, but part of the rhetorician's art is the ability to manage the basic

structure of sentences to produce effects, sometimes by making them elaborate. According to many rhetoricians, the more effortlessly, the less visibly this is done, the better: the best rhetoric is to appear to have none. The purpose of this art is to draw the reader or listener into the world the writer creates. Rhetoric is above all the creation of a verbal world.

Bear with us a moment while we analyze the structure of Giamatti's sentence, to see how he draws us into his world. You can see that the sentence breaks into three parts:

1. When we watch a contest or sport, and internalize the deep fact that this is an activity that has no ultimate consequence, no later outcome, no real effect beyond itself,
2. we invest it with tremendous significance
3. because in this world of history and work and endless, tangled consequence, to have no "real" consequence or sequel is such a rare event.

To use grammatical terms, the second part is the main clause; the first part is an adverbial clause that tells us the conditions under which the main clause operates; and the third is another modifying clause that answers the question of why we invest sport with such significance. There is a powerful logic to this construction. The first clause tells us that sports are ultimately "inconsequential," the second that they are nonetheless "significant." That leaves us with a paradox, an apparent contradiction, and if Giamatti's rhetoric is working, it should have us asking, "How can this be? How can something of little consequence be significant?" The third part, beginning "because," resolves the apparent paradox, and the whole sentence has the structure of a resolved riddle.

Now, notice two smaller elements of rhetoric. One is that the first clause is on the face of it questionable. How does the commissioner of baseball—a "sport" that generates hundreds of millions of dollars of revenue, whose players are paid millions of dollars each year, whose fans live and die with the fortunes of their teams—how can he say that baseball is without consequence? Surely this is an exaggeration—hyperbole, as rhetoricians call it—a deliberate overstatement to make an effect or a point. But notice two important modifiers: Giamatti says that this is a "deep" fact and that baseball has no "ultimate" consequences. And we probably know what he's getting at: baseball isn't important in the way that wars, recessions, drug busts, elections, and the like are; way down *deep*, we know that sports aren't *ultimately* important.

Another rhetorical device is also worth noting: "consequence" and "significance" are terms we would often use interchangeably; they mean about the same thing. Here, though, Giamatti constructs the sentence so that we must contrast them: to be significant, something has to be a *sign*, to have a meaning; to be consequential, it has to have results, that is, things have to follow in *sequence* from it. That's what resolves the paradox: the world of history is a world of sequence, of effects, of things that lead on; the world of sport is not, which is why it is significant.

Repetition—there are three instances of "consequence" and one "sequel"—hammers home the point, and another repetition is particularly powerful: at the end of the first part of the sentence, Giamatti follows the phrase "no ultimate consequence" with two restatements, grammatically appositives: "no later outcome" and "no real effect beyond itself." This triple phrase stops us, makes us reread the words, and adds a nice touch of irony: the lack of consequence of sport must be very important.

Repetition is one of the basic tools of rhetoric, and it is not surprising that part of Giamatti's argument is that repetition is a basic feature of sport. But in the midst of all the repetition that sports are made of, Giamatti says, sometimes there occurs: "a moment when we are all free of all constraint of all kinds, when pure energy and pure order create an instant of complete coherence. In that instant, pulled to our feet, we are pulled out of ourselves. We feel what we saw, become what we perceived" (35). Here Giamatti the rhetorician again uses a parallel construction, the repetition on a large or a small scale of a pattern of phrasing:

we are all free	we feel
of all constraints	what we saw
of all kinds	become what we perceived

He continues: "In that moment of vision, of sensation compounded of sight and insight, everyone—participant and spectator—is centered. No one is eccentric" (36). Here the rhetorical device is called *polyptoton*, which involves playing on different forms of a term, in this case reminding us that the basic meaning of "eccentric" is to be off-center and thus playing off the connotation of eccentric (weird) against the literal meaning, off-center. Similarly, the precise geometrical sense of "centered" also suggests the more mystical or religious sense, as when we say a person is centered, which is what Giamatti's real point is, as he goes on to develop the quasi-ceremonial aspect of sport:

> The essential ceremonial quality of sport, made of anticipation, repetition, and fulfillment, has worked to force the noblest expression leisure can provide—the state of contemplation that is, as Aristotle wrote, "the activity of the intellect that constitutes complete human happiness." It does not last a whole life span, as Aristotle says it should last; it lasts a mere moment. But it is no less authentic for that. The memory of that moment is deep enough to send us all out again and again, to reenact the ceremony, made of all the minor ceremonies to which spectator and player devote themselves, in the hopes that the moment will be summoned again and made again palpable. (36)

If you've gotten into the spirit of this mode, you can read a passage like this aloud, remembering that rhetoric developed from oratory, and get a dramatic sense of the ways in which the repetitions and variations work and how integral they are to Giamatti's point—because, of course, his rhetoric is gamelike, a kind of spiritually significant play.

Variations are as important as repetitions. After the passage just quoted, Giamatti gives us a surprise. The next sentence, beginning a new paragraph, is a simple one: "The gods have fled, I know." Suddenly, he shifts to the personal and, in effect, from baseball to the philosophical. We could say that it is a personal moment in the middle of a rhetorical performance; in fact, it is a daring rhetorical use of an apparently personal moment. The statement is a dramatically simple one: six monosyllable words. It carries a tone of recognition, as if he were saying: "no doubt you will want to say to me that it is silly for me to be talking about gods because we live in an unreligious age"; almost wearily, but with a certain grandeur, he seems to confess: "oh, you don't have to tell me that; I have felt it deeply, and I accept it." Nonetheless, he continues:

> I believe we have played games, and watched games, to imitate the gods, to become godlike in our worship of each other and, through those moments of transmutation, to know for an instant what the gods know. Whether celebrated by Pindar or Roger Angell, sport is, however, ultimately subversive of religion because while it mimics religion's ritual and induces its fanaticism and sensation, sport cares not at all for religion's moral strictures or political power or endless promises. Sport cares not for religion's *consequences*. . . .
>
> If playing sport is akin to another human activity, it is akin to making art. When scholars, like the estimable Guttman, tell me, for instance,
>
> "To the degree that Greek athletic festivals were religious ritual and artistic expression, they had a purpose beyond themselves and ceased to be sports in our strictest definition of the terms. . . . The closer the contests came to the status of art, the further they departed from that of sport." I beg to dissent. (36–37)

You may feel that Giamatti is becoming a little pompous in his rhetoric here, with phrases like "the estimable Guttman" and "I beg to dissent"— terms we might find in the Lincoln-Douglas debates. But it should be noted how much fun Giamatti is having here, affecting the role of public declamation, almost inviting the reader into the performance with him. Let's discuss sport as if we were Chautauqua speakers from a bygone age. The baseball equivalent would be what players used to call "hotdogging," showing off one's skills. But if the skills are real ones and showing them doesn't interfere with the game, and especially if it actually improves performance, showing them off may be welcomed.

✎ **Writing**   Try your hand at some elaborate sentences by starting with a simple construction and adding modifiers or multiplying clauses. Think about how you can keep such sentences under control. Think about how you can use "the drama" of the sentence to achieve effects, for example, by building up to a final point or by constructing parallels.

Now, by writing something fresh or rewriting something you've written before, self-consciously vary your sentence constructions. Use a series of short sentences, followed by a long one or several medium sentences of expanding length, and then a single-word sentence. Use a series of questions that are parallel to each other. In short, play with some rhetorical patterning and see how it feels.

Rhetoric and Individual Styles

Rhetoric has the power to create a world—to draw the reader into that world by sound, by varied cadences, by the power of words—in writing that is apparently far simpler, far less flamboyant than Giamatti's. For contrast with Giamatti's writing, look at an excerpt from a work with a different slant. As it happens, the author, George Will, is paying tribute to Giamatti (the commissioner, if not the writer):

> A. Bartlett Giamatti was to the Commissioner's office what Sandy Koufax [a great pitcher with a relatively short career] was to the pitcher's mound: Giamatti's career had the highest ratio of excellence to longevity. If his heart had been as healthy as his soul—if his heart had been as strong as it was warm—Giamatti would one day have been ranked among commissioners the way Walter Johnson is ranked (by correct thinkers) among pitchers: as the best, period. Baseball's seventh commissioner, who was the first to have taught Renaissance literature at Yale, was fond of noting the etymological fact that the root of the word "paradise" is an ancient Persian word meaning "enclosed park or green." Ballparks exist, he said, because there is in humanity "a vestigial memory of an enclosed green space as a place of freedom or play." Perhaps. Certainly ballparks are pleasant places for the multitudes. But for the men who work there, ballparks are for hard, sometimes dangerous, invariably exacting business. Physically strong and fiercely competitive men make their living in those arenas. Most of these men have achieved, at least intermittently, the happy condition of the fusion of work and play. They get physical pleasure and emotional release and fulfillment from their vocation. However, Roy Campanella's celebrated aphorism—that there has to be a lot of little boy in a man who plays baseball—needs a corollary. There has to be a lot hardness in a man who plays—who works at—this boy's game.
>
> (*Men at Work*, 4–5)

Despite his professed admiration for Giamatti, Will takes precisely the opposite view of baseball: rather than being a release from the world of consequences and history and endless toil, baseball is a game of hard work. Properly, Will's style is workmanlike rather than flamboyant, its control not a liberation but a conquest. Read it aloud, and you will hear the clipped, insistent tone.

The "interruption" in the last sentence—where Will inserts "who works at"—says a great deal. This is another rhetorical device, that of apparent self-correction to get a more precise term. He could have simply said, "There has to be a lot of hardness in a man who works at this boy's game." That would have made the point. But the self-correction under-scores the substitution: "where I almost said *plays*, out of habit, I want to put *works*."

Notice too how Will uses a one-word sentence—"Perhaps"—to comment on Giamatti's talk about the ballpark as "a place of freedom and play." We hear the ironic skeptic here, as if he is looking at you with eyes aslant and a bemused grin, suggesting that he is willing to listen out of politeness but that he really thinks the idea is nonsense. Even when Will is paying tribute to Giamatti he is pursuing his own goal, debunking these fancy ideas about baseball in favor of a meat-and-potatoes approach. And the whole paragraph pivots on the word "perhaps"; you can almost hear him raising his eyebrows, as he moves from admiring Giamatti to disputing his view.

We call Will's piece rhetorical because we feel his exultation in language both as a way of sharing his meaning with the reader and as a medium he can create and manipulate (most, perhaps all, of the examples we quote in this book are in some sense rhetorical). Will relishes developing meaning, honing his sentences, and creating verbal structures. Look at the sentence that begins "If his heart had been as healthy as his soul," and notice how many points Will manages to include, how he strings them along the thread of his sentence: "if his heart had been as strong as it was warm—Giamatti would . . . have been ranked among commissioners . . . the way Walter Johnson is ranked (by correct thinkers) among pitchers: as the best, period."

This isn't rhetorically flamboyant in obvious ways; there is a hard-bitten tone to it, a deliberately antiromantic approach to the game. But it is still rhetoric, well suited to its thesis, as appropriate to its notion of work and vocation as Giamatti's rhetoric is to its notion of freedom and play. The rhetoric creates its whole world; and its viewpoints and its characteristic language and phrasing and metaphors are completely a part of it. That Giamatti was and Will is a public figure allows us to know just how characteristic of its author the rhetoric of each piece of writing is. Will's tribute to Giamatti is the highest tribute a writer can pay: he has used his craft fully, lovingly, and artistically, celebrating in his own words the vitality, the love of baseball, and the love of language that characterized Giamatti.

George Will and Bart Giamatti are realized in the rhetoric they have created. Create your own, not *ex nihilo*, but by experiment, trial and error, borrowing, imitating, inventing. The patterns of grammar, sound, and diction rhetoric needs to create a verbal world for the reader require skill and practice on the writer's part. Nevertheless, the essential elements of rhetoric, its ability to persuade through the arts of language and the comparative simplicity of some of those arts, are adaptable to nearly all styles. In the exercise below we ask you to try your hand at rhetorical writing.

✎ **Writing**   Read over several pieces of your writing, looking and listening for the rhetoric, and the rhetorical self, that emerges. At this point, listen for but don't really try to reject the elements of your own rhetoric that may be part of the discourse of the field in which you're writing. Note any devices or tactics you habitually return to. Where are you most comfortable with the rhetoric, and the rhetorical self, that comes out at you from these pages? Write about your own rhetorical performance.

PART III

Private Voices Made Public

CHAPTER 8

Creating a Public Self

In the last chapter, we discussed ways in which participating in certain discourses define a role for a writer. But we also said that there were choices to make, both in whether you would play those roles and in the ways you could modify them so that they reflect not just the prefabricated roles of a profession or field. In either case, using any of these discourses involves role playing. Here we want to look at role playing across a much broader spectrum of possibilities, with the overall goal of prompting you to think about writing as a dramatic creation of a public self.

Think of the voice that seems to speak to you, to your inner ear, from the pages of what you read. The voice is that of the writer, but it's more accurate to say that it represents a version of the writer, something the writer can create and modify and control for different purposes. From this point of view, writing is personal not only because personal experience and opinions are used but also because a "person" is implicitly created in the act of writing. It is also public in the sense that the persona created exists in order to communicate effectively with another person or group.

As you write, you define yourself for that particular situation. You play a role. In fact you are playing roles during most of your waking time. Think for a minute about all the different encounters you have during the day with different people. You are mother, father, daughter, son, sister, brother, student, teacher, employee, employer, neighbor, colleague, customer, stranger. You are happy, sad, angry, content, aggressive, patient. In each encounter you play a slightly different role, according to the circumstances and according to the person you are talking to. Each role is truly you, but none is the sum of all you can be. You are a combination of roles; you modulate your voice, your words, and your actions to suit the occasion and the audience.

The role you play in any particular encounter will be partly shaped by who you are in all circumstances—by you as a child, a parent, a sibling, a friend, a female or male, a person of a certain ethnic background, a person with or without a certain profession, a person from a certain state or nation, an urban or rural person, and so on. It will also reflect ongoing elements in your personality: friendliness, shyness, outspokenness. Your role will be the product of complex impulses, habits, needs, and traits, as well as of immediate circumstances and reactions to the people you meet. Out of all these and countless other possible factors, your role will be shaped by what you decide to focus on for that particular encounter, at that particular time and place, and interacting with that particular person.

To focus this idea, think about actors you've seen play various roles. Meryl Streep, for example, who seems unusually adept at portraying a wide range of different characters, nonetheless seems also to be Meryl Streep in each role. She has the ability, that is, to dramatize herself in a lot of different ways. But part of her art is that she has developed the dramatic personality Meryl Streep, variations on which appear in each different role.

Writing, of course, offers far less scope for dramatization than acting or speaking does. As a medium it cuts out so many of the obvious means by which we reveal ourselves and perceive others—direct visual and aural means, all sorts of facial expressions and body language—that it may seem that there is little left in writing by which to reveal a person. Usually writers are physically absent from their readers' experience. But words imply speakers, and specific uses of words imply specific kinds of people who use them. You the writer can shape your public presence by varying the degree to which you remove or emphasize aspects of yourself in writing; you can choose how much to dramatize yourself to your reader. In our view, the conception of creating a public voice as inherently dramatic can provide a great deal of power. In the pages that follow, we talk about this public self as a series of roles.

Any verbal character you create reflects not simply who you are or want to sound like but also the imagined interplay between yourself and your reader, defined by the occasion and purpose for which you are writing. In living, you are not simply who you decide to be but rather the result of an interplay between your individual self and other people. In writing, the same is true: the person implicit in your words is the result of an adaptation of yourself to the occasion of your writing and to the reader you imagine reading your words.

1 MAKING A PERSONA

Overtly Implied Selves

In the 1988 presidential campaign, Vice President George Bush took the advice of one of President Reagan's speechwriters, Peggy Noonan, to convey his opposition to any raise in federal taxes and to signal his promise not to raise taxes should he be elected, by using the phrase "Read my lips." The phrase became a hallmark of the Bush campaign and, later, of the early years of his presidency. It was memorable and was cited often during subsequent congressional debates about how to reduce the national deficit. It may or may not tell us something about President Bush's economic theories and commitments, but it does tell us something about the ways in which persons are present in words.

Why was the phrase so effective? Couldn't he just have said, "I am unalterably opposed to any tax increase"? Yes, but somehow "Read my lips" seems to indicate opposition more powerfully than the more literal phrase. Here is Noonan's description of her thinking as she worked on Bush's speech with which he accepted the presidential nomination:

> Jack Kemp [congressman, later secretary of housing] told me, Hit hard on taxes, Bush will be pressured to raise them as soon as he's elected, and he has to make clear he won't budge. (This became, "The Congress will push me to raise taxes, and I'll say no, and they'll push, and I'll say no, and they'll push again. And all I can say to them is read my lips: No New Taxes.") Aides to the vice president later took out "read my lips" on the grounds, I believe, that lips are organs, there is no history of presidential candidates making personal-organ references in acceptance speeches, therefore. . . . Anyway, I kept putting it back in. Why? Because it's definite. It's not subject to misinterpretation. It means, I mean this.
>
> (*What I Saw at the Revolution*, 307; Noonan's ellipses)

The phrase suggests that "the words are so distinct, so plain and simple, that you don't even have to hear them to know what I think; you can see it on my lips; it will be clear in the way things are clear when we talk to the hearing-impaired or when we talk to children, forming the words clearly with our lips." That seems to be the meaning the phrase had for Noonan. This is what some linguists call the "meta-message," the implication that goes along with words and that defines and expands their literal meaning.

But there's something more in this phrase. It was originated, or at least made popular, by a movie character, the police officer called Dirty Harry, played by Clint Eastwood. Dirty Harry is a San Francisco detective who is always fighting two simultaneous battles, one against crooks and the other against the political establishment, which is trying to limit him by oversensitivity to the civil rights of alleged criminals, by restraining him from using force when necessary, and by sheer stupidity. In a series of movies, Dirty Harry is able to defeat bad guys by cutting corners, by taking the law into his own hands and meting out frontier justice.

Harry is tall and raw-boned and rarely smiles. He also talks very little; he distrusts words. He prefers actions and a direct approach. When he does speak, he uses as few words as possible, and the implication is that in doing so, he really commits himself to the words he has spoken. Politicians, he often implies, use a lot of words and end up soft-soaping the electorate and coddling criminals; Harry's terse laconic utterances cut through all that palaver and are a kind of action in their own right. He particularly likes brief, quotable statements, three or four words in the imperative mode. In one movie, he goes into a bank where several crooks are staging a robbery. One of them looks as if he might draw a gun. Harry says, "Go ahead. Make my day." The implication is "if you draw your gun, I'll be happy to draw mine, and I'll kill you." That will "make my day [happy]." He delivers the line softly, with a steely menace and very clear enunciation.

When George Bush says "Read my lips," he not only makes a pledge but also implies something about the kind of person who is making that pledge. He constructs a verbal character or enlarges the verbal character he already has. The words imply an affinity with Clint Eastwood and Dirty Harry. It is not a matter of impersonation; we know that George Bush is George Bush, not Clint Eastwood. But the phrase implies a *kind* of character—someone who does not use many words, who is tough, who doesn't like politicians, and who will go out and get the job done—and makes us look at the speaker, or more literally to listen to the speaker, in a different way. Most listeners of George Bush undoubtedly did not calculate all these implications; the effect would not have been so strong if the listeners had to think all that through. The effect comes as a quick recognition. His words make us conscious of George Bush as a kind of character with whom we have certain associations.

That implied character is what we mean by a *persona.* It is not who George Bush "is" or the movie character he alludes to but the personality, the kind of character, that we re-create in our minds in response to, and shaped by, his words. The persona will not usually be so blatant a device of projection as it is in this example, nor will it usually be created by allusion to another character. But it is the sum of all the impressions you have of the kind of person who might have spoken the words you've heard or read.

Creating a persona is an aspect of writing that you can shape and control. Of course, writing is not the same as speaking, and on many occasions, you will not want to imply a particular kind of persona in the way we have just described. But words imply speakers, human beings of certain sorts who speak the words, and even, as in the Bush/Eastwood example, a whole set of circumstances surrounding them, like a little drama.

On the one hand, using a persona is something you do all the time in your writing, at least in the sense that your readers will draw inferences, perhaps without thinking about it, about what kind of "person" is speaking to them. On the other hand, to shape and modify a persona well is not an easy chore, not a matter of a quickly learned technique. It begins in recognition and awareness, going in two directions. First, you need to pay attention to this aspect of texts as you read them. A good way to begin is to violate a rule you may have learned in grade school, the rule about not moving your lips when you read. Reading silently helps with speed reading, but it allows you to ignore the intonations that define personality and character. Feel free to move your lips as you read (and write), hear a voice in your imagination, and try to visualize speaker and scene. Second, look for signs of your own nascent persona in what you write. Read what you write for sound, voice, and character; imagine what kind of impression, not you the person, but you the character as implied in your writing, is making on your reader. Then, in both kinds of reading, try to identify the sources of your persona—what words and phrases help to create it. Remember, except for whatever might be implied by careful or sloppy or otherwise notable typing or handwriting, the whole impression is being created by the words as you interpret them, so whatever creates it must be coming from the ways in which the words are being used.

✎ **Writing**   Look at the examples throughout the book. Choose two and describe the personae speaking to you. What qualities come through the words the writers choose and the way they arrange them? Identify what is essential to their personae. Be specific.

Implied Selves in Impersonal Writing

Writing allows you to do away with many signs of yourself as the person who has written. But even in nonrevelatory, relatively impersonal writing, traces of the author remain. For example, here are some written comments by George Will that conclude an argument against President Reagan's proposed constitutional amendment to permit prayer in public schools:

> It is, to say no more, curious that, according to some polls, more Americans favor prayers in schools than regularly pray in church. Supermarkets sell processed cheese and instant mashed potatoes, so many Americans must like bland substitutes for real things. But it is one thing for the nation's palate to tolerate frozen waffles; it is another and more serious thing for the nation's soul to be satisfied with add-water-and-stir instant religiosity. When government acts as liturgist for a pluralistic society, the result is bound to be a puree that is tasteless, in several senses.
>
> ("Against Prefabricated Prayer," 177)

We do not know *all* about George Will from this, but we have a distinct sense of a person. Where does it come from? From details of language, phrasing, and metaphor and also simply the way in which he treats his subject. A phrase like "liturgist for a pluralist society," for example, or that rather harsh comparison, ending with the sarcastic statement "most Americans must like bland substitutes for real things," gives a sense of someone with strong opinions and high standards about such things as food. The last phrase, with its tart understatement and its severe irony, suggests a person riding above the scene, observing the political foolishness that even his fellow conservatives can fall into. The extended metaphor of substitutes for real things allied to that of prefabrication suggests a certain aristocratic hauteur: "I am not the sort of person who would eat food that has not been homemade; I am not the sort of person to eat frozen waffles (and I hope you aren't either)." There is also a distinct tone here, a sense of controlled and lightly amused outrage. And the detachment and hauteur are inseparable from Will's argument, that an amendment for prayer in the schools affronts not liberty but prayer. In allowing us to watch himself wrestle with his subject, Will has told us something about himself, has given us materials out of which to re-create an image of him in our minds. He has played a role for us by creating a public persona, with us as his audience.

✎ **Writing**   Read several editorials on a current issue. Imagine what the authors are like, based on what you sense of their personalities in the different columns. In a brief paper explain the source of your impressions. Is it the attitude they take? Are there particular verbal habits or devices or ways of phrasing or choices of words that help suggest a character?

"I" as a Person

Role playing, personal presence, and honesty are not necessarily at odds with one another. Look at what two well-known essayists, E. B. White and Joan Didion, say about the relation of role playing and self-revelation. White's point about the variety of possible personae in essay writing comes from the introduction to his *Essays of E. B. White:*

> There are as many kinds of essays as there are human attitudes or poses, as many essay flavors as there are Howard Johnson ice creams. The essayist arises in the morning and, if he has work to do, selects his garb from an unusually extensive wardrobe: he can pull on any sort of shirt, be any sort of person, according to his mood or his subject matter—philosopher, scold, jester, raconteur, confidant, pundit, devil's advocate, enthusiast. (vii)

White talks about essayists as people who strike a variety of poses, putting on different clothes as befits their mood or the occasion. Even though there is, according to White, a good deal of role playing in writing, it is not a matter of disguise. On the contrary, candor and role playing go together. The mask of the persona worn by the "I" is always a construction, never wholly and truly the actual narrator:

> There is one thing the essayist cannot do, though—he cannot indulge himself in deceit or in concealment, for he will be found out in no time. Desmond McCarthy . . . observes that Montaigne "had the gift of natural candour. . . . " It is the basic ingredient. (viii)

At the heart of all successful verbal role playing, White says, you will find the writer who writes out of experience and out of intellectual and emotional honesty, creating a role true to life but not trying on any one occasion to present the whole that is himself or herself.

Joan Didion takes up this central issue in her essay "Why I Write":

Of course I stole the title for this talk from George Orwell. One reason I stole it was that I like the sound of the words: *Why I Write*. There you have three short unambiguous words that share a sound, and the sound they share is this:

I

I

I

In many ways writing is the act of saying *I*, of imposing oneself upon other people, of saying *listen to me, see it my way, change your mind*. It's an aggressive, even a hostile act. You can disguise its aggressiveness all you want with veils of subordinate clauses and qualifiers and tentative subjunctives, with ellipses and evasions—with the whole manner of intimating rather than claiming, of alluding rather than stating—but there's no getting around the fact that writing words on paper is the tactic of a secret bully, an invasion, an imposition on the reader's most private space.

I stole this title not only because the words sounded right but because they seemed to sum up, in a no-nonsense way, all I have to tell you. (2)

Let's go one step further and read Didion's passage along with the one below by White:

I think some people find the essay the last resort of the egoist, a much too self-conscious and self-serving form for their taste; they feel that it is presumptuous of a writer to assume that his little excursions or his small observations will interest the reader. There is some justice in their complaint. I have always been aware that I am by nature self-absorbed and egotistical; to write of myself to the extent I have done indicates a too great attention to my own life, not enough to the lives of others. I have worn many shirts, and not all of them have been a good fit. (viii)

We can draw several conclusions from these statements. First, the presence of the self, the "I," matters considerably to these two highly skilled writers. You may have been told never to use the first-person singular pronoun in your writing, to remove as many traces of yourself as you can. If we take White's and Didion's word for it, however, "I" lies at the very heart of the writing they do, not just as a matter of whether to refer to themselves in the first person, but also in all the details of their writing. Nothing could make that clearer than Didion's insistence on the rhymes with *I* in "Why I Write" and her stack of *I*'s on the page.

Second, the kind of people White and Didion *say* they are does not necessarily correspond to the *personae* that come through to the reader. Didion calls herself a secret bully who invades and imposes on the reader's space, and she repeats words like *aggressive* and *impose* in different forms; White talks at length about his egotism and self-absorption. But neither piece really sounds invasive, self-absorbed, egotistic, or aggressive. Rather, each author sounds frank and open, friendly and conversational, witty and capable of self-irony. In other words, even in frankly confessional first-person writing, what authors *say* about themselves, about who they truly are (although in each case we have to remember that their self-descriptions actually describe their writing personalities, not their moral, ethical, or social personalities), can and often will differ from the pictures of them we as readers form in our minds. "I" is never the "real" person; it is always a projection of some *part* of the writer.

The self-absorption they claim does not stop them from showing considerable consciousness of their readers. Didion worries about invading the reader's space, White about whether "it is presumptuous of a writer to assume that his little excursions or his small observations will interest the reader." Their words betray just how sensitive they are to their readers' response to them.

Finally, a paradox emerges, perhaps most vividly in White's description of essayists—their "natural candor," their lack of "deceit or concealment," and at the same time their many poses and roles, the different shirts they wear. Your sense may be that role playing has an element of concealment, of pretending to be other than what you are. It is a paradox but not a contradiction. A writer can, and we think must, do both. You play a role, and you reveal yourself. Role playing can certainly involve pretense, but when combined with honesty it can also be self-revealing, an extension of personality by its interaction with a reader. Your persona is a public version of you—more accurately, of parts or aspects of you, dramatized by your words for the purpose and the readers at hand. It is "who you are" for the occasion, projected in a tangible shape.

✎ **Writing**   Begin the work of coming to terms with your own persona. Read several things you've written, covering if possible some variety of modes and occasions: letters, essays, stories, whatever. Read them, to the extent possible, as if you were not their author, and jot down what kind of person you imagine to be speaking. If possible, have someone else read any that you feel like showing. Ask them for their responses along these lines, that is, their picture of what kind of person comes through. Are there any sharply defined roles you or your readers feel are being played here? Write informally for a page or two what you like and do not like, not about yourself, but about the versions of yourself projected in your writing.

2   PRACTICING ROLE PLAYING

Letters offer a flexible medium through which to practice role playing by creating a persona. To write a letter often is to re-create lived experience so that a reader will know what it is like to be you. In many letters that you read, you know the writer and the writer knows you. In most personal letters that you write, you know the reader well and therefore do not have to contrive a personality. Perhaps surprisingly, however, most letter writers do just that, even if without giving it conscious thought. Hence, writing letters is useful practice for the kind of honest role playing that occurs in less obvious ways elsewhere. In writing letters, you reveal yourself, play roles, and calculate your audience's possible reactions—all, for the most part, instinctively. Notice what you do instinctively and think about ways of applying the skill to other kinds of writing.

Creating a Role Through Details

We begin with a letter Margaret Mead wrote in August 1925, when she had just begun her career as an anthropologist. She had been at sea, as she says, "Nearing the Equator" for five days. Apparently she writes this letter to explain why she hasn't written before and why she can't write very much now (a familiar line among letter writers). In doing so she focuses the letter on its readers, by creating for herself the role of rushed, breathless, overladen correspondent:

> *S.S. Sonoma*
> 5th day at sea
> Nearing the Equator
>
> It's no use, dear friends, I just can't write you a nice long descriptive letter on this ship, it rolls too much. To summarize: I had a lovely time in Honolulu, with a whole group of people to see me off and so many leis around my neck that I had to stagger up the gangplank. I got the structure of the language, met all the proper people and was loaded down with more letters of introduction and numerous presents ranging from the picture of a statue of Duke Kahanamoku, the Olympic Games hero, which I am taking as a gift to Tufele, the high chief of Manu'a, to a slip of a palm tree which I am taking to the captain of the *Lady Roberts*.
>
> (*Letters from the Field, 1925–75*, 22–23)

There's very little remarkable about the letter, and that is just the point. Its straightforward style provides information and apology in a lighthearted tone created by the enumeration of several briefly described events. It opens with an abrupt semiapology, moves to absolute statement ("It rolls too much"), and then passes on to summary. All these stages become part of Mead's role as willing but harried correspondent.

Mead's correspondents probably paid no attention to the kinds of things we have been talking about, nor did Mead in writing the letter. But her friends may have had a sense of familiarity in reading the letter: "Isn't that just like Margaret? Can't you see her there, staggering up the gangplank under a load of leis, taking a palm tree to a ship's captain and another gift to a native chief, and writing a letter on the rolling ship?" They quite possibly heard phrases characteristic of her conversation. And she may have had a certain pleasure, even in this quick letter, in presenting herself as she does, as a harried, somewhat comic character who is at the same time on top of things, quickly mastering the structure of a language, distributing gifts, seen off by a large group of people, and writing a letter under adverse conditions. If we are right, these same kinds of recognitions occur to you when you read and write letters, writing in ways that play out your sense of who you are to someone you know. The point, once again, is to begin by recognizing how a persona emerges in a letter, by hearing a voice, visualizing a person, and inferring a character.

✎ **Writing** Make the next letter you write a letter full of details about how you feel and what's been happening to you. Use Mead's format of apology, excuse, and series of evocative details. Chances are you will find it more fun and more interesting to write a letter based on evocative detail than on bland generality.

Using a Persona for a Purpose

Here is a letter the novelist Jean Rhys wrote to her publisher to explain why she had not yet sent him a promised manuscript. The letter illustrates how an accomplished user of language and creator of characters seeks both to get a message across and to shape the reader's expected response. While Rhys appears in control of the situation, she is clearly shaping her role in response to her reader. Notice how both individual details woven into a unified pattern and the form of the letter, in its the brief paragraphing, contribute to Rhys's voice and message:

October 17, 1961

Dear Mr. Wyndham,

Of course you are quite right, I haven't a whole copy of the story—(in spite of my boast that I had fifteen or something!) only a quantity of bits and pieces. I thought of the other start going over it in my head (as I often do) but am pretty sure that if I reread it I would agree with what you say. So—no more of *that* idea[. . . .]

My husband's illness has strained me up rather, but I do feel that with a little will power and so on I'll be able to manage to fix the book up, write it legibly and sooner than you'd believe.

I've got some wonderful pep pills—unfortunately whenever I take one *something happens.*

Yesterday I was all set when a kind neighbour brought me masses of flowers. Instead of dumping them in the bath, I started arranging them. Fatal! All the pep had gone when I had finished trying to show them off. They looked very lovely but I felt finished. (But they *were* lovely.)

Today, another pill, another neighbour who spent hours telling me about a TV writer who has settled in Cheriton Fitz and is going mad with worry because his play or whatever has stuck.

As he has a devoted wife who does all the chores and *creeps* in with cups of coffee when he groans I could not pity him—(Gossip)

In case you don't meet Alec soon—My husband has been ill now for four years—all the same I have got the book done—

As to this cutting, starts, doubts and so on—well that began years and years ago in Paris and I will never lose it now (and I shall never be sure whether it was a good thing or not).

Good for me—but enough to drive everybody else crazy—I know.

"Petronella" started as a 50000 word novel—so did some of the other stories, the best part of Voyage in the Dark was cut. And so on.

But it will be done trust me. I will send the various Chapter I's and you will judge. I guess it'll go pretty quickly after that.

(*The Letters of Jean Rhys*, 206–207)

Rhys may have been more conscious of playing a part here than someone like Mead, who seems to have been writing largely for informative purposes. Rhys begins the first paragraph by exhibiting penitence; in the second and third she is a nurse pushing herself to the limit with pep pills; in the fourth, the victim of well-meaning neighbors. In the fifth, she is again the victim, but this time of another writer who cannot get *his* work done, perhaps letting Mr. Wyndham know that she knows just how he must feel dealing with *her*; in the sixth paragraph, while still seeming to talk about the bothersome playwright, she underscores the difference: "*he* has a devoted wife to take care of him; I not only don't have any such devoted spouse, I *am* the devoted spouse who has to take care not just of a blocked playwright but also of an invalid of four years (and yet I have gotten the book done)." Next she is the penitent who may drive everyone crazy but still gets things done; and finally the maker of a sincere pledge: "It will be done trust me."

Rhys clearly wants her publisher to understand her position, but even more, she wants to have him see her as a certain kind of person so she can solicit his sympathy. Of course, he is never likely to forget that she is Jean Rhys; these roles are not negations of her ordinary personality but extensions of it (and he perhaps responded to it by saying to himself with exasperation, "There goes Jean again, making up excuses").

Probably everyone has had the opportunity to write a letter that offers excuses for not having done something on time, and perhaps you have been still more ingenious than Rhys in offering your excuses. You may find Rhys's excuses either pitiable or laughable (and, of course, for all we know they may be completely true), but whatever their truth and their effect, note that she is not simply offering them up but is shaping a public writing persona through them.

✎ **Writing** Write a letter that makes excuses for some real or imagined offense or neglected chore. Be as ingenious and as believable as you want in your excuses, but think also about the audience for whom you are pretending to write and about the possible roles you might play. Shape your letter accordingly.

Letters written to people you know well, as the exercise above may suggest to you, can produce a symbolic shorthand of references. What happens to role playing when the recipient is not someone you know well but really a complete stranger? This situation corresponds most directly to the usual situation in writing: your audience is not one that has any personal interest in you. Yet, as we have seen, you need to keep yourself, your "personality," in the center of your writing. Role playing becomes even more important when all that your reader knows about you comes directly from what you write. In such cases the writing does not represent a known person, as in the Mead and Rhys letters above, but serves as an ambassador from one unknown person to another. As you can imagine, role playing under such circumstances can offer lots of fun. Once more, letters and letter writers provide accessible and useful models to explore for technique.

You may be familiar with J. R. R. Tolkien, author of, among other works, *The Hobbit* and *The Ring Trilogy*. Besides writing fantasy literature, Tolkien was an Oxford professor and one of the great philologists of this century. The two letters below show how Tolkien was able to create a role for himself in response to a request from his German publisher for information about his racial and ethnic heritage. Notice that Tolkien sounds different in the two letters. The first, written to his English publisher, Stanley Unwin, on July 25, 1938, has a free and easy tone. The role he plays is very close to his "real" self, or at least so we assume from the direct and conversational quality here:

> I must say the enclosed letter from Rutten and Loening [his German publisher] is a bit stiff. Do I suffer this impertinence because of the possession of a German name, or do their lunatic laws require a certificate of 'arisch' origin from all persons of all countries? (37)

In actually writing to the publishers, on the same day, Tolkien is much more controlled but not less angry. Whereas his role above was that of friend writing to friend—open and somewhat colloquial ("is a bit stiff," "lunatic laws")—in his letter to the German publishers he is more circumspect, more controlled. He plays an identifiable role, that of the learned, even pedantic, professor, writing more in sorrow than in anger. This role becomes his public persona for the purposes of writing to the German publisher. We can see that he has selected details from his vast knowledge of languages specifically to ridicule the "lunacy" behind the law he clearly detests:

> Dear Sirs,
>   Thank you for your letter. . . . I regret that I am not clear as to what you intend by *arisch*. I am not of *Aryan* extraction: that is Indo-Iranian; as far as I am aware none of my ancestors spoke Hindustani, Persian, Gypsy, or any related dialects. But if I am to understand that you are enquiring whether I am of *Jewish* origin, I can only reply that I regret that I appear to have *no* ancestors of that gifted people. . . . I cannot, however, forbear to comment that if impertinent and irrelevant inquiries of this sort are to become the rule in

matters of literature, then the time is not far distant when a German name will no longer be a source of pride.

(The Letters of J. R. R. Tolkien, 37–38)

Tolkien points out, on the basis of his extensive knowledge of languages and philology, what the German law seems not to recognize, that the term *Aryan* refers to a number of races and peoples whom the German government of that time regarded as inferior to the German (Aryan) people. For our purposes, however, the letter is interesting because of the role Tolkien chooses to play and because he chooses to speak directly in a dialogic format. He acknowledges that he is writing, creating his role, in direct response to his reader. He addresses the publisher directly as "you" and he characterizes the "I" who is speaking as knowledgeable, in control, and hence speaking from a superior position. He does not exclude emotion but channels it through his knowledge of philology and his personal conviction. Tolkien shows how role playing can create a verbal personality tailored to the reader and the needs of the situation, as the writer perceives them. Without knowing Tolkien personally, the reader of this letter senses a strong personality in the phrasing and the tone.

The principle in Tolkien's letter is the one behind all the letters in this section, the same principle we looked at in the previous section. The repeated "I regret," as well as the repetition of "I," makes the reader aware of the centrality of the person writing. In addition, the details he chooses to focus on are relevant and symbolic. Instead of saying, as the letter clearly implies, "Your Aryan fixation is a lot of unlearned rot!" he suggests that a modest knowledge of languages and heritage (Indo-Iranian) will expose the hollowness of the term *Aryan* as the Germans used it to refer to northern European ancestry. Tolkien lives in this letter and yet he lives behind a role. He uses the role to attack his publisher, his reader, even while he uses the language that fits the role (polite gentleman scholar) conventionally.

✎ **Writing** Try writing a similar letter to someone whose views on a moral or ideological subject you find offensive. Use Tolkien's method of indirection; then rewrite the letter to be openly critical. Here's a place where you can learn something about yourself as a writer. Which was easier to write? More satisfying?

Intimacy and Formality in Role Playing

So far we have had to imagine the responses of readers to correspondence. In this section, we look at some excerpts from the correspondence between John and Abigail Adams, written during June and July 1777, during the American Revolution, at a time when she was at their home in Massachusetts and he was in Philadelphia as a representative to the Continental Congress, very much involved in the prosecution of the war. At first their correspondence may strike you as stilted and old-fashioned, but it illustrates how two people who knew each other well, writing frequently and directly to each other, expressed their innermost thoughts and feelings by consciously creating themselves as living actors in an ongoing drama.

Even though the Adamses, particularly John, often wrote in a style that may seem to us today to be highly formal, the letters reveal the writers' emotions and their heartfelt thoughts through a language that is both dramatic and familiar. The style offered a chance to express deep emotion but at a distance, literally and verbally. We can see the dramatic thrust of these letters both in their content and in the distancing, which results from each referring to the other not as "you" or by name, but almost in the third person, as "friend." We begin with one written by Abigail to John on July 10, 1777.

> About an Hour ago I received a Letter from my Friend dated July 21: beginning in this manner "my dearest Friend." It gave me a most agreeable Sensation, it was a cordial to my Heart. That one single expression dwelt upon my mind and played about my Heart, and was more valuable to me than any part of the Letter, except the close of it. It was because my Heart was softened and my mind enervated by my sufferings, and I wanted the personal and tender soothings of my dearest Friend, that [ren]derd it so valuable to me at this time. I have [no] doubt of the tenderest affection or sincerest regard of my absent Friend, yet an expression of that kind will sooth my Heart to rest amidst a thousand anxietyes.
>
> *(Adams Family Correspondence, 278–279)*

Here Abigail Adams plays the role of a self-observer, a role that allows her to write openly and extensively of her deepest thoughts and emotions, her great love for her husband, with simultaneous restraint and passion. The whole letter, in fact, is a response to his role playing. In his letter he has addressed her as "dear Friend"; she toys with that appellation, plays the game with him, as if they enjoy addressing each other in the third person, conducting a kind of epistolary minuet.

In an age of erotic candor we might find her excitement over being called "dear Friend" a little coy or wonder why she should be so excited by her husband calling her something with which we might rather routinely open a letter to an acquaintance. But we might also imagine that she is responding to what she recognizes as a bit of play acting on his part, in which he intentionally used the slightly formalized expression. Her response is to talk about her feelings and to give him a sense that he has indeed touched her by his tenderness. She writes as an observer of love and of her pleasure in being loved. Wanting her husband to understand both what happens in her life and how the world of emotion and events seems to her, she constructs the role of self-observer, self-scrutinizer, in response. She is central to the letter yet removed, a commentator on her own self.

In his letter of the same day, July 10, 1777, John echoes her sentiment and her role playing:

> My Mind is again Anxious, and my Heart in Pain for my dearest Friend. . . .
>
> Three Times I have felt the most distressing Sympathy with my Partner, without being able to afford her any Kind of Solace, or Assistance. . . .
>
> Oh that I could be near, to say a few kind Words, or shew a few Kind Looks, or do a few kind Actions. Oh that I could take from my dearest, a share of her Distress, or relieve her of the whole.
>
> Before this shall rea[c]h you, I hope you will be happy in the Embraces of a Daughter, as fair, and good, and wise, and virtuous as the Mother, or if it is a son I hope it will still resemble the Mother in Person, Mind, and Heart. (278; Adams's ellipses)

John, like Abigail, refrains from direct address in his writing, creating another dramatic scene in which he projects himself, his wishes, and his love for Abigail into imaginary tableaux sketched in phrases like "to say a few kind Words, or shew a few Kind Looks." We sense not only that the Adamses are playing subtle roles that we can discern in our reading but also that they enjoy playing roles for each other, even at this moment with a war going on and both of them worrying about Abigail and the child she is carrying.

During the eighteenth century the letter form was apparently regarded as a kind of dramatic diary. The Adamses did not question this. While they found letters a poor substitute for each other's presence, they used the letter form as a kind of mental, verbal image, an eighteenth-century videotape of themselves. They imagined themselves each as the dramatic subject of the letter, each positioned in the letter as if in front of a mirror of emotions, writing to describe what they felt.

These letters tell us a great deal about the Adamses, who must have been people of unusual maturity and sensitivity, and yet they also tell us something about letter writing, about the power of dramatic role playing in putting thoughts and feelings into words. The letters reveal the power of a certain formality and distance to convey intense emotion.

The Adamses introduce a problem essential to all letter writing in particular and to writing in general: how to find the tone that will sustain a relationship with the reader over time, how to find a role to play that will convey your message and allow the reader to understand what you write as symbolic of more than what appears on the page. She writes to him to describe how she feels, thinks, and lives, and so does he write to her. They had to live their emotional lives through letters. To do this they chose a significant economy. Each concentrates on and explains what it is like for him or her. Confident in the other's love and aware of a reader whose whole interest is in the writer, each creates a totally self-absorbed role, even to the point of excluding the reader, by referring to him or her in the distant third person. Perhaps we will seldom write such a series of letters to a reader who is so totally absorbed in the writer as the Adamses were in each other. In a way, they are self-absorbed, but it is the same kind of self-absorption E. B. White talked of in his words about the essayist, one that is expressed dramatically to a reader rather than in narcissistic self-regard. The Adamses' technique of self-scrutiny and simultaneous distancing of the other is one that can be profitably adapted to a variety of writing situations that require careful attention to describing the writer's position in relation to the material at hand.

✎ **Writing** Many of you will have kept diaries or journals at some time in your lives; in this age we keep such records for ourselves for the pleasure of recording and for the expectation of pleasure in the rereading. Try writing about yourself, your innermost feelings, as if in a diary written for someone you love, not for yourself. Keep the intense focus on yourself, but construct what you write as a dramatic role designed to be read by a sympathetic reader. You might find this easier to do if you imagine yourself as a character in a novel and imagine the reader as interested in you as in a fictional character. In both cases you want to focus on self-confession and dramatic presentation. As the Adamses do, let the idea of the reader be the idea of the reader of the novel or the viewer of a play rather than the reader of a letter.

CHAPTER 9

Connecting with Readers

1 BREAKING THE PLANE IN PUBLIC WRITING

Role playing in writing is more than creating a public persona to convey intention and elicit a desired response. Role playing also involves defining your relationship to your reader. You will seem a different person if you are formal and distant rather than constantly reaching out to your reader through structure or through modulation of your discourse. We touched on these points in Chapter 4; here we want to talk about how writers create roles based on the calculated control of their distance from the reader.

Direct Conversations

A while back one of us was at a summer theater performance of Oscar Wilde's *The Importance of Being Earnest.* The performance was in a tent, with the players within reaching distance of some of the audience, who surrounded the stage. At one point, while giving an aside—something intended for the audience but not the other characters—the actress playing Cecily put her hand lightly on the knee of a somewhat astounded elderly member of the audience; she really talked to him. It gave a vivid feeling of what an aside really is; it broke the invisible glass that we assume separates audience and stage.

The following is a conversational passage in which you might feel the writer to be on the verge of talking to you. It comes from the beginning of *A Cab at the Door,* a memoir by the British novelist and short story writer, V. S. Pritchett:

> In our family, as far as we are concerned, we were born and what happened before that is myth. Go back two generations and the names and lives of our forebears vanish into the common grass. All we could get out of Mother was that her grandfather had once taken a horse to Dublin; and sometimes in my father's expansive histories, *his* grandfather had owned trawlers in Hull. (3)

Pritchett plunges us immediately into his family history, referring to his mother as if she were our mother, opening up his family's names and histories to us. He feels comfortable using a gentle imperative with us: "Go back two generations," and he starts almost at once revealing family history—his forebears were fishmongers. Note that imperatives and questions often give a sharper sense of interplay and connection between reader and writer than declaratives, which are more often about the relation of the writer to something else. As a writer you can use occasional imperatives and interrogatives, commands and questions, to give your reader a sense of direct communication. Pritchett continues:

> A good many shots must have been fired during the courtship of my parents and many more when I was born in lodgings over a toy shop in the middle of Ipswich at the end of 1900. Why Ipswich? My parents had no connection with the town. The moment could not have been worse. Queen Victoria was dying and my mother, young and cheerful though she was, identified herself, as the decent London poor do, with all the females of the royal family, especially with their pregnancies and funerals. . . . I was to be called Victoria, but now surgery had to be done on the name, and quickly too. (4)

"Why Ipswich?" The question is not so much addressed to the reader as spoken by the author on the reader's behalf. With a sly joviality that is itself a magnet for the reader, Pritchett first answers another question—how he got to be named Victor. But surely this is one more sign of why Pritchett so deftly gives us a feeling that he and we are talking together—he is always thinking of what kind of question the reader may be asking, drawing the reader close. He breaks the normal plane of the text to reach out to the reader because he is playing a role—that of the honest, self-examining, retrospective writer, who looks back over a long and successful career and considers how he became what he is. In this case breaking the plane signals an attempt at absolute honesty, a bargain made with the reader to hold back nothing of consequence.

Questioning isn't the only way of drawing the reader into the texture of the essay. Here is the opening of an essay by another novelist, Alison Lurie, who combines the conversational quality Pritchett achieves with an explicit invitation to enter into the work with her:

> For thousands of years human beings have communicated with one another first in the language of dress. Long before I am near enough to talk to you on the street, in a meeting, or at a party, you announce your sex, age and class to me through what you are wearing—and very possibly give me important information (or misinformation) as to your occupation, origin, personality, opinions, tastes, sexual desires and current mood. I may not be able to put what I observe into words, but I register the information unconsciously; and you simultaneously do the same for me. By the time we meet and converse we have already spoken to each other in an older and more universal tongue.
> ("Clothing as a Sign System," 3)

Note how Lurie immediately turns to you—the reader—and to herself as examples of how we communicate through clothes at a distance. It is playfully ironic that she says, "Long before I am near enough to talk to you" when she seems in fact to be talking to you; she could just have easily said, "Long before one person is near enough to another"—but note what a difference it makes. And note also how effective that approach is in this particular essay, which deals with quite abstract material: semiotics, sign systems, and literary and cultural theory. How good it is for readers to have a writer who is willing to talk directly to them about abstract material, not only using language I can understand, but also using me as an example. The role Lurie adopts here is not that of an analyst of some complex social phenomenon but of a colleague commenting on a lived experience. Lurie may be dealing with an abstract subject tied to semiotic interpretation, but the role she plays, signaled by her attempt at closeness to the reader, is that of one intelligent person talking to another.

Lurie must have begun by imaging her reader and thinking, perhaps with a writer's sixth sense, that she actually *was* talking to someone. That's not a bad place to begin practicing. Have in mind a reader, a kind of imaginary friend. You can also watch the small verbal gestures by which contact is made, phrases that will not only keep the direct line of your exposition going but also reach out toward the reader. It doesn't take many; one or two, strategically placed, can have a strong effect.

An Extended Example

Lurie and Pritchett share a vocal quality in their writing. Good writing can never be the same as speech, but a lot of good writing strikes the ear and mind as "good" because it makes us feel we are listening to, rather than reading, the words. We hear this vocal quality in many places. A good example (often imitated) comes at the very opening of Virginia Woolf's *A Room of One's Own:* "But, you may say, we asked you to speak about women and fiction—what has that got to do with a room of one's own?" (3). Even from the first word we are reoriented, perhaps a little disoriented. We don't expect a piece of writing (or a lecture, which, perhaps significantly, this originally was) to begin with "But"—it gives a feeling of interruption, a sense that something has already happened, that people have been talking. You, the reader, have entered the conversation; you have read the title; you're part of the discussion. Woolf doesn't merely invite your questions; she assumes them. Deftly and economically, she establishes a relationship with the reader in which she conveys her understanding that the reader will participate—will feel free to interrupt. It's almost as if she amusedly shares the reader's uncertainty about her own title.

But Woolf has an answer, or at least a kind of answer:

> I will try to explain. When you asked me to speak about women and fiction I sat down on the banks of a river and began to wonder what the words meant. They might mean simply a few remarks about Fanny Burney; a few more about Jane Austen. . . . But at second sight the words seemed not so simple. The title women and fiction might mean, and you may have meant it to mean, women and what they are like; or it might mean women and the fiction that they write; or it might mean women and the fiction that is written

> about them; or it might mean that somehow all three are inextricably mixed together and you want me to consider them in that light. But when I began to consider the subject in this last way, which seemed the most interesting, I soon saw that it had one fatal drawback. I should never be able to come to a conclusion. . . . All I could do was to offer you an opinion upon one minor point—a woman must have money and a room of her own if she is to write fiction; and that, as you will see, leaves the great problem of the true nature of woman and the true nature of fiction unsolved. (3–4)

Woolf's maneuver here is hardly original—"You asked me to write about this, but I can't"—high school sophomores have been using this as a dodge for a long time. Or, "When asked to write or talk about this, I looked at all the things that might be said and discovered that I could write about only this small, perhaps tangential piece of it." But Woolf's words don't appear to be at all hackneyed here. Why not? Partly because she avoids the pitfall of sounding coy about her device. Rather, she addresses readers as if she really were talking directly to them, and she does it very economically. She isn't trying to get you to say, "My, how clever of her"; she just wants to establish contact. She wants to get you to look at the subject in a certain way, to ask obvious questions. Woolf beckons us to look at the little but significant things that the others have been ignoring, establishing a relationship between reader and writer that is as definite as that between Abigail and John Adams.

One more example from the opening of Woolf's book: she goes on to describe the beginnings of her thought processes, as she sits down beside the river and tries to think about women and fiction. She describes an October scene of beauty and indolence in almost exaggeratedly poetic terms.

> On the further bank the willows wept in perpetual lamentation, their hair about their shoulders. The river reflected whatever it chose of sky and bridge and burning tree, and when the undergraduate had oared his boat through the reflections they closed again, completely, as if he had never been. There one might have sat the clock round lost in thought. Thought—to call it by a prouder name than it deserved—had let its line down into the stream. It swayed, minute after minute, hither and thither among the reflections and the weeds, letting the water lift it and sink it, until—you know the little tug—the sudden conglomeration of an idea at the end of one's line: and then the cautious hauling of it in, and the careful laying of it out?
> . . . I will not trouble you with that thought now, though if you look carefully you may find it for yourselves in the course of what I'm going to say. (5)

She seems to say, "I cannot find the words for this elusive tug, but I don't need to—you, reader, know what I mean," a phrase we probably use often with friends. Quite an amazing thing, if you think a moment, for a writer to say. The gambit works only because of the intimacy that she has been carefully developing with the reader because she has already created a bridge between the reader and the writer and because of her sense of the small gesture, the significant detail. She has used language to break the plane that the printed page often places between them. Woolf's extreme closeness to the reader creates her role as intimate friend, someone whom one virtually strolls with down the gently curving paths of her topic.

That intimacy extends to one of the most difficult areas to gauge: to decide what doesn't need to be said. The signal that you and I are on the same wavelength is that there are things I do not need to explain to you; I can rely on you to understand them—almost as if there were a wink occurring as one goes along. What Woolf has done requires great skill and restraint. To create a feeling of intimacy with the reader is not just a matter of writing what you think or feel; it is also a matter of urging the reader to recognize what he or she thinks or feels, of wondering how far and in what ways the reader's views match the writer's, and of thinking carefully about the small as well as the large verbal gestures by which they are established.

Writing is not just meaning but gesture, verbal equivalents of touching the arm, smiling, frowning, looking surprised. These gestures not only convey their own meaning; they also define roles and establish relationships with readers. How can you use them? You can begin by being aware of them, aware that they are occurring all the time when you are writing, whether you intend them or not. That means, in many cases, that you may be playing a role in your writing that you do not intend, falling into a stereotype. An amazing number of student essays, for example, read as if they were a strained effort to sound professorial.

Partly for purposes of emphasis we have talked mostly about rather overt gestures. If you experiment with such gestures, some readers may find them affected or overly obvious. To begin with, try them on friends for reactions. But also try the small gestures that define roles—the asides, the "proxy" questions of the sort Pritchett and Woolf use, and the changes in form of address, speaking sometimes directly to the reader, sometimes commanding, sometimes questioning. And try particularly to adjust your mind when writing to a dramatic situation, as if you were talking to someone, giving a lecture or sermon, teaching a class, or being interviewed.

✎ **Writing** Below are some roles. Choose a topic, and write a paragraph or two presenting that topic while playing each of several of these roles but without directly identifying the role being played. If you can do this with a partner or colleague, write without identifying which roles you're playing. Exchange exercises, and each reader describe the role being played. Talk about what details do and do not work for each of you.

Judicious critic   Anxious parent
Overeager salesperson   Close friend
Uncertain buyer   Penitent
Insistent supplicant   Arrogant expert
Nursery school teacher   College professor

As you use these roles or others of your choosing, try to refine them, specifying other characteristics as you imagine them in the role you are playing.

Distance

We have been thinking about the relation between reader and writer as
defined by the role the writer is playing. In this section, we look at ways
in which writers create roles based on their distance from both reader and
subject. Knowing how to gauge and modulate these distances for different audiences will make your writing more effective and persuasive.

Think of it this way: you meet someone who stands closer to you
than you are used to or further away. Sometimes this will involve touching: you put your hand lightly on the arm of someone you've recently
met, as a gesture of friendship and sympathy; the person shrinks back,
misinterpreting it as invasion or overfamiliarity. Social scientists—as
well as common sense and experience—tell us that different cultures,
and different individuals within cultures, have different "personal frontiers," based on our assumption that an area around each of us is a part of
us; for someone else to cross that frontier may be a hostile act. Mine may
be 13 inches, yours may be 18 inches, and we may get into all sorts of difficulties if we are not sensitive to each other's spatial frontiers. And sheer
space is not the whole story. Different gestures, and different ways of
reading gestures, different feelings about touch and vocal timbre are also
in operation. A smile that is friendliness to one person or in one circumstance may be a "come-on" or a "put-down" in another.

We can apply this model of distance to writing, where there is not ordinarily any personal contact or proximity but where the verbal signals
may have some of the same effect. For illustration we have chosen articles on the motives and actions of Saddam Hussein, president of Iraq,
during the late summer of 1990.

An article about Saddam Hussein in *Time* magazine begins thus:

> What kind of a man would cold-bloodedly gobble up a neighboring country?
> What kind of a man would try to assassinate a Prime Minister? What kind of
> a man gasses undefended villages or executes his closest colleagues? What
> kind of a man, in short, is Iraq's President-for-Life Saddam Hussein?
>
> The heir, it would seem, of the fierce and bloodthirsty Mesopotamian
> kings who once ruled the civilized world. Many of those ancient potentates
> met terrible ends—when they made the mistake of relaxing their grip for an
> instant. Saddam is determined not to repeat their fate.
>
> (Otto Friedrich, "Master of His Universe," 23)

This is in some ways impersonal prose: Friedrich does not speak in the first person, nor refer to his own base of observation. We don't know much about him. The questions are rhetorical and rapid, and he quickly answers them. We almost feel invaded by the prose, almost feel the threat of this "heir . . . of the fierce and bloodthirsty Mesopotamian kings" in our reading space.

Contrast this approach with an account from the British journal *The Economist*. It begins:

> It was all going a little too dreamily. The cold war was over, the peace dividend on its way to the bank. All that remained was some untidiness on the periphery. In patches of the Middle East, Africa and Asia it was still necessary to win a few more converts to the big ideas of peace, free markets and democracy. Here and there—and especially in the Arab world—small and medium dictatorships persisted. But they would not hold up for long the inevitable march of history.
>
> Wake up, world, after your post–cold-war festivities, and meet your hangover. His name is President Saddam Hussein. In the dead of night on August 2nd, Iraq's dictator sent his army to swallow up Kuwait, his neighbor and former ally, and so bring one-fifth of the world's proven oil reserves under his personal control. . . . The Gulf oil nightmare has at last come true, just when the world was starting to relax.
>
> ("Who Will Stop Saddam?" 13)

The message is quite the same as that in *Time:* Saddam is a menace. But the approach is different. Rather than those almost invasive questions with which the *Time* article begins, this one starts rather lazily, and the tone is chatty and personal, treating international affairs as if they were a minor excursion or a house party. We feel comfortable with the speaker, who seems to be playing the role of a friend who is putting on an amusing imitation.

But then, "Wake up"—as if we were nodding off, just as the world that let Saddam invade Kuwait had fallen asleep—and this is an awakening not *from* but *to* a nightmare. Both articles are trying to give us a sense of menace; but in the *Time* version Saddam is, so to speak, closer, almost marching into our reading space, and the author more distant; whereas in *The Economist*, we are rather comfortably close to the author, with Saddam a rather distant presence.

Now, look at a third article on the subject, also by a journalist, Thomas Friedman:

> Many Western observers of the Middle East do not . . . appreciate the different traditions which make up the politics of this region. They assume that all the surface trappings of nation-statehood—the parliaments, the flags, and the democratic rhetoric—can fully explain the politics of these countries, and that tribalism and brutal authoritarianism are now either things of the past or aberrations from the norm; the lesson of Hama or Halabja or South Yemen [scenes of massacres instigated to stifle dissent and opposition] is that they are not. . . .

> The real genius of Hafez Assad [president of Syria] and Saddam Hussein is their remarkable ability to move back and forth among all three political traditions of their region, effortlessly switching from tribal chief to brutal autocrat to modernizing President with the blink of an eye. They are always playing three-dimensional chess with the world, while Americans seem to know only how to play checkers—one plodding move at a time.
>
> *(From Beirut to Jerusalem,* 103)

Friedman maintains a distance both from the reader and from Saddam and Assad. In the first paragraph quoted, he observes the observers, talking about their wrong assumptions but dealing with them in a rather scholarly and thoroughly analytic manner. In the second paragraph, he invites the reader to see the results of his closer observations, but he still maintains his distance. A phrase like "all three political traditions of their region" helps maintain the distance, giving a sense that Friedman is close enough to know but detached enough to analyze. At all times Friedman's persona and role can be described as judicious, distant, and analytic.

In each of these cases, distance is a complex product of attitude and rhetoric. Each of the writers, we assume, had a goal different from that of the others, aimed to convey a different effect: *Time*'s sense of imminent danger; *The Economist*'s sense of moves on an international chessboard; Friedman's sense of his readers' distance from a locale that is difficult to understand and in need of clarification. Ultimately, the reader's distance from the text results from the role the author chooses to play: Friedrich, almost a prophet, warning his readers of the return of an ancient threat; *The Economist*, a shrewd and witty observer, skeptical and with a keen eye toward factors like the price of oil; Friedman, the knowledgeable observer, explaining the intricacies of Middle Eastern politics to an insufficiently informed outsider.

It is worth remembering that distance is an illusion that writers create: they may create it inadvertently, fall into a familiar pattern of writing that automatically establishes a certain relationship to the reader, or develop a kind of sixth sense that allows them to establish and vary the distance according to the need they sense at a given moment. It is also a creation of the reader. Words do not go directly into the readers' minds but will be re-created by them according to the marks the writer puts on the page. But how do writers establish and maintain or vary the distance they want their readers to sense?

Start by focusing on the readers, imagining them as real people. How close do you want to be to them? How close do you want them to be to your material? Think of your first sentences—in an essay, in paragraphs or sections—as establishing distance, which can, of course, be varied. Note how the writers we've discussed above use their first sentences in that way, Friedrich with his rolling questions, *The Economist* with its breezy wit, and Friedman with his first look at what other observers see.

Try a number of possibilities, and ask of each where it puts you in relation to your reader and your reader in relation to your subject. Which seems appropriate to your purpose, your material, and the kinds of readers you have? Then, not before you write but after, watch for variations. Experiment with sudden shifts, like that in *The Economist*, always calculating in terms of purpose, subject, and audience.

✎ **Writing** Take a position on a topical, controversial subject and argue your point aggressively, occupying the reader's mental space by discounting the other side's arguments. Raise and answer objections to your own argument; construct your argument by asking questions; pursue your reader. Then, try a more familiar approach, implicitly inviting the reader to participate in your reasoning.

2 CULTIVATING EMPATHY

Encounters with Otherness

Here we want to talk about a topic closely related to distance in writing but somewhat more subtle and more difficult to describe: how a writer writes about the difficult experience of facing and coming to terms with something or someone quite alien. It's hard enough to live through such an experience, which may challenge all the settled, comfortable elements of one's worldview. Writing about experiences so that your reader will understand your emotional and intellectual growth, confusion, joy, or distress is even more challenging. We call this process of living, writing, and sharing *empathy*, the ability to enter into someone else's experience, especially when that experience is foreign to one's own.

This subject is closely related to the idea of distance in texts because it requires a writer to adopt a role and to re-create facing, living through, or experiencing something that initially seemed distant or difficult, in such a way that the reader will be drawn into the text to share the experience vicariously. The mere fact of writing about the experience means that to some extent the writer has assimilated it. To talk about it to the reader, though, the writer must play the role of living through it again.

Throughout this book we have said that a writer's awareness of readers' ways of re-creating the writer's words lies at the heart of writing. In writing about what is "other" to you, before you think about how to convey the experience to a reader, you need to face your own relationship to the topic. When you come to talk about empathy, something true of many aspects of writing is particularly noticeable: writing is not necessarily the whole story. Just as to describe you need first to have observed and to write a good argument, you need to think your argument through, so also to write in a way that will both show and enlist the empathy you need to have gone through the experience of reaching out imaginatively to other people. Many of the skills of writing about the experience are extensions of the art of having the experience.

Encounters with "the other" occur all the time, and abstractly, at least, most of us would say that it is a good thing when we recognize the other, when we enter into a new world, when we accept the other as being something that has its own validity. The comic strip character Pogo said, "We have met the enemy and he is us." We can read that line both as a recognition that the other is like us and that, sometimes, there is otherness within us—that part of empathy involves recognizing and accepting forces within us. The next step, a crucial prewriting step, is to sort out the nature of your feelings and thoughts. Why do you believe as you do? What is it that you oppose or once opposed and now understand? Once you can define the position you take, think about why you take it. Once you have sorted out your emotions, the next step is to find a metaphor—a controlling idea—through which to express your thinking.

To illustrate this sequence, consider the following passage from William Manchester's essay "Okinawa: The Bloodiest Battle of All," in which Manchester describes how hard it was for him and the Japanese contemporaries he had fought in that battle to meet even 42 years after the war had ended. We cannot know the thinking processes that led up to this essay, but it describes how hard it was for Manchester to meet his former enemies. As he describes his own difficulty, he pulls the reader into the world of the text. We can see in his narration a controlling metaphor, that of the two former enemies as mirror images of each other:

> On Okinawa today, Flag Day will be observed with an extraordinary ceremony: two groups of elderly men, one Japanese, the other American, will gather for a solemn rite. They could scarcely have less in common.
> Their motives are mirror images; each group honors the memory of men who tried to slay the men honored by those opposite them. But theirs is a common grief. After 42 years the ache is still there. They are really united by death, the one great victor in modern war. (42)

We might think of this as a prototype of an encounter with the other: people who have tried to kill each other trying to meet after a war is over. Notice Manchester's metaphor: "Their motives," he says, "are mirror images." Look in a mirror. The image you see is in some ways an exact replica of the original, of you, and in other ways not. There are reversals: its left hand for example, is your right hand; its right hand, your left. Notice that Manchester is not, at this point in the essay, talking about "us," though he certainly could be. He has chosen to distance himself from himself in order to see the resemblance between his group and the other group. This also allows him to define what the two groups have in common: "a common grief," "united by death." Manchester keeps his style simple and uses sentence structures that underscore the similarity: "two groups of elderly men, one Japanese, the other American." He is establishing a point of view that allows us to look at the two groups looking at each other.

As the essay goes on, Manchester shifts his point of view and lets us see the encounter from his own perspective:

> In 1977, revisiting Guadalcanal, I encountered a Japanese businessman who had volunteered to become a kamikaze pilot in 1945 and was turned down at the last minute. Mutual friends suggested that we meet. I had expected no difficulty; neither, I think, did he. But when we confronted each other, we froze.
>
> I trembled, suppressing the sudden, startling surge of primitive rage within. And I could see, from his expression, that this was difficult for him, too. Nations may make peace. It is harder for fighting men. On simultaneous impulse we both turned and walked away. (84)

Again, the simple style allows us to trace similarities and difficulties. He moves back and forth, from "us" to "me" to "him" and back to "us." For Manchester, the encounter began in perceived similarity and ended with the acknowledgment of difference: if what people have in common is that they have tried to kill each other, they may well end up reasserting their differences, the fact that I tried to kill him, and he me. The art of presenting this encounter originates in the willingness to try to see the other and progresses through Manchester's success in being honest about his reactions and in his willingness to admit that there are limits to how far we can proceed in reconciling differences. Sameness and difference have been sorted out; both remain. The style here is founded on observation. It is detailed, simple, and openly expository; that is, the writer is clearly explaining to the reader what happened. But what is particularly important is the honesty of the accounts. Manchester had available to him two formulas: my enemy is my enemy forever; and we can meet and totally resolve our differences. He was in a situation in which a number of stereotyped responses were available. Instead of relying on them, he not only looked carefully at his own reactions but also gave them a selectively detailed exposition.

When you find yourself in, put yourself in, or remember such a situation, try simply to be honest with yourself about what is happening to you. Notice and remember both physical and psychological details. Then, try to find out—by looking, by talking, by imagining—what is happening to "the other" and how similar or dissimilar it is from what is happening to you. Remember that you have resources in the simplicity and concreteness of language, in the metaphors that emerge out of your experience, and in your ability to tell a story. Then, think about the reader: what does the reader need to know to understand my experience, both of myself and of the other? Again, concrete language, simple constructions, figurative language, specific details, and narrative will help. Particularly, ask what role you are playing with respect to your reader as you come to terms with the experience.

✎ **Writing**   Make a list of who and what is "other" for you. This isn't necessarily what you dislike; include things from which you simply feel estranged, including parts of yourself. Try to describe that separation. Look for metaphors in your experience of it: what images and words spring to your mind? Put all this into an essay. Try to keep the style deliberately simple, following Manchester's model of a controlling idea expressed through details woven into a straightforward narrative.

Role Playing and Self-estrangement

Finally, look at the passages below from *Passage to Ararat*, a work in which Michael Arlen, Jr., recounts how he found his Armenian roots and, through a difficult internal struggle, reclaimed a culture he had been brought up to scorn and to distance himself from. Here is how Arlen introduces himself to the reader:

> At a particular time in my life, I set out on a voyage to discover for myself what it is to be Armenian. For although I myself am Armenian, or part Armenian, until then I knew nothing about either Armenians or Armenia. That is, almost nothing. My father had been Armenian—a child born of Armenian parents—but he had been brought up in England and educated in English schools. His citizenship had been English, and later, American. More to the point, he seemed to have virtually no connection with Armenia. (3)

Here Arlen constructs a series of qualifications and explanations, creating a persona that is somewhat self-deprecating, ingratiating, apologetic. His resistance appears in his style; his honesty about his resistance, we might say, creates the style.

We may feel that we are closer to the Michael Arlen who is narrating these facts than Michael Arlen feels to the Armenian self that he is trying to reach. He has found a simple but serviceable metaphor for the discoveries he will describe, that of the voyage (useful particularly because, in coming to terms with his Armenian past, he will literally be voyaging to his ancestral homeland):

> And so, in due course, I journeyed to Armenia—to Soviet Armenia, or what should be called more precisely the Armenian Soviet Socialist Republic. Armenia *is* there, Saroyan [William Saroyan, a prominent Armenian–American writer whom Arlen has visited to discover more about Armenia] had said. All right, I thought, I will go see it. The passage was not simple to arrange, nor was it extremely difficult. I was told there was a Cultural Committee in

> Soviet Armenia, which might be interested in sponsoring such an expedition. There were letters to be written, and officials to be seen at the United Nations. The Soviet Russians were brusque and noncommittal. The Soviet Armenians brought a bottle of Armenian brandy in a paper bag into the U.N. dining room, and discussed the New York Knicks, and said that the matter would be "no problem." Three months later, it was arranged. (55)

The voyage as metaphor for discovery continues and mixes easily with the semihumorous account of making travel arrangements. Here Arlen has even added a note of brusqueness: "All right, I thought, I will go see it." The reader feels Arlen's emotional distress in sentences like these:

> A flight into the past as well as a flight into that even more startling region of the present—although which past I would find, and whose present, it was hard to tell. I was excited by the prospect of the trip, and also apprehensive about it. With a new anxiety, I realized that although for so many years I had gone without my Armenian background—had gone without it to the point of finally feeling deprived of it—at the same time its very vagueness in my life had been a form of protection: the remote familiarity of a dream. (55–56)

Here and in a long following passage that describes his visit to the Armenian martyrs' memorial, he uses the same style. He writes parenthetically, and seems reluctant to recapture or re-create for the reader the mental difficulty this wrenching experience involves.

In the visit to the martyrs' memorial this parenthetical quality appears not within individual sentences but in the way he constructs his individual paragraphs. Ideas are juxtaposed, disjointed, and piled one on top of the other:

> It seemed as if we drove for hours, but it was less than one hour. The heat was everywhere. There were no people—only yellow fields shimmering in the sun. Sarkis stopped the car—our destination.
>
> We climbed some stone steps. There was a stone walk. "You should take off your coat," Sarkis said. I took off my coat. I felt oddly grateful that he had said that. In front of us, about a half mile away, was an unusual structure. It had the appearance of a kind of Stonehenge—columns, metallic columns rising out of the ground, but angled inward. A Stonehenge of slanted slabs. (70–71)

In fact, the separate sentences and their consecutive, associational relationship provide a stylistic equivalent to the dreamlike state he says he is in. Arlen masters role playing throughout the memoir, re-creating in his writing the different personae that composed his conflicted self during the time of his journey.

He describes his mental state by changing his style. When he is in Armenia, still dubious about the country and the people, for example, his style becomes rather flat, listlessly connecting ideas:

> Some time went by. The days were very hot. Each morning the sun was higher above the olive hills, and warmer—a distant, glaring white circle that hovered over the unfinished pink buildings, the trees, the statues, the jangle of the traffic.
>
> We went to visit old churches out in the dry countryside. There was a place called Garni, on the edge of a cliff, with dark pine forests all around and the racing water of a silvery river far below. Great slabs of black stone overgrown by weeds. (94)

Arlen uses details and sentence structure here to create the reader's response to his writing and to his state of mind. Notice, too, how detailed his descriptions are. The dreamlike state of the land, the hot dryness, and the tumbled stones are all objective correlatives, but he does not develop metaphor or simile here.

It will no doubt prove impractical for you to take a 6000-mile trip to write an essay with empathy, but Arlen's approach to this voyage of discovery provides guidance for smaller journeys, for imaginative and remembered ones as well. Both of the writers we've looked at in this section have framed the experience they are describing by a governing metaphor: warlike encounters as mirror images and making a voyage. You can do the same. Both have used relatively simple language and constructions to draw the reader into the experience they are coming to terms with. In a sense, both have constructed a persona who is a bit wide-eyed, like a tourist who doesn't know what is going to happen, and at the same time a guide who knows where he is going.

There is a great deal of daring in each of these accounts of someone reaching out, trying to empathize with the other, trying to re-create the experience for the reader. The accounts seem to be rather secure and knowing, but one can readily imagine a great deal of anguish that had to be gone through for the writer to create that role. On the one hand, both of them are coming to terms with parts of themselves that are very likely to be submerged: feelings about ethnic identity and wartime experiences remembered from youth. On the other hand, both of them are coming to terms with something large and great in history: a great and terrible war and the terrible Armenian genocide.

Begin by coming to terms with the role you are playing, shaping that role to meet your need for a public persona. Think of yourself as an explorer, a voyager, a peacemaker, an investigator, or whatever. Choose a role and a style that not only draw you toward the experience in question but also allow room for honesty about the complexity of this process and permit your readers to see experiences that might be foreign to them.

✎ **Writing** Use a metaphor of travel or movement to describe your recognition of something about yourself. Describe it in detail for an imaginary reader. Try to identify the things that make this self-exploration difficult.

CHAPTER 10

Finding a Voice

We now want to talk more directly about ways in which one finds a voice in writing, a somewhat paradoxical quest. Print is mute. But the metaphor of voice is powerful, accurate, and apt. Writing can create a sense that we actually hear writers by reading their words. When we do, it is not just a matter of hearing the sounds. Voice goes further, in several directions. It is deeply personal and deeply physical. My voice comes from my breath, through my throat, mouth, and lips. We use our physical bodies as well as our minds when we speak. Voice is a way of gaining a sense of presence in writing. It is deeply individual: my voice speaks my personality, my experience, my interests and purposes. It goes not only toward a listener or a reader but also toward the world in a larger sense. To say that I had a voice in a decision means that I have participated, been heard, been recognized.

Sometimes a given group or a particular individual is not heard in the dominant conversations that define a discussion or an institution. Recent decades have seen a particular awareness of such exclusions through the experiences of various racial groups, of women, of children, of the elderly. Political conservatives in America sometimes say that they have had to struggle mightily to make themselves heard. Radio talk shows fill the airways with people wanting to be heard. How does one make oneself heard? How does one ensure that the essence of one's voice has not been lost in the process of entering the discussion. Questions of voice, we have said, are interesting because they combine some highly personal, sometimes deeply private, aspects of experience (What do *I* sound like? What do I *want* to sound like?) and some very public ones (How do I participate? How can I gain a hearing?). In this chapter we explore these questions about voice in writing.

1 LISTENING FOR CADENCES

One of the most elusive qualities of writing, and yet one of the most central, is what Eudora Welty calls reader-voice:

> Ever since I was first read to, then started to read myself, there has never been a line that I didn't *hear*. As my eyes followed the sentence, a voice was saying it silently to me. It wasn't my mother's voice, or the voice of any per-

son I can identify, certainly not my own. It is human, but inward and it is inwardly that I listen to it. It is to me the voice of the story or the poem itself. The cadence, whatever it is that asks you to believe, the feeling that resides in the printed word, reaches me through the reader-voice. I have supposed, but never found out, that this is the case with all readers—to read as listeners—and with all writers, to write as listeners. It may be part of the desire to write. The sound of what falls on the page begins the process of testing it for truth, for me. Whether I am right to trust so far I don't know. By now I don't know whether I could do either one, reading or writing, without the other.

My own words, when I am at work on a story, I hear as they go, in the same voice that I hear when I read in books. When I write and the sound of it comes back to my ears, then I act to make my changes. I have always trusted this voice.

(*One Writer's Beginnings*, 11–12)

Reread Welty's words, and listen to the reader-voice in your mind as you do, while at the same time following what Welty is saying *about* voice. Welty is dealing with one of the deepest paradoxes of reading and writing, their simultaneous similarity to and difference from speaking and listening. Scratchy ink marks on white paper cannot speak to us. But they do. The skilled writer can choose and arrange those marks in ways that will prompt readers to re-create a voice in their minds, even as they read silently and rapidly and perhaps without conscious awareness of auditory qualities. Just as you have a mind's eye, which allows you to "see" things that you are not looking at, so also you have a mind's ear, by which you can hear what you read somewhat as if it were spoken. A skilled reader hears the voice of the writer and is able to catch the nuances of inflection that one automatically registers in listening to speech. We often think of the imagination primarily in visual terms, but there is also an auditory imagination; we can re-create in our minds with a remarkably lifelike quality the sense of the spoken word.

But Welty is not just interested in the tonal qualities of this reader-voice. In writing, she says, "the sound of what falls on the page begins the process of testing it for truth," and of the sound she hears in her own writing, "I have always trusted this voice." Authenticity and authority, that is, come from voice. It is not that we believe indiscriminately anything that is said in a hearable voice but that voice allows us to hear what is said as a human reality. This sense of a real contact with a real person through the writing opens the door to an acceptance of the world that the writer brings us.

Perhaps the most telling of Welty's statements is that she and we should "write as listeners." You will often hear writers and teachers of writing talk about keeping an eye on the reader, but translating this concept into sound and speech takes the idea further. Keep an ear open to the reader; play the role of listener as you write. Indeed, it must be the case with a highly skilled writer like Welty that as she writes she is *both* reader and writer, both listener and speaker, and that her sense of the intimacy of the connection between speaker and listener is one of the pillars of her success as a writer.

Even in our most prosaic reading we rely on our inner sense of tone to guide our reading. Think of how hard it is to speak a foreign language; sometimes, a nonnative speaker of English who is really quite skilled still has difficulty getting the real meaning of something because the small emphases aren't there. As an experiment, read a piece of prose like the following and distribute your emphases arbitrarily, say on every fourth syllable:

> Three volatile issues—abortion, flag-burning, and the death penalty—could produce tumultuous elections in the United States in 1989 and 1990.
>
> The issues are expected to stir up races in every corner of the country for state legislatures, governorships, and Congress. . . .
>
> Advocacy groups, such as the National Abortion Rights Action League, are promoting no-compromise, black-and-white positions.
>
> Yet politicians, cautious about embracing zealotry, are looking for the middle ground. They are aware that most Americans are ambivalent about these emotional topics.
>
> (John Dillin, "Political 'Big 3' in '89 and '90")

Now read it aloud as you would if you were trying to make it very clear to someone not acquainted with the subject, slightly exaggerating pauses and significant words—trying to represent the meaning fully embodied in your tone of voice. Which words do you emphasize? On what phrases do you drop your voice or build toward a climax? Are subtle modulations of tone necessary to carry out particularities of meaning? How much difference is there between your most emphasized and your least emphasized words? Do you change your pace as the sentence goes on? Read the passage several times, getting its "sound shape" right, and then read it silently, letting your mind re-create the sound. You will probably discover that a few key words and phrases carry the major emphases. You vary your emphasis of certain phrases considerably to indicate their relative importance or unimportance, or as we put it in Chapter 3, you locate the centers of the sentences' energy with small but significant variations in timing and pitch. (You may find it useful—and surprising—to do this exercise with an auditor, asking for feedback. What you think you are exaggerating may not seem so to someone listening to you.)

The goal of re-creating some of the tonality of speaking when writing can be a very difficult one to achieve. It is also a rewarding one because, as we have said, it is a means by which you as a writer can create the conditions for your reader to converse with you, to hear you exploit the full range of meaning available to you. More precisely, it is in these sounds that meaning and person come together. These sounds are necessary to create the meaning of what you're saying, but they also give the meaning its distinctive personal stamp, so that the reader hears not only what the *words* mean but also what *you* mean.

Listen to Welty's voice as she begins her memoir: "In our house on North Congress Street in Jackson, Mississippi, where I was born, the oldest of three children, in 1909, we grew up to the striking of clocks" (3). What defines the voice of this sentence? Partly, it is the pauses, the ones after "Mississippi," "born," "children," and "1909." In fact, we can think of punctuation, particularly commas, partly as signals to the reader to pause. These pauses help focus attention on certain bits of information: place of birth, place in family, year of birth—in short, on some of the most basic information by which we define ourselves. These pauses are voice-lowering signals. Our inner ear hears these pieces of information as just what they are grammatically—parenthetical and subordinate. We may even hear a certain playfulness: the child giving all the information, and running out of breath to get it all in, or the reflections of a mature adult who is remembering. The first phrase ("In our house") and the main clause, at the end of the sentence, call for the most emphasis. Everything up to the main clause is quite routine, an assemblage of information, and we are probably slightly surprised when we get to the oddly phrased words "we grew up to the striking of clocks," as if the sound of clocks orchestrated their upbringing. And that is part of Welty's point as she proceeds. There is even a kind of lilt to the rhythm of the main clause that gives it a musical sense; in fact, this particular phrase can be scanned metrically as three anapests (a pattern of two unstressed syllables followed by one stress, as in "'Twas the *night* before *Christ*mas and *all* through the *house*"), with the main emphasis on the three key words, "up," "strike," and "clocks":

We grew *up* | to the *strik* | ing of *clocks.*

We may think of meter as belonging to poetry, but prose has its own rhythms and accents. Furthermore, those qualities do not belong only to the carefully wrought writing of someone like Welty. We use them in everyday exchanges all the time: "please pass the butter" does not mean the same thing nor convey the same feeling as "*please* pass the butter." Much of the tonality comes from the words we stress. You cannot plan your accents, but you can listen carefully to your written sentences—read them aloud and tinker with them when they just sound wrong.

Welty is keenly aware of the degree to which sounds defined her childhood and hence came to shape her career as a writer. She continues:

> There was a mission-style oak grandfather clock standing in the hall, which sent its gong-like strokes through the living room, dining-room, kitchen and pantry, and up the sounding board of the stairwell. Through the night, it could find its way into our ears; sometimes, even on the sleeping porch, midnight could wake us up. My parents' bedroom had a smaller striking clock that answered it. Though the kitchen did nothing but show the times, the

dining room clock was a cuckoo clock with weights on long chains, on one of which my baby brother, after climbing on a chair to the top of the china closet, once succeeded in suspending the cat for a moment. I don't know whether or not my father's Ohio family, in having been Swiss back in the 1700s before the first three Welty brothers came to America, had anything to do with this; but we all of us have been time-minded all our lives. This was good at least for a future fiction writer, being able to learn penetratingly, and almost first of all, about chronology. It was one of the many good things I learned almost without knowing it; it would be there when I needed it. (3)

Taking this passage from a library copy of the book, we were intrigued to discover that an earlier reader had underlined some words and we were instructed by *which* ones he or she underlined: "time-minded," "chronology," and "a good many things I learned almost without. . . ." Our hunch is that this reader was unconsciously marking what his or her inner ear heard the reader-voice stress as the most important moments or concepts in the paragraph—the central idea—as Welty moves from the particulars of growing up among clocks to the larger ideas of being time-minded and of learning without knowing it.

Tone or reader-voice is something besides stresses and main points. It is also personality and character, the sense we have of a particular person behind the voice. As we "hear" the words, we construct an image of the person who is speaking them. Welty's opening paragraph is a combination of down-to-earthness and a sly, understated wit (as in the long sentence that begins by continuing the enumeration of clocks and ends with something almost from a Tom and Jerry cartoon—baby brother suspending the cat from the cuckoo clock). It is a quiet humor, perhaps slightly mischievous, but not at all satiric. One senses the wit also in the way Welty uses metaphor—when she calls the stairwell a "sounding board," we get a picture of the whole house as an oversized musical instrument and the children as little creatures living enchantedly within its sounds. As the poet Seamus Heaney says, "Finding a voice means that you can get your own feeling into your own words and that your words have the feel of you about them" ("Feeling into Words," 43). To find your voice is partly to find yourself and to find a way of creating that self as someone with whom your readers can feel themselves conversing.

As a writer of fiction, Welty recounts that she found her voice in fiction in the creation of a particular character, Miss Eckhart, a piano teacher in the story "June Recital." Welty notes that Miss Eckhart little resembles either herself or the woman from whom she took piano lessons:

I haven't the slightest idea what my real teacher's life was like inside. But I knew what Miss Eckhart's was, for it protruded itself well enough into the story.

As I looked longer and longer for the origins of this passionate and strange character, at last I realized that Miss Eckhart came from me. There wasn't any resemblance in her outward identity: I am not musical, not a teacher, nor foreign in birth; not humorless or ridiculed or missing out in love; nor have I yet let the world around me slip from my recognition. But none of that counts. What counts is only what lies at the solitary core. . . .

Not in Miss Eckhart as she stands solidly and almost opaquely in the surround of her story, but in the making of her character out of my most inward and most deeply feeling self, I would say I have found my voice in fiction.

(The Golden Apple, 101)

Welty's sense of finding her own voice is inseparable from her creation of a kind of character that both is and is not herself, inseparable from tapping the deepest themes and resources of her inner life ("a passion for my own life work," "exposing yourself to risk") and, perhaps paradoxically, from a sense of the outside world as well: "The outside world," Welty says earlier in the chapter, "is the vital component of my inner life" (76).

Voice, then, in its fullest sense, is not a simple technique that you can immediately mobilize. But it is the goal that every writer, beginner or would-be professional, strives for—the sense that he or she as a person is present in the words written, not because you've been confessional or used the personal pronoun or included bits of personal experience, all of which we think are fair things to do in the game of writing, but because you've gotten in touch with rhythms of your own being and found ways of making them available to your readers.

Hence we urge you, again, to read aloud, to hear the words you are reading. Then, read "aloud to yourself," moving your lips and involving your speech organs, your tongue and lips and teeth and palates. Feel your breath and the way words draw on your lungs and diaphragm. Feel the physical presence of words and the sounds and sound-shapes of sentences and paragraphs. Pay attention to the writers whose voices you like and trust, whose implicit personality is one you like listening to. Collect passages that seem to invite you to converse. As you write, and especially as you revise, listen to your sentences. Make small, or large, adjustments to get them right. As you write, think of yourself as being in a kind of conversation, perhaps with someone else, perhaps with yourself. Above all, trust your ear.

✎ **Writing** Think about an important moment in your life—not necessarily a dramatic one but a time when you felt yourself having an important revelation, a change in attitude, or a new direction. Imagine yourself telling the story of this moment to someone whom you want to know more about yourself. Write a paragraph or two, trying to recapture that moment, using techniques we have discussed, especially in the selection of details. Read your paragraph aloud; perhaps record it and play it back to yourself. Work back and forth between listening to it and rewriting until you have captured the cadence of your voice in writing.

Recognizing Your Cadences

At some time every writer faces this problem: for some apparently inexplicable reason, the words you've written do not sound right. Either they have no style—that is, they don't sound like anything a real person would say, having all the life and interest of a dead fish on a counter—or they seem to circle around the subject, hiding the main point within layers of verbiage. In the latter case you have the feeling that meaning is in there somewhere but that you just can't locate it.

These are among the most frustrating experiences of writing. Moreover, the more you try to correct the problem, the worse it gets. While you can never completely avoid these moments, you can minimize their frequency by learning to recognize the essential elements of your own voice and style. Before you can say what goes wrong, you need to be able to say what goes right in your writing; you need to know who you are as a writing personality. You need to know what kind of impression your writing voice conveys when it's speaking to your satisfaction.

The first step toward this recognition is to find out who you are verbally. You can do this by tape-recording some of your daily conversations and playing them back, listening to how you sound. The rhythms of your conversation will give you a good clue about where you place the emphasis in groups of words and in groups of phrases. While writing this section of this chapter, we hear in the background a broadcast of a Senate hearing. A senator is speaking, and we hear in his speech a quite definite pattern, a rhythm in his cadences that forms a standard pattern in his use of language: three unstressed syllables, usually monosyllabic words, followed by a stressed word, usually a polysyllabic word. He doesn't *always* use this pattern, but it clearly dominates his speech rhythm. Knowing that about himself, he would be able, if necessary, to analyze his writing to see how and in what ways it builds on what is a natural rhythm for him. We'd even go so far as to say that he depends so heavily on this rhythm that it helps to shape his thinking—he clusters ideas and groups them in phrases that build up to a polysyllabic abstraction.

In *Revising Prose* Richard Lanham warns against what he calls "shopping bag sentences," sentences that comprise a string of prepositional phrases, like this one: "The hat belonged to the girl in the car from the yellow house with the green door." Such sentences, he warns, lack focus and energy, seeming like an infinitely expanding series of separate, connectable units. They have no shape and seem to be the product of a mind that is sequentially connecting parts of an idea together, bit by bit. Why is this pattern of construction such a common one? It may be partly because we move through an idea, elaborating it, creating it in parts after the initial thought has occurred to us (see Chapter 5 on movement). But we sense its roots may be deeper: prepositional phrases contain an inherent rhythm of their own; like the senator's anapestic phrasing, they are markedly rhythmic.

As speakers and as writers we are attracted to rhythm, often unconsciously. Have you ever written about something that you care deeply about? Often such writing creates itself, seems to come unbidden from your pen or computer. And very likely you'll find that that writing is satisfying to you, probably partly because it echoes the basic rhythmic patterns of your verbal personality—the way you like to put words together. If you doubt that emotion and emotional commitment can help language, think for a minute about what happens when you become angry and berate someone. If you're not so angry that words fail you, you often find that you use emphasis to underscore your meaning and create a rhythmic pattern: "I can't *believe* you *did* that." Think of the sound of your parents urging you to clean your room: "If you don't clean up that mess. . . ." As common speakers of English, we find that we use rhythm to support our meaning; as individual speakers, we find that each of us adapts the principle of rhythmic emphasis to our own voice and to the way our individual minds work.

As a final step in thinking about understanding your verbal personality, listen carefully to speakers whom you admire. Chances are what you admire in someone else is what you'd like to hear in yourself. Analyzing their patterns may help you to understand how to adapt them to your own language.

When your writing stalls and you have the sense that somehow you're absent from the words you are writing, a time-honored technique to find out what's wrong is to read your writing aloud. We are arguing here that this technique is most useful when you already have a sense of your verbal profile. If you know what you sound like when you speak, you can tell whether your writing has that quality. If you know what combination of rhythm and phrasing constitutes your "sound," you'll be able to spot the presence or absence of these components in your written work. Remember, as Lucille Vaughan Payne says in *The Lively Art of Writing*, good writing must *sound* like speech but can't *be* speech. You're concerned with transferring the essential qualities of your verbal personality—not all the little circumstantial "accidents" of speaking.

✎ **Writing**   After you tape yourself in your daily conversations, make a tape of yourself talking seriously about a subject like politics or the environment that interests you but about which you are not expert. Listen to yourself and ask yourself if and in what ways the rhythms of your daily speech change. Do you still have a rhythm? Again, ask yourself if you can detect a rhythm in your speech and, if you can, how it reflects or differs from the rhythms of your conversation. If you find that your daily conversation is rhythmic but that your serious conversations are not, you might want to ask yourself if in the more serious conversations you have lost your control of your language, if you're relying on the discourse of the verbal marketplace to do your thinking for you, or if you regard thoughtful speaking (and writing too) as fundamentally different from the way you ordinarily use language. Alternatively, you might find that you speak well and convincingly; again, ask yourself whose voice you hear and what "ethos," in the old sense of "character," it conveys.

2 DRAWING ON MEMORY

To find a voice is partly a matter of hearing in a physical sense, but it goes deeper than that. Finding your voice, re-creating your voice in print so that a reader can hear you and sense your presence as a person, involves giving or at least having a sense of who in particular you are. To crystallize your voice draw on your memory. Memory is a gateway to who you have been. Who you have been, what you have experienced, helps define who you are.

Earlier Selves

Here is a dream described by Frederick Buechner, a novelist and minister renowned for his preaching ability:

> I was staying in a hotel somewhere and the room I was given was a room that I loved. I no longer have any clear picture of what the room looked like, and even in the dream itself I think it wasn't so much the way the room looked that pleased me as it was the way it made me feel. It was a room where I felt happy and at peace, where everything seemed the way it should be and everything about myself seemed the way it should be too. Then, as the dream went on, I wandered off to other places and did other things and finally, after many adventures, ended back at the same hotel again. Only this time I was given a different room which I didn't feel comfortable in at all. It seemed dark and cramped, and I felt dark and cramped in it. So I made my way down to the man at the desk and told him my problem. On my earlier visit, I said, I'd had this marvelous room which was just right for me in every way and which I'd very much like if possible to have again. The trouble, I explained, was that I hadn't kept track of where the room was and didn't know how to find it or how to ask for it. The clerk was very understanding. He said that he knew exactly the room I meant and that I could have it again anytime I wanted it. All I had to do, he said, was ask for it by its name. So then, of course, I asked what the name of the room was. He would be happy to tell me, he said, and then he told me. The name of the room, he said, was Remember.
>
> (*A Room Called Remember*, 2–3)

Buechner has much to say about this dream, some of it fairly specifically theological (this is, in fact, a sermon, though he did not preach it). But his argument is not narrowly theological or sectarian, and it is worth pursuing further:

> In one sense, the past is dead and gone, never to be repeated, over and done with, but in another sense, it is of course not done with at all or at least not

done with us. Every person we have ever known, every place we have ever seen, everything that has ever happened to us—it all lives and breathes deep in us somewhere whether we like it or not, and sometimes it doesn't take much to bring it back to surface in bits and pieces. A scrap of some song that was popular years ago. A book we read as a child. A stretch of road we used to travel. An old photograph, an old letter. There is no telling what trivial thing may do it, and then suddenly there it all is—something that happened to us once—and it is there not just as a picture on the wall to stand back from and gaze at but as a reality we are so much a part of still and that is still so much a part of us that we feel with something close to its original intensity and freshness what it felt like, say, to fall in love at the age of sixteen, or to smell the smells and hear the sounds of a house that has long since disappeared, or to laugh till the tears ran down our cheeks with somebody who died more years ago than we can easily count or for whom, in every way that matters, we might as well have died years ago ourselves. Old failures, old hurts. Times too beautiful to tell or too terrible. Memories come at us helter-skelter and unbidden, sometimes so thick and fast that they are more than we can handle in their poignance, sometimes so sparsely that we all but cry out to remember more. (3–4)

We are always remembering, and since from one angle we are what has happened to us, we are what we remember. Or, to make a complicated relationship more precise, the act of remembering continually changes who we are and who we were, but that continually changing reality is one of the primary ways in which we define ourselves.

In the imagery of Buechner's dream, not to remember is to be put in a dark, cramped room; to remember is to reenter a room from the past, spacious and comfortable. But to go into that room called Remember is, as Buechner puts it elsewhere (in a memoir of his growing up), to enter into a different kind of time:

Memory is more than a looking back to a time that is no longer; it is a looking out into another kind of time altogether where everything that ever was continues not just to be, but to grow and change with the life that is in it still. The people we loved. The people who loved us. The people who, for good or ill, taught us things. Dead and gone though they may be, as we come to understand them in new ways, it is as though they come to understand us—and through them we come to understand ourselves—in new ways too.
(The Sacred Journey, 21–22)

Remembering almost inevitably leads us to deal with the experience of someone who may seem to us like a remote ancestor, ourselves as a child. And those ancestors lived in a different world, governed by, as Buechner puts it, "those giants of childhood"—our parents, our siblings, our relatives, our teachers. Remembering, then, often means moving back into contact with parts of ourselves that saw the world very differently from the way we see it now.

How do we bring those selves together? One of the hard parts of writing from or about memories is that our present selves so severely edit and revise them. The goal is to write about the past as a kind of present or perhaps as a kind of dialogue between the past and the present. But you may find that not everything will come at once, that parts of memories especially, including some of the most important parts, will resist your conscious attempts to recall them. Be patient. Try some freewriting as a way of calling up your memories: just take a piece of paper and start jotting down whatever comes to your mind about the matter you are trying to recall, even if it seems irrelevant.

After you've recaptured what you want to remember, you still face the challenge of re-creating for a reader the sense of that earlier self. Sam Hynes, a writer whose work we have looked at before, talks in these terms about a memoir he has written:

> This is the story of a fairly ordinary flying war—of the training and the fighting, and of the growing up that went with it. I have tried to tell it with the voice of the young man who lived it, and to see it with his eyes, and not to impose upon it the revisionary wisdom of age.
>
> (*Flights of Passage*, viii)

In his intentionally simple language, Hynes puts his finger on one of the most difficult parts of writing about memory: how to get the voice of a younger self. Writing from memory is partly a matter of recalling and re-creating what happened to you, but it is also a matter of discovering which *you* it was that the things happened to and how *you* can speak its language in the present. It may well be that what Hynes tries to do is not something that anyone can do fully, that is, speak with the voice of an earlier self. But there are relative degrees of success, and it is worth the effort. Hearing voices of your earlier selves may lead toward writing in your present voice. (Don't forget that senses besides the visual often carry a great deal of remembered emotion. Recall not only what you saw but also what you tasted, smelled, heard, and felt.)

The Voice of Who You Were

Here is the opening of an autobiographical piece by Mary McHenry:

> When I try, I bring up two memories: I was special, and I was alone. Both are memories of feeling, of condition, of a state of being. I choke on the process of remembering. Was I *special* because I was *alone*? or *alone* because I was *special*? My stomach contracts as my head empties and is cleared.
>
> ("Papa's Child," 1)

We have no difficulty in identifying this adult voice that is describing the process of remembering itself. But notice how effectively McHenry uses the simple language of bodily sensation: she chokes, her stomach contracts, her head empties. She continues:

> I was an only child—*the* only child. The only grandchild, too. When I went off to boarding school at thirteen, I sang the words: "One is one, and all

alone, and evermore shall be so." Until that moment of awakening, I had no words to explain how it felt to be alone. And if I was alone, I was also constantly with others: Mother, Daddy, Aunt Helen, Grandma, and Papa. I was always with Papa. There was family everywhere—more aunts and uncles, and people politely called aunts and uncles—than I want to remember. But I was Papa's child. If we had been comfortable with causal language, or if there had been anyone close enough to me to tease me, I would have been called "The Preacher's Kid." Instead I was "Reverend Bennett's Granddaughter," and that house and lineage was to be taken seriously, a sign—perhaps the mark of Cain—to live with, even now. (1)

Memory here is asking a big question: who am I? It works by turning to central relationships and re-creating something of the child's process of working out those relationships. The voice is still predominantly the adult voice, and we hear tones of adult irony in the biblical language ("house and lineage," "mark of Cain") that creeps in. But we also are moving further into the world of re-created childhood vision: "I was Papa's child."

Then comes more explanation, helping the reader by looking back from the present:

Papa was an Episcopal minister. His church was Episcopal, not Anglican. Low Church: no genuflecting, no acolytes, and certainly no incense. The Bishop had called him in 1899 to come to The Nation's Capital and build a church for colored Episcopalians in the District of Columbia, and Papa did just that. No fuss. No stumbling blocks. No conflicts. The church was established by 1901, and by the time I was born in 1933, it had a prosperous congregation that was busy planning to install the equivalent of Tiffany stained glass windows, to the glory of God and the donors as well. There was plenty for me to inherit, within the kingdom and without. (1)

Even in this apparently straightforward passage we hear a delicate play of voices: the second and third sentences, for example, are not in the child's voice exactly but in that of the child who is parroting phrases, important formulas, heard from adults. In the next sentence is the child's memory of an adult, probably her grandfather, repeating the official words of the bishop: phrases like "The Nation's Capitol" and "for colored Episcopalians" carry those tones. "To the glory of God" is perhaps the phrase of the donor or the thankful minister; "and the donors as well" is perhaps the adult making an ironic comment on the earnestly religious church members.

As McHenry goes on to describe Sunday breakfast at her grandfather's table, after lengthy prayers, we see how firmly memory rests on the use of detail:

Papa, a small, elegant man with silky white hair and a neat brush of a white mustache, sits at the head of the table, his black suit immaculately black. Grandma, at the other end of the table, is tiny and meticulously groomed; even at eight-fifteen on a hot summer morning, not a hair is out of place. Her voice is soft and flutters when she talks, like bird sounds; she calls Papa "Mr.

Bennett" or "Husband," and he calls her "Wife." She is wearing a cameo brooch pinned deep in the lace at her neck. She serves our plates, mine first, then Papa's. I always get the pepper—on the scrambled eggs at breakfast, on the carrots at dinner—because I am first, and the pepper is there to decorate, not to season. My aunt is across the table from me. She smiles and winks at me from time to time. She is my friend; when I stay at Grandma's, I sleep in her room, with her. My parents are not at the table. Saturday night is the night I spend at Grandma's, and their night to be alone. I stay over, not to give them a free evening, but to be on hand early for Sunday School and Church.

My plate is smaller than the rest, and the china is so thin I can see the shadows of my own fingers through the rim. I know there are pink roses on the plate, under the great flow of hominy grits with a yellow pool of melting butter; when I have been a good girl and eaten everything on my plate, I will see the roses. Curved around the edge of the hominy is one link sausage, cut into six or seven pieces, but left in an orderly line, as though it were whole. (2–3)

Memories are made up of details—of sounds and sights, tastes and smells, gestures and habits and tiny rituals. Here, the details are lined up as parts of an overall impression: a certain kind of orderly, purposeful household, in which every detail is governed by a carefully defined purpose and a carefully defining personality. The pepper on the eggs, the cutting of the sausages, and the choice of the china all convey the sense of life that surrounds Papa. The adult who remembers the little girl is careful to filter the remembered details through the child's eyes. These details are not just observed bits of external reality; they are signs, and the child is, we might say, a primary semiotician, decoding these signs and grasping the message that has been offered, partly a religious message, partly a social one. We look over the shoulder of the adult writer and take a further step in the decoding process, understanding slightly broader motives than the young girl could immediately articulate, but it is important that we see first through the eyes of the child.

Notice the sentence structure. As in a great deal of writing from memory, the sentences are simple, the connectives coordinating, by and large, rather than subordinating. We have a sense that they are childlike, though not necessarily childish, constructions. They also have the effect of freeing the details from the more intricate patterning of grammatical relationship so that we may perceive them more directly.

Such memory work puts us in touch with our earlier selves, our most basic perceptions of the way the world is; it also may define us in terms of our most fundamental relationships. Looking through our memories is often a search for moments when particular relationships crystallize or perceptions become clear. In this memoir, after Sunday dinner and a session of planning summer sewing, the little girl visits her grandfather's room:

I sit beside him on the bed, almost floating in the silence between him and his book. With my finger, I stroke his moustache and trace the V shaped scar that marks the center of his mouth and disappears into the hair under his nose. He told me once that he was bitten by a dog when he was small, and the scar never went away. I am tickling his nose now, and he stops me; he stops reading, too.

"Tell me a story," I say. "Tell me about when you were a little boy. Tell me about your Papa and your Daddy. What did you do with them? Did they play with you?"

Papa's eyes are suddenly so full of pain that I think he is going to cry. Instead, he turns red, and he sits up straight on the bed and looks at me hard. "Don't you *ever* ask me about my father," he says. "I didn't have a father. Talk about something else. Don't *ever* say that again."

I am stunned, hurt and frightened. *Everyone* has a father, even if he's dead. And there is God. He's *everyone's* Father, and Papa's Father too. What does Papa mean? What happened to Papa's father? I have seen a picture of Papa's mother, Grandma Bennett, and my mother has her rocking chair at home, where we live. I remember the picture: the dark dress with lace at the neck; the grey hair pulled back and pinned up; the face. . . . For the first time, I realize that the face was black. What does that mean? What *did* it mean? Is that why Papa didn't have a father? Because he was black? Didn't she know who Papa's father was? Didn't she tell Papa? Or was it a secret? Then God must have known, because He knows all secrets. Why didn't God give Papa a father he could know and play with? Did Papa do something wrong? Or did Grandma Bennett do something wrong? Somebody must have done something wrong—that was why God punished Papa and didn't let him have a father. And we can't talk about it because, whatever happened, it was wrong.

Papa knows I do not understand. "I'm sorry," he says, and he looks sad. He hugs me, and brushes his nose against mine, our special game, his moustache tickling *me* this time. He says I will understand later and I must not talk about it with anyone but him. He promises to tell me later, when I am older. "It will be *our* secret," he says. (11–12; McHenry's ellipses)

This is a moment of partial insight, into personal, family, and racial identity. McHenry resists the temptation to explain; she stays with the child's questions. In fact, much of this passage is made up of questions. It is also a moment of perception of weakness and pain on the part of grown-ups. Until now, Papa has been godlike, magisterial, the person everyone looks up to; here he is touchy, uncertain, unfair, and in pain.

But again, we only see this happen; we are, for the most part, shown, not told. Because it is easy to imagine that we are right there and part of the scene, we might not be aware of how carefully the writer has selected and focused the details, much as did the writers we discussed in Chapter 1. Consider the little girl's gesture of touching her grandfather's moustache and him tickling under his nose: these details say a great deal about their relationship. The scar tells us about Papa's weakness, about the wounds of his spirit, before the girl or we are consciously aware of them. These details may not have come to the writer immediately in their finished form, or they may have been so crowded by other details, other images, and other memories that they were not at first the clearly focused

images that they are in the final version. The process of composing probably started with some fairly idle meandering in memory, with fusing a
specific incident with more general memories. The scene was probably
visualized and heard before it was put into words. When we deal with
such memories, two somewhat opposing forces are at work. We often
tend not so much to forget as to layer over some of the crucial elements
of our memories; the memories do not always spring back to us at our
bidding. At the same time, a few central images or words or other sensa-
tions may well lie at the heart of our remembered scene and may reveal
the essence of the feeling, the relationship, or the realization.

Notice how McHenry focuses her material. The whole story takes
place in one day, a Sunday at her grandfather's house. A good deal of repeated or habitual memory is probably compressed into the narrative of
that one day, the day that she discovers Papa's vulnerability, the day in
which her specialness and loneliness were focused. Each scene is as
fresh as a memory of an individual occurrence, but it also represents essential relationships. Although this is by no means the only use of remembered material, it is surely one of the most powerful: to represent
moments when something terribly important to our development occurred to us, when a crucial change occurred, or when we understood
things we had not known before. Here is a paragraph near the end of
McHenry's memoir:

> Papa kept his promise and told me what there was to know about his father
> the last time I saw him before he died. I was going back to boarding school
> after Christmas Vacation in the middle of that first important year away
> from home, a year in which I found out that I was colored, too, and no better
> than any other colored person. Papa was dying of a broken heart: his real
> heart was broken, and he was suffering wave after wave of pain as each heart
> attack swept him further from us. His priest's heart was broken, too. His
> successor at the church turned out to be High Church after all, and there
> were drippings and bowings that Papa didn't believe were necessary, and lit-
> tle boys underfoot at the altar at communion, and a funny smell in church
> that we all recognized. Papa told me to be careful and not to talk about us, so
> people wouldn't misunderstand and think we didn't know who we were. We
> were *colored* people, he said, and I should never forget that fact. He died in
> 1946. Being "colored" was simpler to understand in those days. (13–14)

McHenry doesn't tell the reader what Papa's secret was, though we may
guess it. The mystery increases our sense that it really was a very important secret, that her relationship with Papa was special, and that she
would not think of telling it to her reader. Here, too, though perhaps in
different harmonies, she mixes several voices. When she says that in her
year away from home, "I found out that I was colored, too, and no better
than any other colored person," acceptance, irony, and defiance are
mixed together. One senses the writer remaining loyal to her grandfather
and his vision, as it included religion, class, and race, and yet distancing

herself from it, not totally acquiescing in it. Think of the wars fought over just these issues: class, religion, race. Here, they are treated with quiet delicacy; the writer lets us follow a young woman into her awareness of them as she explores a central human relationship.

We may not always want to write about such vital and central experiences; the range of possibilities is enormous, and we would not want to restrict ourselves. We can use this passage, however, as the basis for several practical suggestions. Spend time remembering in the sense of visualizing, letting your mind roam freely through time. As you compose the story, think of a few moments that crystallize the importance of the event you are working with. Listen as carefully as you can to the voices of earlier times within yourself. Present the experience by using a lot of details, referring if necessary to the discussion in Chapter 1; give the reader a chance to see and hear and smell and touch and taste. Try to be as honest as you can, first with yourself and then with your readers. Memories that are all marshmallow fluff and chocolate are apt to be both unrealistic and cloying; as Charles Schultz's Snoopy says, "Nostalgia is the rust of memory." Let the reader hear the voice of the person who experienced (but perhaps didn't understand) the earlier event. It is often preferable to the voice of the older, "understanding" narrator, who may be reshaping the experience to fit current occasions: Aunt Milly's current weight problems may convince you to make her eat continually in remembered scenes, whereas she may in fact have been a spottier eater than is needed for the current moral you want. Finally, as we emphasized in Chapter 1, train yourself to remember many details. As you walk down the street, notice the colors of things, the heights, the shapes and shades—whatever is there. When you begin to work from memory, put that observational training to work. Let the details come up as they will, and you will probably find that they carry with them the emotions and meanings you want.

✎ **Writing** Write about an important incident from your adolescence. Begin simply with "I remember" and let the scene unfold as you remember it now, as if you were explaining to someone—a friend, one of your children, a spouse—what happened and why it was important. Speak as an adult remembering, not as a child experiencing, but try to recapture the images and other sensory events.

Set this piece aside for a while, and then return to it. Imagine showing it to someone who wasn't there at the time and think about ways of explaining to them what it is like for you now, as well as what it was like for you then. This means that you will be remembering not only the scene but also the child who experienced it. What do you need to tell your imaginary (or real) auditor to make clear what it was really like for you? Imagine that your reader wants to hear about these things that happened to you but might fall asleep if you are indiscriminate in your catalog of every little detail.

For the second part of this exercise, rely on some of the devices we've talked about in this book. Begin by visualizing the scene and focusing on the details that carry the feeling of the experience. Site your readers—let them know what it was like to grow up in Watertown, Massachusetts, in the 1960s or in Kansas City, Missouri, in the 1940s. Use simple sentence structure and simple, concrete diction. Try to get your voice right by listening carefully to its rhythms.

3   HEARING DIFFERENT VOICES

Mixed Style in a Single Text

McHenry's memoir suggests that we may have different voices from different stages of our lives. To find one voice may require the discovery of several. That discovery may not be restricted to the difference between childhood and adult voices, and we may become aware of this multiplicity of voices in contexts besides intense exploration of our lives and selves. Listen, for example, to the voices that can be heard in the following letter from a western Massachusetts newspaper:

> I live . . . on a mountain road alongside Mountain Road and Sunset Rock Road. For three months I have watched a beautiful doe, and her two fawns, come into my backyard daily to eat apples that have dropped from our trees. It was a beautiful sight to see, every day for five minutes or so.
>
> On the afternoon of Sept. 18th, I heard one shot in the woods. For two days I didn't see the doe or her fawns. Then, on Sept. 26th, I saw the two fawns enter the backyard, but with no mother.
>
> I don't know if these beautiful babies can make it without their mother this fall and winter.
>
> I am so angry! I wish that whoever shot that poor doe will choke on the first bite. I will be listening and intend to find out who would shoot a doe with babies.
>
> Where are the game wardens anyway, when there is a no-hunting law in . . . ?
>
> (*An Incensed Neighbor*)

This letter is interesting for a number of reasons. First, it is a clearly written statement of a scene and an event. The first two paragraphs give the reader a good sense of what the writer saw and how he or she felt, largely through the repetition of the word "beautiful," which, although it is not specific, lets us know that the writer feels deeply about the subject. The writer uses the word in the third paragraph, too, but even as she does, something happens to the letter. A tone of sadness, almost of resignation, briefly takes over. "Beautiful" now expresses the vulnerability of the "babies," a word that makes them sound like human infants.

Then, almost like the echo of the shot, comes the explosion of the writer's anger. Something happens to the writing. Instead of the careful placement of the scene—the geography, the time of day, the specification of the event—there's a grammatical crash of sorts. A different voice is heard, perhaps two. It is as if the writer did not quite know where to go once the anger is voiced and she lapses into a somewhat clichéd rhetorical question: "Where are the game wardens anyway?" The letter gives the impression of a writer carried away by anger, so carried away, in fact, that style and control break down and the message—"someone should stop this"—gets lost in another message, "I am so angry." What happened? In large part, realizing that it was time for a voice shift, the writer lost control of her style.

This happens to experienced and inexperienced writers alike. While there is no obvious writing "up to" the occasion in the diction of the first two paragraphs—the language is direct and straightforward—there is an attempt to be factual and objective, to present the writer as a person in control of details and, by implication, of emotion. Notice the setting of the scene and the time of day, as well as the mention of the dates, which except for indicating whether it is hunting season don't matter. This attempt at filling in facts gives the impression of a police log or a "Dragnet" interview—"Where were you on such and such a date?"—and stands in contrast to the feeling and lack of "facts" of the rest of the letter. The writer doesn't seem quite to have control over the voices in which she speaks, yet some of the effectiveness of her letter comes from the sharp contrast of factuality and anger.

Consciously Shifting Voice

Next, look at a pair of passages by Lewis Thomas, a physician who has written essays on many subjects; we discuss one of them in the section on emotion in Chapter 3. Thomas is an engaging and learned writer who combines wit and knowledge with a deep concern for the craft of writing. Here is an example of a witty, familiar style that opens an essay as a conversation with the reader (notice the interwoven scientific style, discussed in Chapter 7):

> When you are confronted by any complex social system, such as an urban center or a hamster, with things about it that you're dissatisfied with and anxious to fix, you cannot just step in and set about fixing with much hope of helping. This realization is one of the sore discouragements of our century. Jay Forrester has demonstrated it mathematically, with his computer models of cities in which he makes clear that whatever you propose to do, based on common sense, will almost inevitably make matters worse than better. You cannot meddle with one part of a complex system from the outside without the almost certain risk of setting off disastrous events that you hadn't counted on in other, remote parts. If you want to fix something you are first obliged to understand, in detail, the whole system, and for very large systems you can't do this without a very large computer. Even then, the safest course seems to be to stand by and wring hands, but not to touch.
>
> ("On Meddling," 110–111)

Thomas begins with a statement that rapidly shades into humor, "an urban center or a hamster," which on reflection evaporates as the reader realizes the truth of what at first seems an outlandish comparison. We then move to an example, in this case Jay Forrester's mathematical modeling. Thomas then reflects on the implications of this mathematical model from the first example he has given, the "urban center," thus coming full circle and orienting the reader to the topic of the "problem of cities," which in turn will become a metaphor for understanding the goals and processes of modern medicine: "The analogy between a city undergoing disintegration and a diseased organism does not stretch the imagination too far" (111), he goes on to say.

Compare the tone and manner of this essay to those in another of Thomas's essays, "On Medicine and the Bomb," wherein we hear a professional voice more readily identified as that of a scientist:

> In the complicated but steadily illuminating and linked fields of immunology, genetics, and cancer research, it has become a routine technical maneuver to transplant the bone-marrow cells of one mouse to a mouse of a different line. This can be accomplished by irradiating the recipient mouse with a lethal dose of X-rays, enough to destroy all the immune cells and their progenitors, and replacing them with the donor's marrow cells. If the new cells are close enough in their genetic labels to the recipient's own body cells, the marrow will flourish and the mouse will live out a normal life span. Of course, if the donor cells are not closely matched, they will recognize the difference between themselves and the recipient's tissues, and the result, the so-called graft-versus-host reaction, will kill the recipient in the same way that a skin graft from a foreign mouse is destroyed by the lymphocytes of a recipient. (114)

This passage is certainly accessible to the nonscientist, and few would mistake it for a scientific paper in a professional journal. It nevertheless differs stylistically from the first one you read. First and most obviously, it is full of passive constructions and of medical terms like "irradiating." The mouse that might die, if the cells are not closely matched, is the "recipient." The prospect of its death is buried in a nonparallel analogy: in the case of the theoretical mouse's death, the host dies as a result of a transplant; but in the case of the grafting, the transplant will die, not the host. Thomas goes on from this paragraph to expand his point, using this mouse tale, like the urban center and hamster example, as a jumping-off point to talk about his real subject—the possibility of such procedures in humans and whether the Defense Department of the United States has ever realized the extent to which, in the case of nuclear war, the country will need such procedures to save some proportion of its population.

In both essays Thomas begins with an arresting instance that he then builds into an analogy. In the second, though, he never quite develops his typical edge of humor. Writing about nuclear holocaust, the destruction of life, and the spread of disease and suffering seem in this essay to require an adaptation of style. The humor and the offhand quirkiness is gone. In its place is a clear but impassioned style that reflects both his knowledge and his commitment to the point he is arguing:

> If there were enough money, these things [research and development of medical science to treat trauma, especially radiation and burns] could be scaled up to meet the country's normal everyday needs with tailor-made centers for the treatment of radiation injury, burns, and massive trauma spotted here and there in all major urban centers, linked to outlying areas by helicopter ambulances. It would cost large sums to build and maintain, but the scores, maybe hundreds, of lives saved would warrant the cost.
>
> The Department of Defense ought to have a vested interest in enhancing this array of technologies, and I suppose it does. . . .
>
> But I wonder if the hearts of the long-range planners in DOD can really be in it.
>
> Military budgets have to be put together with the same analytic scrutiny of potential costs versus benefits that underlies the construction of civilian budgets, allowing for the necessarily different meanings assigned by the military to the terms "cost" and "benefit." It is at least agreed that money should not be spent on things that will turn out to be of no use at all. The people in the Pentagon offices and their counterparts in the Kremlin where the questions of coping with war injuries are dealt with must be having a hard time of it these days, looking ahead as they must look to the possibility of thermonuclear war. Any sensible analyst in such an office would be tempted to scratch off all the expense items related to surgical care of the irradiated, burned, and blasted, the men, women, and children with empty bone marrows and vaporized skin. What conceivable benefit can come from sinking money in hospitals subject to instant combustion, only capable of salvaging, at their intact best, a few hundred of the victims who will be lying out there in the hundreds of thousands? There exists no medical technology that can cope with the certain outcome of just one small, neat, so-called tactical bomb exploded over a battlefield. As for the problem raised by a single large bomb . . . with the dead or dying in the millions, what would medical technology be good for? As the saying goes, forget it. Think of something else. Get a computer running somewhere in a cave, to estimate the likely numbers of the lucky dead.
>
> The doctors of the world know about this, of course . . . but it has dawned on them only in the last few years that the public at large may not understand.
>
> ("On Medicine and the Bomb," 117–118)

Thomas's characteristic humor is here transmuted into a more sharply ironic manner ("the numbers of the lucky dead," "dawned on them only in the last few years"). As a result, the tone is almost caustic, conveying a sense of professional frustration and personal, moral outrage at the system currently in place. Both this passage and the one above are equally Thomas's voices. Both voices are his, but they are adapted to different circumstances and purposes. In the former he is the witty scientist whose mind, as Jacob Bronowski says of scientists' minds generally, is full of connection, looking for metaphor and analogy. In the latter he is the re-spected professional, arguing a point of moral earnestness with a style suitably attuned to his purpose.

Multiplicity of Selves and Voices

In reading our discussion of the different voices emerging from the letter about the doe, you might have wondered which of the voices was the au-thor's *real* voice. The answer is that both are authentically the writer's. That is, our assumption here, as in the discussion of roles in Chapter 8, is that each of us has many inner voices, many different personae, and that the search for one's own voice is most likely to end in an awareness of multiplicity. The point is to be aware of and in conscious control of this multiplicity.

It is not surprising that a writer like Thomas, who adapts his voice readily to different topics and occasions, has a lively sense of the multi-plicity of his voices. In a witty yet ultimately serious essay called "The Selves," he begins by referring to "psychiatric patients who are said to be incapacitated by having more than one self. One of these, an attractive intelligent young woman in distress, turned up on a television talk show a while back . . . to reveal her selves and their disputes" (135). Thomas confesses, "I've had, in my time, more [selves] than I could possibly count or keep track of." And he closes with a wonderful picture of his "self" as a kind of wild bureaucratic meeting of all his different selves:

> What do we meet about? It is hard to say. The door bangs open and in they come, calling for the meeting to start, and then they all talk at once. Odd to say, it is not just a jumble of talk; they tend to space what they're saying so that words and phrases from one will fit into short spaces left in silence by the others. At good times it has the feel of an intensely complicated conver-sation, but at others the sounds are more like something overheard in a crowded station. At worse times the silences get out of synchrony, interrupt-ing each other; it is as though all the papers had suddenly blown off the table.
>
> We never get anything settled. In recent years I've sensed an increase in their impatience with me, whoever they think I am, and with the fix they're in. They don't come right out and say so, but what they are beginning to want more than anything else is a chairman.
>
> The worst times of all have been when I've wanted to be just one. Try walking out on the ocean beach at night, looking at stars, thinking. Be one, be one. Doesn't work, ever. Just when you feel ascension, turning, wheeling, and that whirring sound like a mantel clock getting ready to strike, the other selves begin talking. Whatever you're thinking, they say, it's not like that at all.
>
> The only way to quiet them down, get them to stop, is to play music. That does it. Bach stops them every time, in their tracks, almost as though that's what they've been waiting for. (43–44)

Thomas not only speaks in different voices but also has a home-bred philosophy of many selves, a view of the self as a contention, and occasionally a harmony, of different selves. That is probably why he is so comfortable projecting different selves as a writer. His essays show that a careful, conscious blend of styles can often produce an effect of humor, familiarity with the subject, and correlative control both of the material at hand and the words chosen to describe it.

✎ **Writing** Write an essay about the selves and voices within you, in which you identify them, give them names, and "quote" them. Let your reader hear the different voices. Feel free to disagree with the premise or to make your own metaphor of multiplicity.

CHAPTER 11

Writing with Responsible Authority

1 SPEAKING TO THE WORLD

People write for many reasons. Some find pleasure in the simple act of putting down on paper the thoughts that fill their minds about various subjects. The mere process of linking, connecting, subordinating, or high-lighting the various ideas that have filled our minds, coming and going like the patterns in a kaleidoscope, somehow helps to create order, helps to tell us what we really think. Writing acquaints us with ourselves. For many of us, that seems to be enough. We are our own readers; we write for ourselves, for the joy of knowing ourselves and for the happiness that the right words in the right order can bring.

In this book we assume, however, that all of us at one time or another want to address a larger world, want to take the order, the sequence, and the thinking that writing gives us to a wider readership. In this we are like the poet Emily Dickinson, who wrote for her own small world, declining publication yet always aware that publication was the ultimate goal of her work. (She even shaped her poems into little home-made booklets—fascicles, she called them.) Dickinson did not oppose publication in the sense that she wanted no one to see what she wrote, but, fearful of misinterpretation, she wanted to control the "public" that read it. She showed her work widely to her own friends and others in her world. The uncertain reactions of one of the foremost literary critics of her time to whom she showed some unpublished poems and the doctor-ing of her posthumously published works by her first editors indicate that she was correct in her assessment of the larger public world. Yet she wanted to be read.

Dickinson may seem to be the extreme case, the lonely poet writing privately in idioms for which the world was not ready. But we suspect that there are similarities between Dickinson's experience as expressed in the poems and that of her less brilliant and less isolated readers, which is perhaps why her work became so popular once it was made accessible. Dickinson wrote personally of the worlds within and around her as they seemed to her. But she also wrote to the world and expected and desired that at some point her work would be widely read.

That this intensely private, personal poet who lived a reclusive life in a small Massachusetts village should have struggled so with the issue of where, how, and for whom to publish makes us realize that it is the nature of writing—as opposed to thinking or talking—to exist in a real, tangible, public form. Whether it be on computer printout, yellow legal pad, or even the scraps of household paper Dickinson used, putting words down in order is a gesture to the wider world. Writing makes a gesture to time and to circumstance, an acknowledgment that the material world reifies thought and fixes it, captures it in existence and being. It is also a gesture to the community we share with others. The very fact of writing is a reaching out of the self and mind to something other, to your reader, to express, persuade, convince, or merely to raise a thought. As we have said before, writing is building a bridge and asking your reader to meet you in the middle, to see the world from your perspective and to respond. Dickinson was aware of the tremendous leap of faith that unites the writer and the reader in this enterprise. The writer fears the bridge will not be strong enough, will not be easy to find, will be mistaken, or will not offer a view worth the trouble. The reader may be willing enough to cross the bridge but unable to find it. Building the bridge is the essential work of the writer. If she does it well, both she and the reader will have learned something new. This is the point we want to make—that the personal exploration of ideas in language is ultimately tied to the public, to your reader. It's profoundly true that you cannot know if what you think and write have meaning without the experience of your readers' responses.

Many writers would go one step further and say that you cannot know what you think or even really know yourself until you write. Writing is conversation among your several selves. You are your own first reader. Writing fixes, first for ourselves and later for readers other than ourselves, what we think. There's a multistep sequence that Dickinson seems to exemplify. We write to know, to locate, what we think about the world; we read this and learn about the world and ourselves; we share this with people likely to "understand," either because of personal sympathy, like-mindedness, or similar experience; then we move to the wider audience. Writers can stop anywhere in the sequence, but most of us, for various reasons, need to go through the steps to the last step—the world.

Living Out Loud

Anna Quindlen, whom we have quoted often, writes about her own experience of finding herself in her writing and finally finding her public:

> For there are two parts to writing a column about yourself, about your life and your feelings. One is, naturally, the writing itself, the prose, and if you've got it in you, the poetry.
>
> But the other is the living, and that is the harder part. When I was twenty-two, I wanted badly to do such a column, but the managing editor of the newspaper for which I was working said that I was a good enough writer,

but that I hadn't lived enough to be qualified for "living out loud." At the time I was enraged by his attitude; now I know he was right. My prose may have been adequate, but my emotional development was not.

(Living Out Loud, xv-xvi)

Living out loud is, to say the least, a difficult task; it is also as precise a definition as we know for writing of the sort we are talking about. Being able to do so comes not just from Quindlen's "being able to write" in some technical sense but also from her own decision to trust her own life, her own experiences, and her ability to render them symbolic rather than individual. Of her final ability to write the column she proposed at age 22 she says,

> One of the most exhilarating parts of [the turmoil in my life] was that my work became a reflection of my life. After years of being a professional observer of other people's lives, I was given the opportunity to be a professional observer of my own. I was permitted—and permitted myself—to write a column, not about my answers, but about my questions. Never did I make so much sense of my life as I did then, for it was inevitable that as a writer I would find out most clearly what I thought, and what I only thought I thought, when I saw it written down. (xix)

Writing was an enlargement of her life through words, and it became a bridge that connected her to other people, in two senses. Through her words, she could convey her experiences to other people, and in doing so she came to recognize the essential similarities between herself and others, that she in fact was representative:

> I had often felt alone with these feelings because of the particular circumstances of my own life. But over the last two years, as I wrote my columns and read the letters they evoked, I realized more and more that what has happened to me has been typical. (xix)

We want to underscore the connection Quindlen draws here among writing, personal experience, her readers' letters, and self-knowledge. She has moved through the steps of the writer-reader relationship, finally, after years of apprenticeship, arriving at the place where she wanted to be—addressing the public world through her own personal experience. Of course, she is atypical in that she had the opportunity to *publish* her thoughts and experiences on the pages of major newspapers twice a week. But she could do that because she has found ways of making her private experience *public.*

To do so cannot have been easy because our culture assumes, in part because of our academic division of writing into creative and noncreative, that there is a split between the world of nonfiction publication and the world of the personal. (An ironic reflection of that split occurred when—after we had originally written this section—Quindlen stopped writing her column to devote herself full time to writing fiction.) The world of nonfiction publication is generally thought to require a disinterested, impersonal style and example. It is a world of analysis, persuasion, and exposition. It is a world in which "I" and its attendant emotions have been submerged in the myth of impersonal, unbiased discourse. The world of the "personal" is relegated to "creative" writing courses for which it's okay to bring in examples from your own life, to draw on your own experience. Naturally this world of creative writing leads to publication, too, but reception of its publication is always tempered by the expectation that emotion and personal experience will underlie the writing. Quindlen and others like her have challenged these oppositions; think about the model she presents of how to combine personal experience and public statement and about what this book says about the interrelationship of self, experience, reader, and persuasion.

A final point: Quindlen's model is increasingly attractive to writers largely for what we may broadly term "political" reasons. It is a model that casts off external authority and empowers experience. It comes out, as Anna Quindlen says, of years of turmoil—in her own case, personal turmoil shaped by the cultural turmoil that followed the social and academic revolutions of the late 1960s. It is a model of the impetus to reclaim language for personal use and to share personal experience, lived and thought. It does not accept the identifications of *personal* with *private* and of *public* with *impersonal*.

Public Worlds Made Personal

We can think of Dickinson and Quindlen as two very different examples of people who build bridges from the worlds of their own personal experiences to their readers. Other writers move in the opposite direction. That is, writers used to working in the idioms of quite impersonal discourses sometimes find it useful to draw on their personal experiences, their persons, and language of a more personal sort to convey their thoughts to readers. Even within the discourse of literary theory, an arena in which obfuscation, jargon, and nonreferentiality often perform to delighted audiences who know its secret rules, we hear calls to use language more simply, to relate it more closely to individual experience and to remembered cadences. Here is Terry Eagleton, a powerful Marxist critic who has been notable both as a theoretician and as a clear expositor of theory, explaining "the significance of theory":

> But of course this sharp polarity between "theory" and "life" is surely misleading. All social life is in some sense theoretical: even such apparently concrete, unimpeachable statements as "pass the salt" or "I've just put the cat out" engage theoretical propositions of a kind, controvertible statements about the nature of the world. This is, admittedly, theory of a pretty low level, hardly of an Einsteinian grandeur; but propositions such as "this is a beer mug" depend on the assumption that the object will smash if dropped

from a certain height rather than put out a small daintily coloured para-
chute, and if it did the latter rather than the former then we would have to
revise the proposition. And just as all social life is theoretical, so all theory is
a real social practice.

What distinguishes the human animal from its fellow creatures is that it
moves within a world of meaning—or, more simply, that it inhabits a *world*,
rather than just a physical space. Human life is sign-making—"significant"—existence. It is not that, unlike other animals, we have physical activities but signs as well; it is that living among signs transforms the whole
meaning of the phrase "physical activity". The activity of the human animal
is not behaviour plus something else; because we have that something else—
language—our biological behaviour is transfigured into history.

(*The Significance of Theory*, 24)

Look both at Eagleton's argument and at his language and phrasing. If the
sharp distinction people often make between "life" and "theory" is mis-
leading and even invalid, then so might be the separation between the
language of theory and that of ordinary life. Hence, Eagleton carries out
his rather abstract argument *about* theory and social life in language that
is *not* highly theoretical. Eagleton is presenting a rather abstruse argument about theory in down-to-earth, rather humorous language. People
have been doing that for a long time. But that kind of writing has not, by
and large, been officially taught or sanctioned, and there are great institu-
tional pressures not to bridge the verbal gaps between theory and practice. You need not always observe the strictures that separate these
worlds of language.

In an interview printed in the same book, Eagleton talks about these
matters of style directly:

I've always been very concerned with writing in the quite narrow sense, with
the style and quality of writing, perhaps because like some other critics I'm a
creative writer *manqué*. The deconstruction of humour and seriousness for
me now comes down to a matter of finding a particular way of writing that
can be at once committed and, one hopes, more companionable than the
somewhat alienated rigours of certain traditional male Marxist discourse.
The other influence, I suppose, is that I am of Irish provenance, and the Irish,
of course, have always preserved a tradition of wit and humour—largely, I
may add, because they've had very little else. . . . I would like to think that
my own writing had increasingly been able to unrepress that element in myself. . . . Perhaps when I first began to write "serious criticism", I never really
saw a way of hooking that up with more popular kinds of cultural activity. I
would hope that, now, there's in my writing an attempt at a greater conver-
gence between the two. . . . So, once again, to try to write, as they say, creatively, but also intellectually, would be a desirable stylistic and political
goal. (88–89)

Several things strike us about this passage. When Eagleton talks about
"the deconstruction of humour and seriousness," we hear the discourse
of the theorist, even as he talks about moving away from such a mode.

Where he wants to move, however, is to a place where several widely made distinctions no longer hold sway over our writing, distinctions between humor and seriousness; between being committed to political causes, even revolutionary ones often described in very abstract language, and direct contact with readers; between highbrow writing and popular culture; and, interestingly, between a style and way of thinking he characterizes as "male" and one that has been liberated by feminism. Where he wants to end up is with a way of writing that is both politically and stylistically desirable, both highbrow and popular, both male and female.

As a final example we want to look at the end of an essay by David Bromwich about the William Wordsworth poem popularly called "Tintern Abbey." To read the passage you need to know that in this poem the poet muses about his loss of a spontaneous relationship with nature as he has grown older, replaced by a more thoughtful though less magical response, and that the poet ends by addressing someone not named but universally assumed to be his younger sister, whom he sees as having, but someday also losing, the kind of intimacy with the natural world that he once had. Bromwich writes:

> I believe that Wordsworth was jealous of the strength Dorothy could enjoy without his wisdom. He took his revenge by proving how much she would need his wisdom—"matured/Into a sober pleasure"—when at last her childlike powers gave out like his. I once asked a class what was happening in these lines between the poet and his sister, and will never forget the intensity with which one gifted student replied: "He's taking *everything* from her." If there is a touch of bad faith in the poem, it comes in here and not [as some critics have argued] in the concealments of the landscape. But one can see why it had to happen. Wordsworth was never as sure as we suppose in retrospect that his kind of internalization or sublimation would succeed—whether it would be understood by many readers; and whether, even if it was, it could ever lead to many poems that would have the power of his greatest conceptions. He turned out to have been well advised to harbor both of these doubts. Yet he wanted to survive. To survive, that is, as the individual and reflective mind he had already become, and to be recognized as a person of some good to his society. The truth is that Wordsworth, in the late 1790s [when the poem was written] even more than at other moments of his life, needed very much to feel indispensable. At the end of "Tintern Abbey," he makes himself necessary to Dorothy, without being asked to, under a pretense of showing why she is necessary to him. The better one gets to know "Tintern Abbey," the more the reversal grates. Maybe it goes some ways to vindicate this last turn of the poem if one recalls that in suffering such a fate, Dorothy stood for all the remoter persons by whom Wordsworth could no longer be touched as closely.
>
> ("The French Revolution and *Tintern Abbey*," 22–23)

Notice how subtly Bromwich personalizes his discussion. He breaks out of the ordinary text-and-author-focused discourse of literary criticism to identify the people inside the poem as ones outside the poem. That distinction between literary text and lived life used to be insisted on in a good deal of literary criticism, but here Bromwich talks about Dorothy and William Wordsworth as living people, inside and outside the poem, without distinction—and he talks about them as quite ordinary people in most respects. Notice, too, that Bromwich is willing to judge: Wordsworth is too concerned with his own benefits and not concerned enough with what's going to happen to Dorothy—indeed, that the ending of this much revered poem comes out of Wordsworth's jealously of his sister's youth.

Bromwich draws readily on his own experience. He quickly admits that the student's remark in class has guided his interpretation, for example, and offers a bit of dialogue that suggests not the learned pronouncements of the expert but the back-and-forth conversation of someone willing to admit uncertainty. Indeed, the whole essay is framed in terms that do not describe what he has found the poem to be concerned with but rather the process by which he found it. He begins, in fact, by referring to the traditional interpretation of the poem: "Tintern Abbey has been read for a long time as a Romantic poem about landscape and consciousness" (1). The problem is not that this interpretation is wrong:

> I repeat these familiar judgments with much complacency and no satisfaction because I believe they are right, and I am sure they say nothing interesting about the motive of this poem. By the motive of the poem in general, I mean what it feels like, the way it wants to move or persuade the reader, and above all why the poet wrote it. (1)

Bromwich puts himself in a striking intellectual position. Believing that the standard views are correct but challenging them because they don't feel right, he is willing to trust his own reactions to the poem and to reveal them to his readers as grounds for questioning standard opinion.

Bromwich describes the basis for his interpretation of poems in terms similar to those that we have wanted to use in describing your relation to your readers: "what it feels like, the way it wants to move or persuade its readers, and above all why the poet wrote it." While Bromwich clearly admires Wordsworth's genius, he does not see it as being different in kind in its operation from that which you and I do when we try to write anything. We try to move and persuade our readers, to realize our intention in their reactions.

✎ **Writing**   Think about some of the academic, professional, or avocational fields in which you work. Are there in any of them established positions about which, on the basis of your experience, you have felt uneasy, without necessarily being able to mount a full-fledged critique of them? It may be something relatively minor—how long to cook a turkey, how to warm up for a swimming meet, how often to water plants—but it should be something wherein what you have experienced is at odds with the way it "officially" is or is supposed to be done.

Assuming you can find such a precept or technique, write about your experience of it in relation to the established view. Summarize the established position, and then recount the experience you have had that makes you doubt it. The purpose here is to explore the connection between what is generally accepted as a public truth and your own experience of it.

2   ESTABLISHING AUTHORITY

At various times and in various circumstances, we invest certain kinds of writing with authority: in sacred scriptures, in scientific textbooks, in $100 bills, in minutes of meetings, in lottery tickets, and so on. Sometimes, the fact that the words are written gives them authority, as with contracts; sometimes, as in the exchange of wedding vows, the opposite seems to be the case: the occasion gives the words their authority.

But where do the different kinds of authority come from? What makes particular pieces of writing authoritative? Is it only a matter of external power, that is, of power external to the writing? Or are there ways of writing that give it more or less authority?

Authority and authorship, as we might expect, are tightly connected. Both words (along with *authorize, authoritative,* and *authoritarian*) come from the Latin word *auctor,* which means "creator." In writing, authority can be *created* by an author. True, a good deal of the authority of any given kind of writing comes from circumstances external to it. An instructor assigns a reading from an astronomy textbook; you accept the information in that book because you accept the whole system of assignments and scientists and institutions that it is a part of. Or you see a parking ticket on your car, and whatever you decide to do about it, you know that a whole system of penalties and enforcement stands behind it. Discourses, as we suggested in Chapter 7, lay claims to authority—which is one of the major reasons they exist; one asserts one's point, for certain readers, by showing mastery or at least competence in handling the conventions of a given field or set of readers' expectations.

But authority also can come from particular choices made by individual writers. If I support my arguments by saying "scientists have proven . . . ," I claim one kind of authority. If I say, "God told me in a private message that . . . ," I have claimed another. If I support my arguments by signaling that I have investigated the up-to-date sources of information or that I have done original research that the reader can repeat, I assert another kind of authority, that of accumulated knowledge. If I create authority by drawing on my own experience, signaling a conversational relation with my reader, and opening up the processes of my own discovery, I draw on still other sources of authority. There are many kinds of authority, then, that clamor for our acquiescence and shape different discourses. They are not mutually exclusive. In this book we argue that strong writing comes from careful and considered use of these discourses and, in many instances, from offering the reader a clear view of the personal stake one has in the question being discussed and from awareness of the readers' possible needs and responses—a willingness to coordinate external with personal authority. People test authority in their personal lives all the time, and sometimes to challenge it, sometimes to choose among competing sources, and sometimes to check their own thinking against someone else's experience. We want to advise that a similar sorting should go on in one's writing.

Writing with authority is both important and difficult to achieve. It is often difficult to assert your authority if you're a relative beginner writing for "experts," such as your instructors. You may feel totally unauthoritative. Yet, for the particular job at hand, the linguistic connection between author and authority holds. To be the author requires claiming a certain amount of authority. To recognize that fact seems a necessary first step to gaining it. There are many sources of authority. To draw on experience, to make the person of the writer known to the reader, to create interplay between the reader and the writer, to temper the discourses of expertise, to re-create a recognizable voice—all of these are ways of claiming authority, ways that in many circumstances are not only effective but desirable on other grounds as well.

✎ **Writing**   Take stock. Whom do you invest with authority? Are there any writers or speakers who are authoritative to you? Are there modes of writing that carry authority—verse, the editorials of certain newspapers, encyclopedias? Spend some time looking at advertisements on television or in magazines. What kinds of authority do you see being invoked by the various advertisements? Try to sort out the kinds of authority that have an effect on you, being as candid as possible. Is it a matter of position? Power? Wealth? Looks? Are there styles of writing or speech that have an authoritative ring for you? Try simply to describe and annotate the sources of authority in your writing and reacting. In doing so, don't try to edit or censor your responses.

Institutional Versus Personal Authority

An essay by John Janovy in *Keith County Journal* begins as follows:

> *Stagnicola elodes* is the snail king of Keystone Lake. The animal is slightly less robust than the terminal joint of an average human little finger, and it thrives in astronomical numbers just below the surface of Keystone Lake cattail marsh. It's a large conical snail for the area, and fit food for any number of higher as well as lower species. The words *Stagnicola elodes* translate from an ancient language into modern English as "one who dwells in the stagnant marsh," and few animals have ever been named so truly. Snails move with dignity and detachment along the submerged and rotted stems of last year's cattails, in the center of the marsh, where it's warm and still. (12)

We sense right away that the writer is a scientist. We have no way of knowing from the text how bad or good a biologist he is, unless we happen to be biologists ourselves and can see that he has made a dreadful error or wonderful discovery. His authority here comes from the reader's sense of his willingness to move easily back and forth between the kinds of language and details scientists use, on the one hand, and a straightforward conversational mode, on the other, as we have noted with other writers in Chapter 4 and earlier in this chapter. The comparison of the snail to "the terminal joint of an average human little finger" establishes not only the rough size of the snail but also a connection between us and the writer: we can measure this creature simply by looking at our hand. It gives us a sense of proportion, of scale—of being able to measure the thing being talked about against the reader's own body.

The quiet humor in Janovy's writing also expands his authority. He slightly inflates his descriptions, as in "an ancient language" (rather than Latin) and "one who dwells in the stagnant marsh," a nicely overblown phrase that emphasizes the incongruity between the elegant Latin and the probably grubby environment of this snail. All of this gives Janovy an authority that comes from accessibility, willingness to explain, and familiarity with his readers, without seeming to diminish his more quietly asserted authority as a scientist. He might have been tempted—and in certain circumstances it might have worked—to claim authority by limiting access, making the reader feel that he, Janovy, understands and needs to be taken at his word. But Janovy has chosen to enlarge the authority we recognize in him as a scientist by playing the role of explicator of technical matters, as someone whose experience of the natural world is available to us.

Witness as Authority

Janovy also gets authority from our sense that he is an honest observer, which in terms we have used before is a role he plays and part of his ethos, part of the moral character that comes from his words. Closely related is a source of authority that we can call *witness.* Here is Paul Fussell describing some of his experiences in World War II with an extraordinary combination of irony and gravity, of distance and immediacy:

> Everyone knows that a night relief is among the most difficult of infantry maneuvers. But we didn't know it, and in our innocence we expected it to go according to plan. We and the company we were replacing were cleverly and severely shelled: it was as if the Germans a few hundred feet away could see us in the dark and through the thick pine growth. When the shelling finally stopped, at about midnight, we realized that, although near the place we were supposed to be, until daylight we would remain hopelessly lost. The order came to stop where we were, lie down among the trees, and get some sleep. We would finish the relief at first light. Scattered over several hundred yards, the two hundred and fifty of us in F Company lay down in a darkness

so thick we could see nothing at all. Despite the terror of our first shelling (and several people had been hit), we slept as soundly as babes. At dawn I awoke, and what I saw all around were numerous objects I'd miraculously not tripped over in the dark. These objects were dozens of dead German boys in greenish-gray uniforms, killed a day or two before by the company we were relieving. If darkness had hidden them from us, dawn disclosed them with open eyes and greenish-white faces like marble, still clutching their rifles and machine-pistols in their seventeen-year-old hands, fixed where they had fallen. (For the first time I understood the German phrase for the war-dead: *die Gefallenen.*) Michelangelo could have made something beautiful out of these forms, in the *Dying Gaul* tradition, and I was startled to find that in a way I couldn't understand, at first they struck me as beautiful. But after a moment, no feeling but shock and horror. My adolescent illusions, largely intact to that moment, fell away all at once, and I suddenly knew I was not and never would be in a world that was reasonable or just. The scene was less apocalyptic than shabbily ironic: it sorted so ill with popular modern assumptions about the idea of progress and attendant improvements in public health, social welfare, and social justice. To transform guiltless boys into cold marble after passing them through unbearable fear and humiliation and pain and contempt seemed to do them an interesting injustice. I decided to ponder these things. In 1917, shocked by the Battle of the Somme and recovering from neurasthenia, Wilfred Owen was reading a life of Tennyson. He wrote his mother: "Tennyson, it seems, was always a great child. So should I have been but for Beaumont Hamel." So should I have been but for St. Dié.

("My War," 257–258)

Authority comes here partly because Fussell, having been part of this scene, can now write of it so that he—and the reader—seem clearly to be there. We know this from the details he uses and from his honesty about his feelings. But the witness is subtler than that. It comes also from his willingness to take other than the obvious view of what he has seen, from his reflections, and from our sense of his radical honesty. The sights he saw as he awoke that first night in combat were horrible, and he conveys that horror; but though it only lasts a moment, he also witnesses a certain beauty in the bodies of his dead adversaries. The clarity also comes from the narrative shape of the piece. Fussell uses a traditional form for his story: the moment of disillusionment. That perhaps seems too mild a term. This is a moment of total revolution, of the world being turned over, so that everything that looked one way now looks totally different. Fussell uses a blend of detachment and involvement to give us the sense of this moment. We are deeply involved in his experiences, and yet we move back from them as he thinks about the German word for the dead or sketches a comparison with Michelangelo's sculptures.

✎ **Writing** Read some other accounts of battle, whether in formal wars or elsewhere, or other scenes of encounters with disaster. Try to classify some of the different ways in which the writers present what they witnessed. If possible, interview some veterans—of Vietnam, World War II, Korea, the Persian Gulf—or survivors of other disasters. Try to ask questions that elicit details about what they saw. Without probing into painful moments or intruding into private matters, try to get those you interview to talk about moments in which they suddenly saw the world in a different way. Don't restrict yourself to warriors in the most military sense. You might find a conscientious objector who has "fought" the battle to stay out of war. You might find someone who has been involved in a civil rights march, an antiabortion or political campaign, or a strike. You might decide to find interviews in a film library or an oral history project. Write up one interview in the words of the interviewee, trying to gain the authority that comes from presenting to readers a witness born out of struggle.

Fussell's life placed him in a position to have witnessed what may seem to be extraordinary events. But some of the same spirit can govern the witnessing of quite unspectacular happenings. Following are some excerpts from Annie Dillard's *Pilgrim at Tinker Creek*, other parts of which we looked at in Chapter 5. Here Dillard describes a praying mantis that is hatching its eggs:

> She was upside-down, clinging to a horizontal stem of wild rose by her feet which pointed to heaven. Her head was deep in dried grass. Her abdomen was swollen like a smashed finger; it tapered to a slushy tip out of which bubbled a wet, whipped froth. I couldn't believe my eyes. I lay on the hill this way and that, my knees in thorns and my cheeks in clay, trying to see as well as I could. I poked near the female's head with a grass; she was clearly undisturbed, so I settled my nose an inch from that pulsing abdomen. It puffed like a concertina, it throbbed like a bellows; it roved, pumping, over the glistening, clabbered surface of the egg case testing and patting, thrusting and smoothing. It seemed to act so independently that I forgot the panting brown stick at the other end. The bubble creature seemed to have two eyes, a frantic little brain, and two busy, soft hands. It looked like a hideous, harried mother slicking up a fat daughter for a beauty pageant, touching her up, slobbering over her, patting and hemming and brushing and stroking. (57)

This, too, is witness and more similar to Fussell's witnessing of war than we might imagine. Dillard gets right in there (looks at the mantis hatching and tries to sort it out), but she tries also to keep herself from seeing only what the language she has available can describe. (Coincidentally, she uses the very same device Janovy does: she compares the bit of zoological life to what is close at hand, her finger—which does not show that fingers are particularly important in observing but does demonstrate a shared awareness of writers for relating their observations to their readers' immediate experience.) Her authority is not just a verbal matter. It also comes from her commitment to seeing in its broadest sense and her willingness to embrace a large and confusing range of visions. As she puts it elsewhere, talking about the creeks near her house:

> Theirs is the mystery of the continuous creation and all that providence im-
> plies: the uncertainty of vision, the horror of the fixed, the dissolution of the
> present, the intricacy of beauty, the pressure of fecundity, the elusiveness of
> the free, and the flawed nature of perfection. (3)

Seeing and talking about what one has seen is demanding work. Authority comes from a strenuous honesty and questioning that many of us will
not often be able to achieve, certainly not at the level of Fussell or Dillard. But there is much to be said for shooting high in writing. Dillard had
to free herself from some of the words she had for nature in order to see
nature more fully; war for Fussell meant not freeing himself voluntarily
but being shocked into a new recognition. The authority also comes
partly from the ways in which the authors create a new kind of authority
that does not deny the near chaos they have witnessed.

Think for a moment about war as Fussell sees it and nature as Dillard
sees it. Are there similarities? What about that chaos that both see,
Fussell on a grand scale, Dillard in this particular instance on the minute
scale of the mantis's birth? Think about chaos, not only as an aspect of
the subjects that these two writers happen to be describing but also as
something whose recognition, the result of careful observation, empowers their writing. We posit that a kind of authority comes when you recognize that the world is not a neat and orderly one to which your words
have a simple one-to-one relation. Instead, there are chaos, brutality, conflict, war, pain, or—as Dillard puts it—uncertainty, horror, dissolution,
intricacy, pressure, elusiveness, and flawedness. Out of that chaos you,
the author, create order.

✎ **Writing** Try to recall moments when you have felt yourself close to
the kinds of perception Fussell or Dillard describes in the passages
you've just read. Remember details; remember your feelings. Construct a
detailed description of one or more such experiences. As you recall them,
were there any stirrings of authority in you? As you write about and gain
control of an experience by presenting it to someone else, do you feel any
sense of power or control emerging—if from nothing else, then from your
ability to look chaos in the eye and not be undone by it?

Moral Authority

Martin Luther King's "Letter from Birmingham City Jail" was written
when he was serving a sentence for participating in the civil rights
demonstrations in Birmingham in 1963. An historically important instance of witnessing, it replies to a statement made by a group of white
Alabama clergy, all of them sympathetic to King's goals of breaking down
legalized racial segregation but critical of using civil disobedience, even
though it was nonviolent, rather than fighting the battle in the courts.
Even the title is richly paradoxical: a religious leader who is writing from

jail. This particular jail has been memorialized in a verse from an old song, "Down in the Valley":

> Write me a letter,
> Send it by mail;
> Send it in care of
> The Birmingham Jail.
>
> Birmingham Jail, dear,
> Birmingham Jail;
> Send it in care of,
> The Birmingham Jail.

The song suggests not the learned and reverend but the downtrodden, the peripheral, the outcast; the title somehow combines folksiness and dignity. King chose to cast his response to his fellow clergymen in the form of a letter, to address them directly and as people who share his beliefs:

> In deep disappointment I have wept over the laxity of the church. But be as-sured that my tears have been tears of love. There can be no deep disappoint-ment where there is not deep love. Yes, I love the church. How could I do otherwise? I am in the rather unique position of being the son, the grandson, and the great-grandson of preachers. Yes, I see the church as the body of Christ. But, oh! How we have blemished and scarred that body through so-cial neglect and through fear of being nonconformists.
>
> (*Why We Can't Wait*, 95)

Throughout the letter, King talks directly to these clergymen. Whether or not he originally intended the letter also to be widely read by other people, it gains enormous power from the directness of address, from the aware-ness that he is talking to clergymen about profound religious and ethical questions and that he uses their objections as the basis of his answer. The letter's arguments are powerful ones, concerning both the civil and the re-ligious imperatives of desegregation. Moreover, they are powerful in mak-ing the case that there is agreement between the civil and the religious imperatives. And they are powerful in delineating not only the abstract rightness of King's cause but also the concrete importance of direct action to accomplish his goals. All that is a source of considerable authority.

A good deal of its power comes from King's full exploitation of the personal situation in which he found himself. Indeed, his moral genius was bound up with his dramatization of his case in this literary form. Be-ing a letter from jail, from a prisoner, it represents just the situation King is talking about: unjust laws are wrongfully imprisoning, enslaving, and denigrating the innocent. By being open about his cause, King is saying that he has nothing to hide; he is proud to be where he is. Because this is a letter to the clergy, full of references to great ethical heroines and he-roes, it has a clear grounding for its own authority, which it establishes by quotations, references, and allusions—and even by its rhythms, which suggest the preaching style that King used so effectively. Being a letter, it is always clearly a personal statement, so that King's discussions of public issues are always grounded in personal experience:

> Perhaps it is easy for those who have never felt the stinging darts of segregation to say, "Wait." But when you have seen vicious mobs lynch your mothers and fathers at will and drown your sisters and brothers at whim; when you have seen hate-filled policemen curse, kick, and even kill your black brothers and sisters; when you see the vast majority of your twenty million Negro brothers smothering in an airtight cage of poverty in the midst of an affluent society; when you suddenly find your tongue twisted and your speech stammering as you seek to explain to your six-year-old daughter why she can't go to the public amusement park that has just been advertised on television, and see tears welling up in her eyes when she is told that Funtown is closed to colored children, and see ominous clouds of inferiority beginning to form in her little mental sky, and see her beginning to distort her personality by developing an unconscious bitterness toward white people; when you have to concoct an answer for a five-year-old son who is asking, "Daddy, why do white people treat colored people so mean?"; when you take a cross-country drive and find it necessary to sleep night after night in the uncomfortable corners of your automobile because no motel will accept you; when you are humiliated day in and day out by nagging signs reading "white" and "colored"; when your first name becomes "nigger," your middle name becomes "boy" (however old you are) and your last name becomes "John," and your wife and mother are never given the respected title "Mrs."; when you are harried by day and haunted by night by the fact that you are a Negro, living constantly at tiptoe stance, never quite knowing what to expect next, and are plagued with inner fears and outer resentments; when you are forever fighting a degenerating sense of "nobodiness"—then you will understand why we find it difficult to wait. There comes a time when the cup of endurance runs over, and men are no longer willing to be plunged into the abyss of despair. I hope, sirs, you can understand our legitimate and unavoidable impatience. (83–84)

In one sense, this is highly fashioned rhetoric. King deliberately draws on authority recognized by his audience as supreme—he wraps himself and his argument in the Bible and the classics; he also draws on a wide range of rhetorical devices of the sort we discussed in Chapter 4. Note the long, elaborate, beautifully controlled set of parallelisms, in which we sense the author's long-strained patience in the very rolling out of the clauses; patience and impatience seem to vie within the sentence structure. Note also that this is the letter of a great orator, a great preacher in a certain style that is both magisterial and personal, showing itself in a rhythmic accumulation, in metaphors, and in repeated sounds ("your tongue twisted and your speech stammering"); we might imagine that even in these extreme circumstances, both of jail and of general mistreatment, King was almost enjoying the opportunity to preach to preachers, in a kind of virtuoso display of his art. But in this sermonic, rhetorical passage, there are deeply personal vignettes of his family, even of some of his fears and humiliations. These, too, are part of what creates King's authority.

We can look at this piece of rhetoric in terms of some of the tools we have discussed elsewhere in this book. It is a brilliantly sited piece, both in the use it makes of Birmingham jail, with all its reverberations, and in the common moral and political vocabulary it tries to establish with those to whom it is immediately addressed. Its details and its metaphors are finely realized. The "person" of the author is with us all the time. It uses the letter form to make itself—even with its powerful, almost grandiose rhetoric—into a kind of conversation, which King brilliantly dramatizes as a conversation of love between disagreeing brothers. Addressing his immediate readers, the Alabama clergy, directly, he is also able to make us, his other readers, feel as if he were actively in conversation with us. The cadences drawn from King's particular tradition of learned Southern Baptist preaching make us hear the voice when we read it.

Much of its authority comes simply from the depths of its ethical engagement, or we might better say, its ethical engagement is inseparable from the other aspects of it that we have discussed. In this case, it is not the particular morality that King espouses that makes it so powerful but the depth of feeling and intelligence with which he espouses it. This is authentic and authoritative writing not because King is "right" but because he is totally committed; King was writing from the depths of his being. It is a multidimensional piece of writing. The passion, the character, and the argument are both rich and richly coordinated, one with the other. King is fully present as a dramatized person; his arguments are carefully established and rigorously presented; his passions are directly perceptible. We hear his voice, and we are aware of his deepest convictions.

The same is true of what we have read by Annie Dillard and by Paul Fussell and by other writers we have looked at. The best personal writing begins not when we decide to write well but when we decide to write about what we feel strongly and to submit our views to the kind of scrutiny entailed by putting them into publicly available form.

✎ **Writing**   Find another piece of writing that you feel to be ethically authoritative or that is generally considered to be, whatever your own personal view of it. This might be a Supreme Court decision, a personal statement, a political speech, a poem, a letter from someone you know, or a learned article. Analyze its authority as a piece of writing, thinking about the various dimensions authority can draw on. What persuades you, and what fails to?

Use this exercise as a launchpad for writing an essay of your own in which you try to achieve the kind of authority you admire. You may decide, as many have, that impersonality is more authoritative for you than the kind of personality that comes through the writings of someone like King. If so, think about how you want to achieve that impersonality. Choose a subject that is important to you, and write an essay about it in which you establish your authority with respect to a group of readers you know—say, a few of your friends or some teachers you admire. If you have time, go through several drafts, showing them to your intended readers as you go along and asking for their responses along the lines of authority. That is, ask them not to tell you whether they agree but to give you candid feedback about the kinds of authority they discover your writing has or does not have. Think carefully about who "you" are in the piece—how you put yourself forward and how you want yourself to be seen and heard by your readers.

Bibliography

Adams, Henry. *The Education of Henry Adams.* Ernest Samuels, ed. Boston: Houghton Mifflin, 1973.

Arlen, Michael J. *Passage to Ararat.* New York: Farrar, Straus & Giroux, 1975.

Austen, Jane. *Emma.* In *The Novels of Jane Austen IV*, R. W. Chapman, ed. London: Oxford University Press, 1933.

Baker, Russell. "Life with Mother." In *Inventing the Truth*, W. Zinsser, ed. Boston: Houghton Mifflin, 1983.

———. "Getting Tired of High-culture Humility." *New York Times*, 28 December 1988.

———. "The Bad Bugs." *New York Times*, 16 October 1990.

———. "Flying with a Heavy Heart." In *There's a Country in My Cellar.* New York: William Morrow, 1990.

———. "So Happy in Omaha." *New York Times*, 23 October 1990.

Baldwin, James. *The Fire Next Time.* New York: Dell, 1988.

Bettelheim, Bruno. *Freud and Man's Soul.* New York: Vintage, 1984.

"Bewitched, Bothered . . . and Bewitched." *New England Monthly*, 7:9, September 1990.

Bromwich, David. "The French Revolution and *Tintern Abbey*." *Raritan*, 10:3, Winter 1991.

Bronowski, Jacob. *Science and Human Values.* New York: Harper & Row, 1956.

Buechner, Frederick. *The Sacred Journey.* San Francisco: Harper & Row, 1981.

———. *A Room Called Remember: Uncollected Pieces.* San Francisco: Harper & Row, 1984.

L. H. Butterfield, ed. *Adams Family Correspondence, Vol. II: June 1776–March 1778.* Cambridge, MA: Belknap Press, 1963.

Campbell, Jeremy. *Winston Churchill's Afternoon Nap.* New York: Simon & Schuster, 1986.

Churchill, Winston. Official Report of the House of Commons, 8 October 1940, *Parliamentary Debates*, Fifth Series, vol. 365. London: HMSO, 1940.

Desai, Anita. "India: The Seed of Destruction." *New York Review of Books*, 38:12, 27 June 1991.

Dethier, Vincent G. *To Know a Fly.* San Francisco: Holden Day, 1962.

Devlin, Polly. *All of Us There.* London: Pan Books, 1984.

Didion, Joan. "Goodbye to All That." In *Slouching Towards Bethlehem.* New York: Farrar, Straus & Giroux, 1968.

———. "Why I Write." *New York Times Book Review*, 5 December 1976.

Dillard, Annie. *Pilgrim at Tinker Creek.* New York: Harper & Row, 1985.

———. *The Writing Life.* New York: HarperCollins, 1990.

Dillin, John. "Political 'Big 3' in '89 and '90: Flag, Abortion, Death Penalty." *Christian Science Monitor*, 18 July 1989.

Dinesen, Isak. *Out of Africa.* New York: Random House, 1938.

Dorris, Michael. *The Broken Cord.* New York: HarperCollins, 1989.

Duke, Paul, Jr. "Survey Finds Limp Economy on Eve of War." *Wall Street Journal*, 24 January 1991.

Eagleton, Terry. *The Significance of Theory*. Oxford: Basil Blackwell, 1990.

Ehrenberg, Victor. *From Solon to Socrates: Greek History and Civilization During the Sixth and Fifth Centuries B.C.* London: Methuen, 1986.

Eiseley, Loren. *The Immense Journey*. New York: Vintage, 1957.

Elbow, Peter. "Reflections on Academic Discourse." *College English*, 53:2, February 1991.

Flores, Camille. "Tierra Amarilla." *New Mexico Magazine*, 69:2, February 1991.

Franklin, R., and R. G. Gosling, "Molecular Configuration in Sodium Thymonucleate." *Nature*, 171, 25 April 1953.

Friedman, Thomas L. *From Beirut to Jerusalem*. New York: Doubleday, 1990.

Friedrich, Otto. "Master of His Universe." *Time*, 13 August 1990.

Fussell, Paul. "My War." In *The Boy Scout Handbook and Other Observations*. New York: Oxford University Press, 1982.

Galbraith, John Kenneth. *Economics in Perspective*. Boston: Houghton Mifflin, 1987.

Gates, Henry Louis. "The Case of 2 Live Crew Tells Much About the American Psyche." *New York Times*, 15 July 1990.

Gelb, Leslie. "Policy Monotheism." *New York Times*, 17 March 1991.

Giamatti, A. Bartlett. *Take Time for Paradise: Americans and Their Games*. New York: Summit Books, 1989.

Gombrich, E. H. *Norm and Form: Studies in the Art of the Renaissance*. London: Phaidon, 1966.

Hawking, Stephen. *A Brief History of Time*. New York: Bantam, 1988.

Heaney, Seamus. "Feeling into Words." In *Preoccupations*. New York: Farrar, Straus & Giroux, 1980.

Heat Moon, William Least. *Blue Highways: A Journey into America*. Boston: Little, Brown, 1982.

Hoagland, Edward. *The Courage of Turtles*. New York: Random House, 1968.

Hogan, Edward A., Jr. "How a Law Professor Tells His Children the Story of the Three Bears." In *Trials and Tribulation*, 3rd ed., Daniel R. White, ed. New York: Penguin, 1989.

Howarth, William L., ed. *The John McPhee Reader*. New York: Farrar, Straus & Giroux, 1976.

Hynes, Samuel. "The Whole Contention Between Mr. Bennett and Mrs. Woolf." In *Novel*, Fall 1967.

———. *Flights of Passage: Reflections of a World War II Aviator*. New York: Frederic C. Beil. Annapolis: Naval Institute Press, 1988.

"Imelda Marcos Not Guilty." *The Economist*, 316, 7 July 1990.

An Incensed Neighbor. "Who Shot Defenseless Doe?" *Springfield Union News*, 25 September 1990.

Jacobs, Jane. *The Economy of Cities*. New York: Random House, 1970.

Janovy, John, Jr. *Keith County Journal*. New York: St. Martin's Press, 1978.

Khan, Hashim. *Squash Racquets: The Khan Game*, with Richard E. Randall. Detroit: Wayne State University Press, 1967.

King, Martin Luther, Jr. "Letter from Birmingham City Jail." In *Why We Can't Wait*. New York: Harper & Row, 1963, 1964.

Lanham, Richard. *Revising Prose*, 3rd ed. New York: Macmillan, 1991.

Lasch, Christopher. *The Culture of Narcissism.* New York: Norton, 1979.

Lewis, C. S., quoted in Barzun, Jacques. *Simple & Direct.* San Francisco: Harper & Row, 1975.

Lewontin, R. C. "Fallen Angels" [Review of Stephen Jay Gould, *Wonderful Life: The Burgess Shale and the Nature of History*]. *New York Review of Books,* 37:10, 14 June 1990.

Lurie, Alison. "Clothing as a Sign System." In *The Language of Clothes.* New York: Random House, 1981.

McCloskey, Donald N. *The Rhetoric of Economics.* Madison: University of Wisconsin Press, 1985.

McFeely, William S. *Grant.* New York: Norton, 1981.

McHenry, Mary Williamson. "Papa's Child." Unpublished manuscript.

McPherson, James M. "How Lincoln Won the War with Metaphors." In *Abraham Lincoln and the Second American Revolution.* New York: Oxford University Press, 1990.

Manchester, William. "Okinawa: The Bloodiest Battle of All." *New York Times Magazine,* 14 June 1987.

Mead, Margaret. *Letters from the Field, 1925–75.* New York: Harper & Row, 1977.

Minnis, Alistair. *Chaucer and Pagan Antiquity.* Cambridge: D. S. Brewer, 1982.

Narbonne, G. M., and Aitken, J. D. "Ediacaram Fossils from the Sekwi Brook Area, Mackenzie Mountains, Northwestern Canada." *Paleontology,* 33:4 1990, 945–980.

"Nasty Little Stowaways." *The Economist,* 316 (7 July 1990).

Nemerov, Howard. "On Metaphor." In *New & Selected Essays.* Carbondale: Southern Illinois University Press, 1985.

Nixon, Richard M. *In the Arena.* New York: Simon & Schuster, 1990.

Noonan, Peggy. *What I Saw at the Revolution.* New York: Random House, 1990.

Orwell, George. "Looking Back on the Spanish War." In *A Collection of Essays by George Orwell.* New York: Doubleday, 1954.

———. "Politics and the English Language." In *A Collection of Essays by George Orwell.* New York: Doubleday, 1954.

Payne, Lucille Vaughn. *The Lively Art of Writing.* New York: Follett, 1965.

Petro, Pamela. "The Ripe Age of an Island." *New England Monthly,* 7:9 September 1990.

Pomeroy, Sarah B. *Goddesses, Whores, Wives and Slaves: Women in Classical Antiquity.* New York: Schocken, 1975.

Pritchett, V. S. *A Cab at the Door.* London: Chatto & Windus, 1968.

Quindlen, Anna. "Life in the 30s." *New York Times,* 24 February 1988.

———. "Life in the 30s." *New York Times,* 28 April 1988.

———. *Living Out Loud.* New York: Ivy Books, 1988.

———. "A Bias Crime." *New York Times,* 6 May 1990.

———. "At the Circus." *New York Times,* 11 October 1990.

———. "Grand Juries." *New York Times,* 25 October 1990.

———. "Getting in the Door." *New York Times,* 20 July 1991.

Rhys, Jean. *The Letters of Jean Rhys,* Francis Wyndham and Diana Melly, eds. New York: Viking, 1984.

Rich, Adrienne. "When We Dead Awaken: Writing as Re-vision." In *On Lies, Secrets, and Silence.* New York: Norton, 1979.

Ricoeur, Paul. "The Metaphorical Process as Cognition, Imagination, and Feeling." *Critical Inquiry*, 5, Autumn 1978.

Rodriguez, Richard. *Hunger of Memory*. Boston: Godine, 1982.

Russett, Cynthia. *Sexual Science: The Victorian Construction of Womanhood*. Cambridge, MA: Harvard University Press, 1989.

Safire, William. "Fourth of July Oration." *New York Times*, 3 July 1989.

Schultz, Christine. "A Sister's Gift." *Yankee Magazine*, June 1989.

Shakespeare, William. *The Complete Plays and Poems of William Shakespeare*, William A. Neilson and Charles J. Hill, eds. Cambridge, MA: Houghton Mifflin, 1942.

Steele, Shelby. *The Content of Our Character*. New York: St. Martin's Press, 1990.

Steiner, George. "Eros and Idiom." In *On Difficulty and Other Essays*. New York: Oxford University Press, 1978.

Stieber, Tamar. "L-Tryptophan—A Medical Puzzle." In *The Pulitzer Prizes 1990*, Kendall J. Willis, ed. New York: Simon & Schuster, 1990.

Tannen, Deborah. *That's Not What I Meant! How Conversational Style Makes or Breaks Relationships*. New York: William Morrow, 1986.

Thomas, Clarence. "Climb the Jagged Mountain." Commencement Address at Savannah State College, Georgia, June 9, 1985. *New York Times*, 17 July 1991.

Thomas, Lewis. "On Meddling." In *The Medusa and the Snail*. New York: Viking, 1979.

———. "The Selves." In *The Medusa and the Snail*. New York: Viking, 1979.

———."Late Night Thoughts on Mahler's Ninth Symphony." In *Late Night Thoughts on Mahler's Ninth Symphony*. New York: Viking, 1983.

———. "On Medicine and the Bomb." In *Late Night Thoughts on Mahler's Ninth Symphony*. New York: Viking, 1983.

Thurow, Lester C. *The Zero-Sum Society*. New York: Basic Books, 1980.

Tolkien, J. R. R. *The Letters of J. R. R. Tolkien*, selected and edited by Humphrey Carpenter with the assistance of Christopher Tolkien. Boston: Houghton Mifflin, 1981.

Tompkins, Jane P. "Sentimental Power: *Uncle Tom's Cabin* and the Politics of Literary History." In *Sensational Designs*. New York: Oxford University Press, 1985.

Watson, James. *The Double Helix*, Gunther S. Stent, ed. New York: Norton, 1980.

Welty, Eudora. *One Writer's Beginnings*. Cambridge, MA: Harvard University Press, 1983.

White, E. B. *Essays of E. B. White*. New York: Harper & Row, 1977.

"Who Will Stop Saddam?" *The Economist*, 316 (4 August 1990).

Will, George F. "Against Prefabricated Prayer." *The Morning After: American Successes and Excesses 1981–86*. New York: Macmillan, 1986.

———. *Men at Work*. New York: Macmillan, 1990.

Winerip, Michael. "Our Towns." *New York Times*, 13 November 1990.

Woolf, Virginia. *A Room of One's Own*. New York: Harcourt Brace Jovanovich, 1929, 1957.

Zinsser, William. "Writing & Remembering." In *Inventing the Truth: The Art and Craft of Memoir*, W. Zinsser, ed. Boston: Houghton Mifflin, 1981.

Zoretich, Frank J. "Silver City: Mining Its Historic Past." *New Mexico Magazine*, 69:2, February 1991.

Credits

Pages 3–4: From George Orwell: *A Collection of Essays.* Reprinted by permission.

Pages 8–9: From *Grant: A Biography,* by William S. McFeely. Copyright © 1981 by William S. McFeely. Reprinted by permission of W. W. Norton & Company Inc.

Page 10: "India: The Seed of Destruction" by Anita Desai. Reprinted with permission from *The New York Review of Books.* Copyright © 1990–91 Nyrev, Inc.

Pages 18–19, 19–20: From Polly Devlin: *All of Us Here.* Reprinted by permission.

Pages 24–25: Copyright © 1989 by The New York Times Company. Reprinted by permission.

Page 25–26: Reprinted with the permission of Simon & Schuster from *Pulitzer Prizes* by Kendall J. Willis. Copyright © 1990 by Kendall J. Willis.

Pages 26–27, 32–33: © 1988 by The New York Times Company. Reprinted by permission.

Page 28–29: "A Sister's Gift" by Christine Schultz. Copyright © 1989. Reprinted by permission of *Yankee Magazine.*

Pages 38–39: Reprinted by permission of Henry Louis Gates, Jr.

Page 41: Copyright © 1991 by The New York Times Company. Reprinted by permission.

Pages 42–43: Copyright © 1991 by The New York Times Company. Reprinted by permission.

Pages 47–48: From Russell Baker, "Flying With a Heavy Heart," in *There's a Country in My Cellar.* Copyright © 1991. This article first appeared in The Observer column of The New York Times. Reprinted by permission.

Page 49: Copyright © 1988 by The New York Times Company. Reprinted by permission.

Page 50: Copyright © 1990 by The New York Times Company. Reprinted by permission.

Page 51: Excerpt from *Economics in Perspective.* Copyright © 1987 by John Kenneth Galbraith. Reprinted by permission of Houghton Mifflin Company. All rights reserved.

Pages 52–54: Copyright © 1990 by The New York Times Company. Reprinted by permission.

Page 55: Copyright © 1990 by The New York Times Company. Reprinted by permission.

Pages 55–56: Copyright © 1990 by The New York Times Company. Reprinted by permission.

Page 56: Copyright © 1990 by The New York Times Company. Reprinted by permission.

Pages 59–60: Excerpt from *The Fire Next Time* by James Baldwin. New York: Dell, 1988. Reprinted by permission of Bantam, Doubleday, Dell.

Pages 61–62: Copyright © 1990 by The New York Times Company. Reprinted by permission.

Page 64: Excerpts from *Late Night Thoughts on Listening to Mahler's Ninth* by Lewis Thomas. Copyright © 1983 by Lewis Thomas. Used by permission of Viking Penguin, a division of Penguin Books USA Inc.

Pages 70–71: From *The Content of Our Character* by Shelby Steele. Copyright © 1990 by Shelby Steele. Reprinted with permission by St. Martin's Press, Incorporated.

Pages 71–72, 214–215: Excerpts as submitted from *Pilgrim at Tinker Creek* by Annie Dillard. Copyright © 1974 by Annie Dillard. Reprinted by permission of HarperCollins Publishers, Inc.

Pages 77–79: Excerpt as submitted from *The Broken Cord* by Michael Dorris. Copyright © 1989 by Michael Dorris. Reprinted by permission of HarperCollins Publishers, Inc.

Pages 82–84: Copyright © 1990 by The New York Times Company. Reprinted by permission.

Page 100: From George Orwell: *A Collection of Essays.* Reprinted by permission.

Page 118: "Molecular Configuration in Sodium Thymonucleate" by R. Franklin and R. G. Gosling. Reprinted by permission for *Nature* vol. 171, pp. 740–741; Copyright © 1953 Macmillan Magazines Limited.

Author Index

Subject Index